ARTFUL COLOR MINDFUL KNITS

artful mindful *mindful* artful

Laura Miltzer Bryant

Photography by
Alexis Xenakis

To Kanella,

*who infused my life
with creativity.*

I love you, Mom.

ARTFUL COLOR · MINDFUL KNITS

BOOKS

PUBLISHER Alexis Yiorgos Xenakis

EDITOR Elaine Rowley

MANAGING EDITOR Karen Bright

TECHNICAL EDITOR Rick Mondragon

INSTRUCTION EDITOR Traci Bunkers

INSTRUCTION PROOFERS Sarah Peasley, Ginger Smith

ART DIRECTOR Natalie Sorenson

PHOTOGRAPHER Alexis Yiorgos Xenakis

STYLIST Rick Mondragon

ASSISTANT TO THE PUBLISHER Lisa Mannes

CHIEF EXECUTIVE OFFICER Benjamin Levisay

DIRECTOR, PUBLISHING SERVICES David Xenakis

TECHNICAL ILLUSTRATOR Carol Skallerud

PRODUCTION DIRECTOR & COLOR SPECIALIST Dennis Pearson

BOOK PRODUCTION MANAGER Greg Hoogeveen

MARKETING MANAGER Lisa Mannes

BOOKS DISTRIBUTION Mavis Smith

MIS Jason Bittner

FIRST PRINTING, 2013

PUBLISHED IN THE USA IN 2013 BY XRX, INC.

ISBN 13: 9781933064260

Produced in Sioux Falls,
South Dakota by XRX, Inc.
PO Box 965
Sioux Falls, SD 57101-0965
USA

605.338.2450

Visit us online — knittinguniverse.com

Printed in Hong Kong

A personal color journey

Have you ever had a V8 moment? I did, in 1983—one of the many epiphanies a young adult experiences. Walking the aisles at The National Needlework Association wholesale trade show, I stumbled upon Dyed in the Wool and Cheryl Schaefer, one of the pioneer hand dyers. Fresh out of art school (where I had studied textiles and color), I had worked in a local yarn shop as clerk and finisher, then moved on as sales representative for several fashion yarn lines, including Tahki Yarns and Berroco. It was a great position for me: life-long knitter and crocheter; textile artist; young, eager, and willing to drive hundreds of miles every week. But back to that V8 moment…

I felt as if a comet had struck me. People were willing to buy hand-dyed yarns? Why had I not known this? It was the early days, there weren't many dyers yet, and there seemed to be room for another. I had knowledge. I had desire. And I guess I had moxie: I convinced Diane Friedman of Tahki Yarns that I should hand dye a line of their existing product. Thus was born Prism and a fascination that has engaged me for decades. Eventually Prism went solo with our own products. Stores loved the yarn and colors, but inevitably asked, "What can I do with it?" Out of necessity, I evolved into a knitwear designer. Fortunately, having been an avid sewer since my teens, I had lots of hands-on experience with clothing construction. But from sweater to sweater I repeatedly observed that, although I might adore a color combination I had dyed, traditional stitches and sweater shapes might not cast those colors, or my dyeing, to best advantage. Often striping or random areas of pooling and patterning popped up and then didn't continue elsewhere, and sometimes colors that looked good in blocks next to one another lost their punch when mingled together in rows of stitches.

Thirty-five years of thinking about color (first as art student, then art weaver, then dyer and knitwear designer) have led to this book. Twenty-five of those years have been spent knitting and designing for Prism. My natural curiosity and my art-school experience using ongoing critique have turned me into an inveterate questioner: What worked? What didn't work? Why did that happen, and how can I control/repeat/neutralize it? I observe both good and bad results and seek to understand why they occur; I refer to this as "the scientific-inquiry method of knitting and design."

The first time I noticed that a turtleneck collar worked in the round produced a spiral of color, my world was rocked. It was the mid-1980s, and that one observation has led me down a path of designing specifically to take advantage of everything hand-dyed yarns have to offer. My hope with this book is to share with you as much of this process and my accumulated knowledge as possible, so you can go on to achieve stunning results with hand-dyed yarns.

Laura B

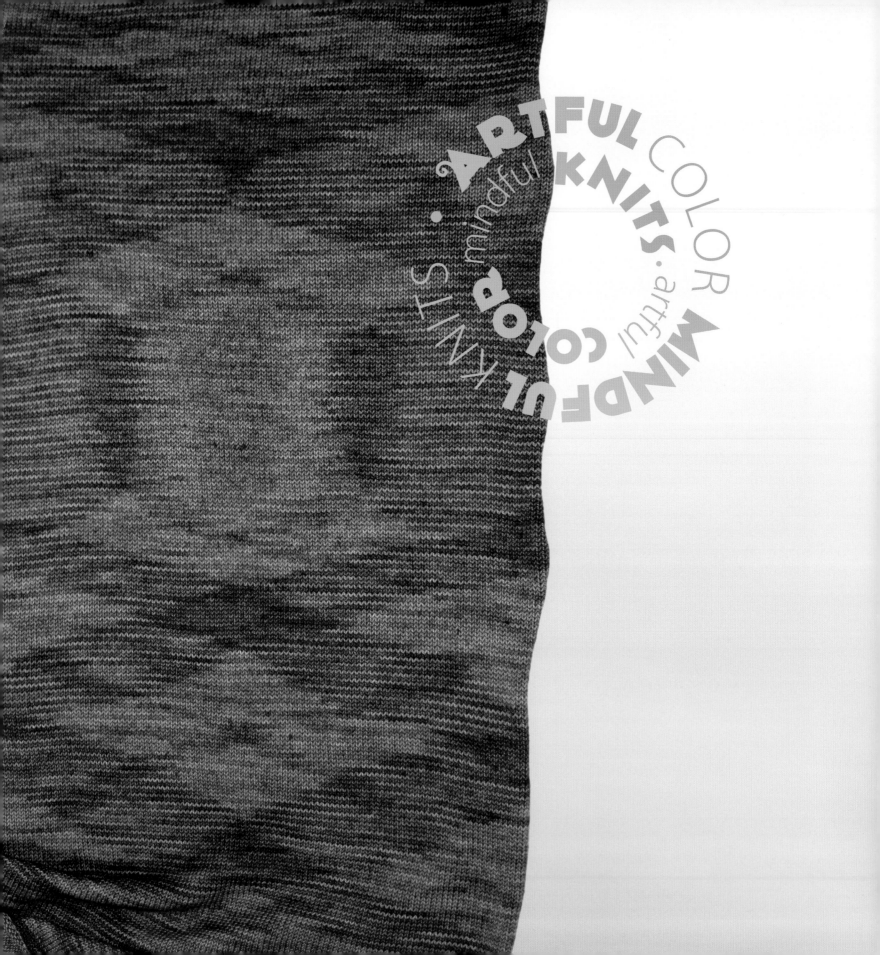

Why hand-dyed yarns?

The first and most obvious answer is that the maker's hand is apparent in every skein of hand-dyed yarn. An individual artisan applies dye to fiber in a personal expression of color. Inspiration arises from many avenues: the beauty of one's own personal environment, whether mountains, desert, prairie, or ocean; the brilliant perceptions of fine artists as expressed in their work; couture fashion; riotous flower gardens; trays laden with beautifully arranged food—you name it, a dyer will be inspired by it.

While factory-dyed yarns come in a huge array of solid and multicolored combinations, they do not have the same intimate qualities. Factory yarns are dyed efficiently in very large batches, so colors chosen must appeal to a large group of consumers. Factory methods of creating multicolored yarn are quite different than hand dyeing and most often produce either much shorter bursts of color or very long color repeats that result in self-striping effects. Factory-dyed yarns follow color trends to justify their large quantities, so your favorite colorway may go out of production as trends change.

Hand dyers have the luxury of producing small, artisanal batches. That means you won't see infinite multiples of a colorway, which offers a much greater chance for a truly unique knitting or crocheting experience. Hand dyers can produce unusual color combinations that might not have universal appeal, but could be just right for you. And they can include a much larger variety of colors, as many hand-dyed yarns are dyed to order and so don't need to be inventoried—a step which adds to cost and often dictates limited palettes.

Most important, hand-dyed yarns have a subtle beauty that can't be duplicated through factory processes. There are variations in tone and shade. Even hand-dyed solids aren't really solid, but have light and dark areas within the same skein. Dyers apply color in a variety of ways, producing distinctly different effects. Color can be applied in multiple steps, producing layers of color. The list of possible variations is almost infinite.

One last distinction is unique to hand-dyed yarns: yarn for dyeing comes in a small range of skein circumferences, and the size of a skein to be hand-dyed determines the length of its color repeat and governs how that skein will work up. While very few factory-produced yarns share this quality, virtually all hand-dyed yarns have it. This is the single most important concept to understand and will become your guidepost by which to knit and crochet. Artful Color will teach you how to read a skein, to determine its style of dyeing, and to choose the best possible technique and pattern to turn your work-of-art skein into a work-of-art fabric.

Color

It's what draws our eye, but too often we purchase a lovely skein of hand-dyed yarn only to be terribly disappointed when it is made into fabric. That disappointment stems from the interaction of colors within the yarn as it is stitched, not the specific colors themselves. We share a natural tendency to think that if a yarn is that beautiful, then only simple stockinette or a basic crochet stitch is required. But if the colors gather together, creating blotches, pools, and undesired patterns, they can be the worst choice.

Hand-dyed yarns come to us either in an original dye skein, where large areas of color clearly show how the dye was applied, or rewound into a different-sized skein, where colors blend in thread-thin lines. Neither skein represents how the yarn will look when it is knit or crocheted. Colors that look good next to one another in large blocks may not be as attractive when they intermingle in fabric. Colors that are appealing in thin lines may not be as effective when stitches shape those colors into taller, shorter runs. In all cases, as colors gather during stitching we may see unpleasant random blotches. Every one of these occurrences can be compensated for—and the beauty of any skein of hand-dyed yarn can be coaxed out—with the right knowledge and a willingness to experiment. Let's start on our journey by seeing just what the possibilities are.

Variety of hand-dyed skeins.

The Butterfly Effect and Knitting

To control a thing, you must first understand it.

*I remember my initial exposure to Chaos Theory in the 70s. Wikipedia defines it thus: "Chaos theory studies the behavior of dynamical systems that are highly sensitive to initial conditions, an effect which is popularly referred to as the butterfly effect. Small differences in initial conditions…yield widely diverging outcomes for chaotic systems, rendering long-term prediction impossible in general. This happens even though these systems are deterministic, meaning that their **future behavior is fully determined by their initial conditions, with no random elements involved.**" (Emphasis added.) When knitting or crocheting with hand-dyed yarn, it is not unusual to have seemingly random stripes suddenly become argyle-like diamonds, particularly as stitch counts change. This seems to fit Chaos Theory—why, oh, why did that happen?—especially when tiny differences seem to make big changes. It is worth noting that hand-dyed yarns are deterministic: their future behavior (how they will look when knit or crocheted) is fully determined by their initial conditions (size of dye skein). There really isn't anything random at all, and it certainly pays to know how to read those initial conditions correctly.*

Learning the Ropes: A Vocabulary for Hand-Dyed Yarn

Since there isn't a science of hand-dyed yarn, there isn't a precise language. The following are terms that I have developed or that are commonly used, and I think it will be helpful to specify what they mean. Later chapters will elaborate on the how and why, but with this information we'll all visualize the same effect when we think about a specific term.

Repeat is the length of a unique sequence of colors before they begin again (or repeat). Repeat is determined solely by dye-skein circumference and is not altered by the number of colors or their placement. Some hand-dyed yarns do not have a reliable repeat as a color may not be present throughout all of the strands of a skein.

The following terms describe how the colors appear when knit or crocheted into fabric.

Magic Number is the number of stitches that will use an entire repeat of color exactly once. Magic Numbers and fractions or multiples thereof are used to intentionally pattern hand-dyed yarns in a variety of ways.

Dyed-around skein repeat.

Stripes are thick or thin, depending on where the colors meet on the next row.

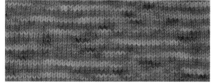

Orange and green are forming stripes, while blue is tending to pool.

Colors in a dyed-across skein stack well.

Striping is an easy concept to grasp—it is the tendency of long runs of color to read as stripes. Stripes are more noticeable in narrow pieces such as socks, scarves, and entrelac.

Pooling happens when colors gather together, and is a general term for a variety of effects that will be described more specifically. Pooling happens when a color occurs in the same place on several rows.

Stacking occurs when gauge, repeat, and stitch count all conspire so the full repeat is used within one row and then begins again, causing colors to stack on top of one another. The number of stitches needed to cause stacking is what I refer to as the Magic Number. Precise stacking requires constant small adjustments to stay as close to vertical as possible, so attention must be paid to tension.

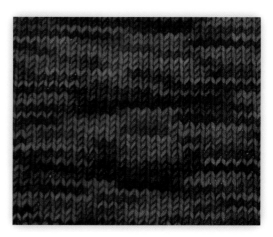

Small stripes become blotches when colors appear on top of one another in the next row or rows.

Blotching or splotching is pooling at its worst: colors that gather seemingly at random, interrupting stripes but not really resolving into any coherent pattern. Splotching makes strongly contrasting colors more noticeable, with thick yarns creating more distinct splotches as the large stitch size reinforces colors where they touch.

Stacked colors in double crochet, dyed-across skein.

Spirals are circular stacks that lean either to the right or to the left so the columns of color move on a diagonal. Spirals are worked on slightly more or fewer stitches than the Magic Number. Worked with consistent tension and mindfulness, clean diagonal stripes can be formed.

Spiral, dyed-across skein. Notice the end colors, gold and dark brown, appear once, with two sets of narrower orange and brown stripes from the dyed-across portion.

Flashes are spirals that are allowed to move back and forth slightly, producing lightning bolts of color more or less vertically. These zigzags can be controlled by the subtle increase or decrease of a stitch or two, or by slightly tightening or loosening tension.

Argyles are diamond-shaped patterns that occur when a Magic Number, plus or minus 1 or 2 stitches, is worked flat (back and forth). As the colors move diagonally, they will hit the edge and turn, just as a pool ball striking the table side will bank the other way and travel to the next edge, where it will bank again. This regular zigzagging motion produces interlocking diamonds that often won't show up until many inches have been completed. They are more forgiving to knit or crochet than vertical stacks, reading well even with small variations. Highly contrasting colors often make the most striking argyles.

Circular flash, dyed-around skein. Each color appears once.

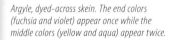

Argyle, dyed-across skein. The end colors (fuchsia and violet) appear once while the middle colors (yellow and aqua) appear twice.

Dyed-around yarn at 7 stitches per inch stacks (center) at the Magic Number and argyles at both 4 stitches fewer (bottom) and 4 stitches more (top). The difference between the two argyle sections is 8 stitches, or about an inch in width.

Argyles, stacks, and yarn weight
Argyle-like patterns will occur when the stitch count is just a few stitches off from the Magic Number. Since the amount of yarn used in each stitch is quite different from thick to thin yarns, thick yarns will turn from stacks to argyles with a difference of just 1 or 2 stitches, while thin yarns may require a difference of 4 or more stitches.

Meanders are how I describe less-than-precise argyles. Worked on a number that would argyle with mindfulness, but worked with no regard for how colors are actually patterning, meanders feature grouped colors that gather but that also travel around enough so that they don't create crisp argyles. I find this effect to be more noticeable with thinner yarns.

Ribbed scarf in dyed-around fine-weight yarn has meandering colors.

Half-stacks are patterns produced on half the Magic Number. Half-stack argyles are more elongated than those worked on a whole Magic Number. Half-stack columns look just like a full Magic Number divided vertically down the middle — whether dyed-across or dyed-around. Dyed-across skeins retain clean color columns, while dyed-around skeins produce every-other-row sections coupled with solid sections — reflecting both the number of colors and where in the repeat the work is begun.

Half-stack argyle, dyed-around skein.

Intentional patterning is the purposeful use of repeats to cause any of these patterns, and is also known as **planned pooling**.

Randomizing
Any strategy intended to neutralize these effects.

Color again

Since understanding how colors interact is crucial to predicting how a hand-dyed colorway will look when knit or crocheted, we also need a color vocabulary. This book was printed using a four-color ink printing process known as **CMYK**, which is more similar to dye behavior than to pigment such as oil paint. We were all taught that the primary colors are blue, red, and yellow, which is true for pigment. But ink and dye are somewhat different: their primaries are **C**yan (turquoise), **M**agenta, and **Y**ellow, with the addition of blac**k** (CMYK).

It is also helpful to understand how we see color. Our eyes have two sets of light receptors: rods and cones. Rods are sensitive to light and are located more densely around the outside of the retina. This is why, in low-light situations, you often see something more distinctly from the corner of your eye: on a starry night, for example, I can always find the Pleiades more easily if I don't look directly at them—they appear much brighter from the corner of my eye. Three types of cones are located centrally and sense long (**R**ed), medium (**G**reen), and short (**B**lue) wavelengths of light (**RGB**, the color system your computer uses). Cones require much greater amounts of light to function, which explains why we don't see color well in dim light.

We perceive color that is reflected back to us: white is the total of all light reflected (none is absorbed by what we see); black is the total absorption of all light, with none reflected. In pigment, the total of all colors mixed together gets darker and muddier, going toward black; in light, the total of all colors is white. Dye and ink are translucent, with no "white" except for the original fiber or paper.

Primary colors in pigment are blue, red, and yellow; in ink (or dye): cyan (turquoise), magenta (fuchsia), and yellow; in light: blue, red, and green. The differences lie in how a particular medium functions. All other colors derive from the primaries. White lightens color to pastels, and black darkens color.

Secondary colors are mixtures of primary colors: yellow and magenta (red) make orange, yellow and cyan (blue) make green, cyan (blue) and red make violet.

Hue refers to a color itself: red, orange, olive, and aqua are all examples of hues. Hues all derive from the primaries plus black and white (paper or yarn color). Every hue can be placed in its appropriate spot in relation to the colors that create it.

Color names beyond primary and secondary colors are basically marketing concepts. We all know what olive looks like, but ask ten individuals to select olive from a group of yellowish/blackish greens and you will likely get ten different choices. And who knows what color "puce" really is? (It's the color of dried blood and comes from the French word for "flea.") Of far more importance than naming a color is using our eyes to actually **look**, to be able to see what makes up that color. Seeing is what matters!

100% of each CMY, print and dye primaries.

Primaries and secondaries.

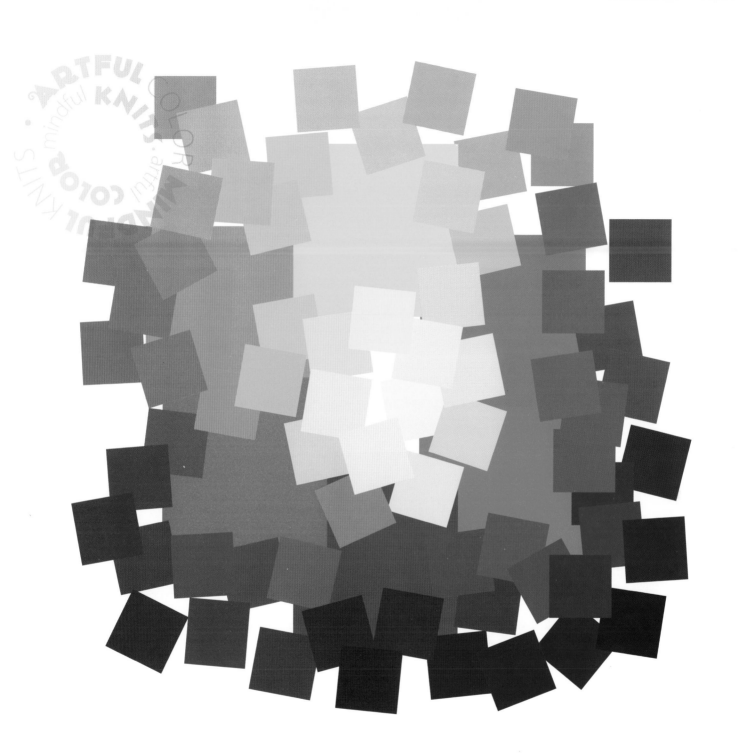

Value

refers to relative lightness or darkness on a gray scale—that is, the quantity of black present. Grayed colors are less saturated and will be relatively lighter or darker depending on the amount of black added. Printer's ink and dye are translucent media (the white of paper or fiber shows through to make pale colors), as opposed to opaque media such as pigment (which completely covers what is underneath, as happens when painting a wall). So we never add white to ink or dye, we simply use less color, allowing the original white to show through and create tints or pastels.

Saturation

is the amount of pure color that is present. Pastels and grayed colors have low saturation. Highly saturated colors are brilliant, pure hues such as fuchsia and lime green. Saturation can be equated to brightness, but is not exactly the same thing.

Color weight

refers to the relative lightness or heaviness of a color. This is not the same as value and is a bit more difficult to comprehend, particularly in the middle ranges. (It is an odd quirk of the English language that **light** is the top end of either scale, but **heavy** and **dark** are not synonymous.) In any given pair of colors, one will be lighter and one will be heavier. Lighter colors move forward visually. Heavier colors recede. The same is true for value: lighter values move forward; darker values recede. The reason we draw a distinction between value

VALUE

Value scale at 10% steps.

SATURATION

100% magenta at center is reduced 20% per step at right, allowing more and more white to show through; 20% black has been added per step at left. Using less magenta produces less saturated color; the addition of black (or other hues) also desaturates.

COLOR WEIGHT

Colors arranged from heavy (left) to light (right). Within the strip are very close pairs, like magenta and red, and pairs whose weights are further apart; like light blue and bright yellow.

Highly saturated colors.

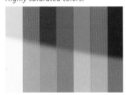

The same colors, desaturated to varying degrees.

and weight is that pure colors such as saturated yellow or turquoise don't fit well into a gray scale—they really don't have either white or black in them. A weight scale such as the one shown allows us to place highly saturated colors with other like-weighted colors. This is particularly true for the middle of the scale. Even though bright or highly saturated colors might pop visually, they still have a home at some point on the weight scale—a place where each will stand out the least and is most comfortable.

Tip: One of the best things every knitter can do is to keep a white pillowcase in their knitting bag, especially when swatching. The distance from which we most often view our knitting is about 14"–18". No one else—except maybe your knitting friends or a judge at the county fair—will ever view the work from that distance. Everything looks different from a longer perspective. After a few inches of swatching, and before you rip in disgust because "it just isn't working," place the pillowcase over a chair or sofa back, place the knitting on the pillowcase, and walk away. Now turn and look at it from across the room—the distance from which others will see it. It often looks entirely different. Try to get into the habit of doing this, and you'll observe more and more how visual perception works and how changeable it is. There is a reason artists have large studios and easels. They can't judge their work from up close when creating it—they must constantly walk away and look.

Contrast is the visual difference between one color and another. Contrast can be present in hue, such as green and violet; in value, such as black (dark) and white (light); in weight, such as fully saturated yellow (light) and red (heavy); or in all three at once. Contrast can exist in hues with no contrast in value or weight: there are colors that are distinctly different in hue, yet they read on the same level. Contrast can exist in value with no contrast in hue: two shades of the same color, one with more black or white.

Contrast
is the key
to everything.

CONTRAST
CONTRAST

The pair at either end have contrast in both hue and weight; the 3 center pairs are similar in weight but have hue contrast. Notice the sharp vertical line between colors with weight contrast versus the softer line when weights are closer.

Color pairs showing saturation contrast, which can also be read as weight contrast.

Color pairs showing hue and weight contrast.

Optical mixture

is a phenomenon that occurs when the eye sees—and then the brain interprets—small bits of different colors as one; the colors are mixed optically, in the brain. They don't mix the same way as dye, pigment, or light mix. Instead, the new color we perceive is slightly grayed, but luminous. Optical mixture was first exploited by the Impressionists. The old newspaper style of printing, with tiny dots of color, also relied on optical mixture. Computer screens use optical mixture to mix their 256 colors into millions of shades. Knitting, with its pixel-like stitches and thread-thin strands, is an ideal medium for optical mixture. The effect is particularly noticeable from greater distances, and less so when looking closely at the work in your hands—just like photographs viewed at normal range on a computer screen look different than they do when blown up, allowing individual pixels to be seen. Hand-dyed yarns, by their nature, present optical mixtures.

Highly contrasting colors produce fabric with more splotching, pooling, and striping.

High-contrast colors have a more energetic and distinct pattern than low-contrast colors.

Color is unique to each dyer. Choice of color is not only an expression of the artisan using it, but also a personal expression of the stitcher who falls in love with and purchases a skein of yarn. Each dyer has their own individual approach to color, and while there is no single correct path, there are predictable outcomes. And there is one controlling, overriding facet that applies to color use, particularly in hand-dyed yarn:

Take a look at the photos of commercially made fabric. The weave is identical except for color choice. Black and cream (high contrast) reads very differently from black and royal blue (low contrast).

Colors with similar weight appear more harmonious and read as one surface, particularly from a distance.

Take a good look at the two sets of stripes. Both have exactly the same colors in exactly the same proportion, but they present very different faces. One is a random series of colors, with no thought to relative weight. The other has been ranked from heavy to light. Some individual colors may be switched, but the overall trend is from heavy to light. It is almost impossible to get an exact gradation, particularly with yarn.

One is difficult to look at, with lines jumping all over. It is hard to perceive individual colors, with several heavy colors all tending to read as black. The other flows from one side to the other, leading us to see each color in succession, and proving that there is in fact only one strip of black. From these illustrations we can draw the following rules of thumb:

To make a pattern story, choose colors of contrasting weight.

To make a color story, choose colors of similar weight.

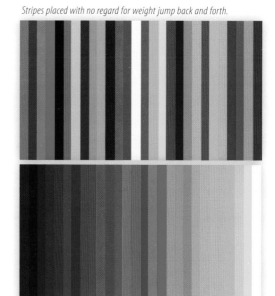

Stripes placed with no regard for weight jump back and forth.

The same colors placed in a weight scale flow from one to another.

Because it is a difficult concept, let's talk some more about weight. Colors from the spectrum are not equal in terms of visual impact. Highly saturated, pure colors, which have no white or black in them, do not necessarily sit in the same position on a color-weight scale. Yellow is, by nature, much lighter than red or blue. Highly saturated yellow sits in the top quarter of the scale; highly saturated red and blue are much further down, below the halfway point. Yellow pops visually, not only because it is bright, but also because it is light. Of course brightness enters into it, but a brilliant saturated turquoise will never be as light as anything with yellow in it—until you add lots of white, and lose the saturation.

Saturated turquoise is much heavier than saturated yellow, left. To bring the turquoise to a similar weight level as the yellow, very little turquoise is diluted with lots of white, right.

Again, notice that the vertical line between colors gets much softer as the turquoise lightens. The greater the contrast, the sharper the line. Less contrast equals a softer division, which leads to more harmony and less definition of shape.

All color is relative

We don't view individual colors in a vacuum. Colors are always seen with other colors, where they have a tremendous effect on one another. Imagine a sociable friend who suddenly becomes a wallflower when surrounded by a noisy bar crowd, or a person of medium height who seems incredibly short at a convention of models. It's all about contrast, and the more contrast present, the busier a surface will appear. Our eyes are drawn to contrasting edges, where color meets color. The sharper that edge is, the harder it is to discern the different colors. Conversely, the softer the edge, the easier it is to read the colors.

Our brains also seek patterns, and they are very good at supplying missing information. Tr rdng ths sntnc—rlly nt s dffclt, s t, spclly n ths dy f txtng? Even with all of the vowels missing, our brains supply the information needed. One reason we tend not to like hand-dyed yarns worked in simple stockinette or basic crochet stitches is that the unavoidable splotching doesn't have a readable pattern. Our brains try to make sense of the splotches…but there isn't any real pattern to make sense of. We need to grab the reins and impose a pattern, but with this in mind: The key to either a pattern or a color story is to control contrasts so that there is enough to make it readable, but not so much as to create cacophony.

Colors placed randomly.

The bright blue is obviously too heavy on the left, and too light on the right. Although it is still noticeable for being a bright, saturated color, when it sits in its proper place in the middle, it does not stand out.

Here are two arrangements of yarn samples. Each board has exactly the same colors, yet one is visually chaotic, with colors popping and receding at random, not allowing the eye to rest and absorb. Multiple dark colors seem to be black, even though they are not. Light colors are dull and lifeless. Saturated colors are garish and loud. The other board has been arranged according to visual weight, and colors flow from one end to the other even though no attention has been paid to hue. We can see the dark/heavy colors as individual colors, not just as black; what seemed to be light neutrals are revealed in all of their nuance and tints. Saturated colors continue to attract our attention, but they are playing nicely with their neighbors. Relationships are harmonious and pleasing. When you have a tricky bright color that seems to pop, you can simply move it along the board: at one end, it is definitely too light, at the other end, it is too heavy. Eventually we find the appropriate place for it to sit. It isn't a shy wallflower, so we will still see it, but it isn't popping like it did when it was out of place.

The same colors, placed in a weight-derived gradation.

Again:
To make a pattern story, choose colors of contrasting weight.
To make a color story, choose colors of similar weight.
Keep it simple: adopting the above as your color mantra will go a long way toward guiding you to appropriate yarn selection.

Dyeing styles and their effect on patterns

Each dyer has many facets to control. They must choose the initial fiber and skein size (both circumference and net weight), type of dye, number of colors, order of colors, style of dyeing…the list goes on. Each selection then affects the fabric's final appearance. Let's look at some of the initial choices and their effects:

Fiber Hand dyers can comfortably and safely dye a wide range of fiber types in their studios. Polyester and acrylic are typically dyed only by industrial mills because the chemicals are strong and require special equipment and handling, but animal fibers (wool, mohair, alpaca, camel, llama, angora, etc.), cellulose fibers (cotton, rayon, bamboo, Tencel®, corn, soy, etc.), silk, and nylon are all easily dyed and are, therefore, fair game. Cotton tends to absorb dye with less vibrancy than other fibers, but mercerized cotton (cotton that has been treated with lye for strength and sheen) is more vibrant than raw cotton. Fibers can be matte or shiny, and this also can affect how a color reads. Dye type, too, can affect vibrancy.

Skein circumference determines the repeat—how many stitches will be worked before the same sequence of colors begins again. Repeat determines how a yarn will appear when knit or crocheted. As skein circumference increases, more stitches will occur within a repeat. This is a neutral factor, neither good nor bad, but necessary to know for planning.

Skein net weight determines how much yarn is in a given dye skein. Many dyers dye pre-wound skeins and do not rewind before selling them. These skeins are the easiest to read—you can see which colors are next to one another and can also tell how the skein was dyed. Others dye large dye skeins and then rewind to smaller skeins, usually at a different circumference, causing colors to intermingle and give an idea of how they might look when knit or crocheted. In either case, there may be color variation within the same dye lot, as strands deep within a skein may not have as much dye penetration as strands on the outside.

Type of dye There are several that are most often used by hand dyers.

Direct dyes, such as those available in the grocery store, dye most fibers but are not particularly light- or wash-fast. Direct dyeing produces a mechanical bond between dye molecule and fiber molecule, and that bond is easily broken. Food coloring, often used by home dyers for fun, is a direct dye.

Fiber-reactive dyes are most often used for cellulose fibers and silk. There are several brands available, and dyers make selections based on their particular process and choice of colors. Fiber-reactive dyes are superior to direct dyes for light- and wash-fastness. A chemical reaction takes place through the addition of an alkali such as washing soda, forming a chemical bond between dye and fiber molecules that is less easily broken than a mechanical bond. Heat is generally required to set the dyes, either by using a hot-water dye bath or by steaming the dyed skeins.

Acid dyes are similar to fiber-reactive dyes but are formulated for animal fibers, silk, and nylon. The reaction occurs through the addition of a weak acid (acetic or citric) to the dye bath. Animal fibers can also be dyed with fiber-reactive dyes in an acidic bath. Heat is required to set these dyes.

Natural dyes derive from plants, invertebrates, or minerals, whose colors are teased out through the addition of chemicals (mordants) specific to the dyestuff. They produce lovely, subtle colors but are more labor intensive, have more variables, and are often less light- or wash-fast than synthetic dyes.

Vat dyes are related to fiber-reactive dyes but have a more complicated process and so are rarely used by production hand-dyers. They require a chemical agent to become soluble in a reduced (oxygen-free) form. Fiber is immersed repeatedly into an oxygen-free dye bath and then exposed to air, whereupon the reduced form changes color as oxygen interacts with it. Indigo is an example of this dye class—it changes from yellow in the dye bath to green and then to blue as it is allowed to sit in the air. Some vat dyes use light rather than oxygen to effect this change.

Selection of color is the most personal aspect of hand-dyed yarns and the dominant factor that sets dyers apart from one another. Not only does each dyer consider the beauty of a particular combination, but we pay special attention to colors that will maintain their integrity during the dyeing process — you can't include a color that will contaminate others when washing out, for instance. The order of color placement is also critical — regardless of dyeing style, there will be an overlap where one color meets another, which becomes…yet another color.

Repeats Equipment available for winding skeins is only made by a few manufacturers. The circumference of a dye skein typically ranges from 42" to about 72". Some specialized equipment exists that produces much larger skeins and thus longer repeats; dyers employing these winders generally state that fact as part of the marketing effort for their yarn. Yarn is plastic — no, not synthetic, but not hard like metal or stone. Therefore, yarn wound into a dye skein under tension will probably not stay the same size when dyed, washed and dried. Twist, fiber content, prior handling, steam finishing — any and all of these factors will affect the difference between the original circumference and the actual finished circumference of a dye skein.

So why does it matter? You can't base calculations on an **original** dye skein measurement. Prism has one yarn with such an energetic twist that it shrinks from 72" to 64" after dyeing. That final measurement is the repeat, and the repeat will determine the Magic Number and everything about how the colors will look when knit or crocheted. If you choose to experiment with your own dyeing, make sure you know how the final yarn will behave.

Crocking is a term that refers to excess dye that has not been properly set. It happens occasionally to most dyers, usually with dark colors on protein fibers (particularly superwash wools), and generally can't be removed by simple washing. Crocking is noticed while stitching, as the friction of yarn passing through fingers causes dye to transfer to hands, needles, or hooks. If crocking is severe, dye might also come off onto clothing when the garment is worn, so the yarn should be set before wearing. Setting involves using a mild ammonia bath (half a cup of ammonia diluted in 2–3 gallons of water) to loosen the excess dye. Allow the yarn to soak for 10 or 15 minutes, then wash in mild soap to remove the ammonia. A cup of vinegar in the rinse water will restore the proper pH to the treated yarn.

Different skein circumferences = different repeats.

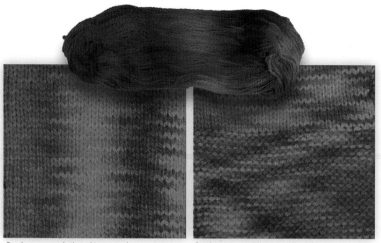

Dyed-across stacked stockinette and garter on half the Magic Number.

Dyed-across argyle garter and stockinette on half the Magic Number.

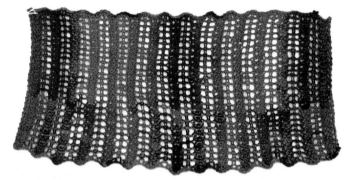

Dyed-across colors on top of swatch started at one edge of the skein, so colors are stacking in clean columns. Colors on bottom third are staggered every other row as this portion was begun in a different place in the skein. This is a full Magic Number.

Dyeing across the skein is the most common style. Dye skeins are laid flat, and then dye is applied across multiple skeins using a variety of methods unique to each dyer. The size of each color can vary, as can the number of colors applied. Color runs tend to be shorter than in dyed-around skeins, in turn leading to less striping when worked. Dyed-across skeins typically have one color at each end, with all other colors appearing twice on the skein. Sometimes colors will be repeated, so a color may appear three or more times. If your work begins in the middle of an end color, dyed-across skeins stack in clean vertical columns; begin at another spot and the colors will stack in an every-other-row manner, producing vertical stacks of color that are optically blended within each column. Complex argyles occur on a stitch count that is 1 or 2 off from the Magic Number; these argyles have both large diamonds formed by the single end colors and smaller diamonds formed by the center colors which appear twice in each skein.

Because dyed-across skeins are symmetrical from side to side, the appearance on a full or half Magic Number is essentially the same. You can think of the repeat as beginning in the center of one side color and ending in the center of the other side color. If a dyed-across skein varies much from one side to the other, as often happens, the total circumference (the full Magic Number) should be treated as the repeat.

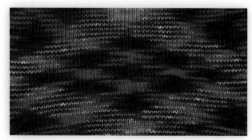

Dyed-across argyle on full Magic Number.

Notice that the end colors, gold and brown, appear once while plum and orange appear twice. Brown and plum are very close in weight, so read as the same.

Myriad styles of dyeing exist,
  with many different ways to apply dye.

Dyed-around full argyle. Each of the 4 colors takes a turn as a solid center diamond, with all 3 diamonds composed of every-other-row blending.

Dyed-around half argyle is essentially the full argyle cut in half vertically. The diamonds appear slightly taller, and the solid colors congregate at the sides instead of the middle.

Dyeing around the skein (also known as **dip-dyeing**). Skeins are suspended in a dye bath for the required length of time, then removed, turned, and immersed into the next color. Each color appears only once on the skein. Color runs tend to be longer, producing fabrics with more striping. Worked circularly, dyed-around skeins stack in clean vertical columns, as dyed-across skeins do. Worked flat, however, they produce stacks where some columns blend in every-other-row stripes. Argyles appear with symmetrical diamonds, as each color occurs the same number of times, often in the same size.

Dyed-around skeins create stacks where some columns are staggered with every-other-row stripes, while others are solid. From a distance, these stripes form optical mixtures and read as one color.

Stacked colors in double crochet, dyed-around skein. Colors stack every other row. Since double crochet stitches are taller than knit stitches, the colors are much less likely to optically mix, and the resulting pattern is more complex in its color interaction.

Each style has its attributes and its drawbacks.

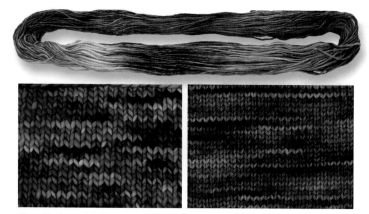

Hand-painted skeins often begin life as dyed-across skeins, where some amount of dye is applied as a ground. More colors are added in much smaller bursts that do not necessarily carry through all adjacent strands of the skein — there are often paint-brush-sized dots of color. Hand-painted skeins have many more colors within each skein, and since the color is not consistent across every thread, they will not reliably stack or pattern. Some minor pooling can occur, but rarely stripes or argyles. A lot of optical mixture is present, and colors may get muddy as color is applied on top of color. Great skill is required to cover all of the white yarn and still maintain the integrity of the color intention.

Magic Number—slight diagonals can barely be detected.

Kettle-dyed, sandwashed solids.

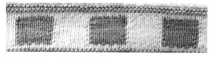

Kettle-dyed, sandwashed solids.

Sandwashed solid squares more closely match hand-dyed colors than a factory-dyed yarn would.

Kettle-dyeing or sandwashing While "kettle" generally refers to a dye pot into which yarn is placed, in hand dyeing it applies to skeins that have been fully submersed in a dye bath. Depending on specific choices that are made by the dyer, streaking and uneven tones are often encouraged, producing distinctive tonal semi-solids that are beautiful in their own right, and are very useful for combining with multi-colors. When worked, the fabric most closely resembles sueded or sandwashed woven fabrics. Some dyers use multiple baths of different colors to create subtle layered effects. Kettle-dyed yarns are easy to coordinate with ready-to-wear separates, since an exact shade needn't be matched. They also pair beautifully with multicolor hand dyes, and most dyers offer both types of colors for this very reason.

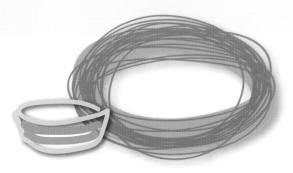

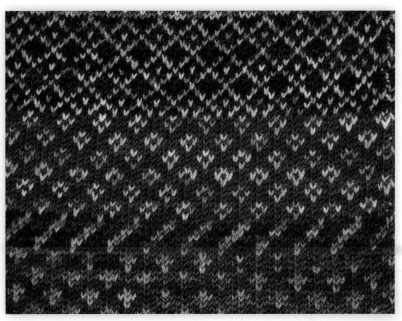

Layered colors (also known as **glazed** colors) are related to sandwashed solids. Instead of tonal variations of one color, however, more than one color is layered onto the entire dye skein, creating sophisticated, nuanced shades of each parent color and all of the combinations between them.

Layered colors are more complex then sandwashed solids, yet still read as mostly monotone.

Layered colors are a good background for Fair Isle, where the soft tonal variations add depth.

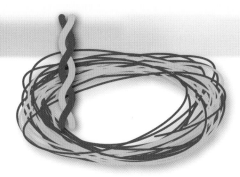

Double-dyed skeins.

Double-dyed rayon and kid mohair in Fisherman's Rib scarf—each element patterns separately, creating more complexity.

Double dyes This sub-class involves combining two separately dyed elements. Within any of the styles above, a dyer may choose to combine two or more strands of dyed yarn into a single entity. This may be done by dyeing 2 singles that are then plied together, such as Mountain Colors River Twist, or that are loosely twisted, such as Prism Kid Slique. Another method involves yarns that are mill-spun with cellulose and protein or nylon elements; since each fiber requires its own dye type, two colors can appear side-by-side on a strand as they are dyed with their respective dye type and remain unaffected by each other's bath. In any case, the colors are more optically mixed and muted, with fewer stripes and blotches. Depending on the dyeing method, however, stacks or argyles can sometimes still be attained.

Two plies that have been dyed first and then twisted together. Where colors align, we see more regular striping as at bottom. Where plies are offset, the appearance is tweedy, as at top.

How do I tell?

If a skein of yarn has been rewound, it is more difficult to determine the exact method of dyeing. There are clues, however, that lead us to some pretty good guesses. If there are small bits of color noticeable on each strand, it probably is a hand-painted skein and will not pattern. If you can see more than one color on the same place in a strand, it is probably a double-dye. If there seem to be fairly long runs of color—at least several inches—then it was most likely dyed either across or around the skein. Look also for how many colors are apparent—more colors tend to suggest dyed-across or hand-painted. You can also ask the dyer, if they are present. Tell them why you want to know, so they don't think you are stealing secrets, and I suspect most would be happy to share with you.

Each dyer chooses a dyeing style based on their vision and the finished effects most important to them.

Dyed-across skeins have shorter runs of color, and thus can have more colors in each skein. They stripe less frequently and with shorter color runs but may still blotch, pool, and pattern. They stack easily and cleanly on either full or half Magic Numbers. Argyles are complex. Consistency in size of each color may vary within a skein and from dye lot to dye lot.

Dyed-around skeins have longer runs of colors, and thus usually fewer colors. They tend to stripe, pool, and pattern. The colors are very clear and repeatable, with crisp edges and consistent lengths of each color. They stack with every-other-row stripes, and produce the crispest argyles.

Hand-painted skeins contain many colors and work up with little patterning or striping, but can vary radically from skein to skein and even within a single skein.

Kettle-dyed and layered colors can vary from the inside to the outside of a single skein or, based on position in the dye pot, from skein to skein.

No one method is foolproof in producing totally consistent, even skeins. Each style has its strong points and its weaknesses.

Dyed-across skeins have both short and long runs, often of many colors.

Dyed-around skeins have long runs of fewer colors.

Hand-painted skeins have shorter runs of many colors, and some colors that are almost never there, such as the orange in the skein to the left.

Kettle-dyed colors, top, have light and dark variations in one hue. Layered colors, bottom, have tonal variations of more than one color.

Patterning versus randomizing

Effects such as pooling, striping, stacking, and patterning can become vexing when not planned for. Hand-dyed yarns will do what they will do, and pooling, striping, stacking, and patterning are natural results as stitches are formed. We can't change the essential nature of a hand-dyed yarn: my parents could have spent a fortune on voice lessons, but I would never have become a singer! Knowing how a yarn has been dyed, singling out the specific colors within a skein, swatching with intent, observing color behavior, and most of all, *having a game plan* will all lead to a successful project, whether you choose to exploit the built-in patterning or mask it. The following chapters detail many different approaches, both to intentionally pattern and to randomize. The beauty is that the choice is yours. Never again do you need to experience disappointing results!

Dye-lot and skein variations It is the nature of the beast: almost all hand-dyed yarns have variations from skein to skein, and certainly from dye lot to dye lot. Rather than considering this a negative, let's accept it as fact—it's the price we must pay for all of that beauty. But rather than accept an abrupt change in the middle of a project, let's look at some strategies for neutralizing the effect, whatever the style of dyeing and whether you are intentionally patterning or randomizing.

• Always lay out all skeins for a project in good light and take a close look. If you can see any differences in light and dark or color intensity, or you notice a more dominant color in one skein than another, you need to take action. Divide the skeins into groups that are most alike. Make a game plan based on what your intended project is.

• Wind the skeins, making sure that the colors are going in the same direction. This is not as important in dyed-across skeins (where the colors are symmetrical) as it is in dyed-around skeins (where the colors have a specific order). If the skeins are not in the original dye skein, simply follow a strand for a few yards, noting the sequence of colors. When winding the next skein, begin with the end that maintains the same color sequence. This is crucial if you are patterning in any way, less important if you are not.

• For projects using a single yarn, whether intentionally patterned or randomized, alternate two rows each from the most highly varied skeins as you work, blending the differences throughout the fabric. Contrary to popular lore, this will not reduce patterning, pooling, or striping. Remember, the repeat for those skeins is essentially the same, so the colors will repeat at the same rate. Even if you are intentionally patterning, as long as the skeins begin in the same place, they will act the same in each row, but the variance in color will be blended and, therefore, less noticeable. If you are striving to randomize, start the second skein in a different place to encourage even more randomization.

• Alternatively, if differences are subtle, finish one skein by simply alternating two rows each from the old and new skeins for an inch or two, so there isn't an abrupt change.

If your project includes other colors, solids, or pattern stitches, the differences in skeins won't be as prominent, but it is still worth having a look. Better to spend a little extra time up front than to have unfortunate surprises later.

Magic numbers

HARNESSING REPEATS FOR SELF-PATTERNS

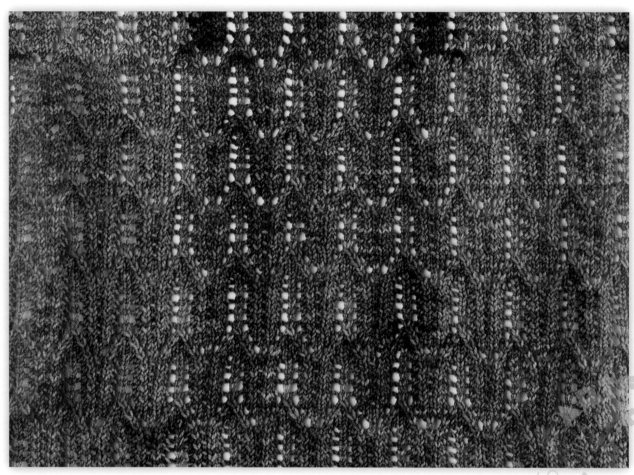

*Dyed-around skeins stack with some columns
mixing colors in every other row.*

3-color

4-color

5-color; all dyed-around skeins, same yarn, same stitch count.

Another notable V8 moment came in the early days of Prism, way back in '85, when I was designing with mohair and observed that a circularly worked turtleneck produced a noticeable spiral as the colors stacked. That first piece was entirely fortuitous, but it started a journey of inquiry. I now know how to reliably make colors stack, flash, or argyle, and you are about to know, too.

Stacks of color are simply the result of a Magic Number that is derived from length of repeat, amount of yarn used for a single stitch, and total number of stitches. That's it: three factors. While dyeing methods cause variations in the appearance of stacks or argyles, a yarn's appearance when stitched still comes back to those same three factors.

Visual variables

As shown earlier, dyeing style determines how stacks or argyles will appear. In addition to style of dyeing (across or around the skein), the number of colors within a skein will affect the final appearance. Here is a series of 3 swatches worked in the same type of yarn on 2 stitches fewer than the Magic Number. All are dyed-around skeins. The first has 3 colors, the next has 4 colors, and the last has 5 colors. You can see that, as the number of colors increases, the argyles become less distinct. The crispest argyle occurs with 3 colors, the argyle is a little less distinct with 4, and even less so with 5. Dyed-across skeins (which often have even more colors) produce argyles that appear less and less distinct. On the other hand, stacks are much clearer from dyed-across skeins, where each color, no matter how many there are, can stack upon itself. Dyed-around skeins may have some colors stacking upon themselves, but others will appear as every-other-row columns.

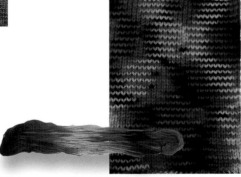

Dyed-across skeins have more complex argyles; in this half-argyle, within the larger movement of pink and brown there are 2 diagonals each of cream and olive.

Dyed-across skeins stack with clean pure columns of color.

For any type of yarn, the best way to measure the repeat is on 8-10 reconstructed loops.

Note *No matter how accurately you measure, there will always be some variations since yarn is…well…plastic. The measurement can vary from the inside to the outside of a dye skein. Picture yarn being wound around rigid arms—as the yarn piles up, strands on the outside are marginally longer than those on the inside — or, as tension increases, the outside strands might actually become shorter. And during the dye process, strands can move. A little movement is not an insurmountable problem, as adjustments can be made during knitting or crocheting. For these reasons, however, I recommend that a measurement be taken over an average number of strands, either from the original dye skein or from 8–10 reconstructed loops. It can actually be easier and more accurate to work on reconstructed loops even for a skein in its original condition, as the larger the group of yarn strands, the harder it is to decide on an average size; often there is just too much volume of yarn in a dye skein.*

Determine the repeat

A repeat is simply the measurement between when a color sequence begins, and when it occurs again. It is the same as circumference. Skeins that have not been re-wound show clearly how dye has been applied, and the repeat seems relatively easy to determine (simply measure the skein), however, it can be difficult to decide exactly where to measure. For the steps that follow, I recommend working on a white fabric surface (or a black one if your colors are very dark—they will be easier to see). The fabric allows the dye skeins or loops of yarn to be stretched and then released, providing a bit of drag so they don't spring back into a less than straight line. Measurements should be taken with the skein or loops as straight as possible, as any curves will distort the final measurement.

Recreating the color repeat

1 Wind the skein into a ball and then work from the outside of the ball; the inside will acquire some crimp that can distort measurements.

2 Identify one color to track—the most noticeable color of the group.

3 Holding the yarn in your hand, wind loops that hang down, aligning the selected color and paying attention to the cleanest color break. Don't worry about the other colors—where one color goes the others will follow—although you must make sure that the color selected is either unique to the skein (appearing only once) or that you are catching the full repeat. If it occurs more than once, make sure all of the colors align.

I recommend working on a fabric surface (beds are perfect for this; plain-colored sheets are helpful). The fabric provides a bit of drag so that, when the dye skeins or loops of yarn are stretched and then released in Step 5, they won't spring back into a less-than-straight line, which might happen on a slippery surface. The loops should be as straight as possible, as any curves will distort the final measurement.

4 When you have 6–8 loops, lay them on a flat, cloth-covered surface. If the yarn is dark, try a dark fabric; if light, on white—remember, contrasting edges make it harder to see the interior colors.

Lay the loops down to measure. Identify a clean color break--in this case, where olive meets pink.

5 Now stretch the loops as straight as possible, then release, allowing them to relax, and take a measurement of the average from one end to the other. Double this number to get the skein circumference.
This circumference is the **repeat length**.

6 Determine how the colors read: **across** or **around** the skein.

Align colors of dyed-across skein in back and forth loops. Measure the average. Place locking stitch markers or pins in the middle of each side color.

7 If across, locate the 2 end colors, and mark the center of each strand with locking stitch markers or pins, inserted directly through the plies of the yarn.

Determine Your Magic Number

We have now identified the style of dyeing that was done to our skein and the length of its repeat. The next step is to determine your Magic Number, and there are several ways to accomplish this. Our minds can work in astonishingly different ways, so I will describe the 3 most common ways of finding the Magic Number. You may then select the method that appeals to you the most. For learning purposes, we'll stick to stockinette, garter stitch, or single crochet. In every case, identify a target color—something that is most easily recognizable, probably the same color that helped you measure the repeat.

Doing the math

Color repeat = _____ " (A)
See page 25.

From marker
to stitch   =   _____ " (B)

B ÷ 20 =   _____ " (C)
Yarn per stitch:
Do not round.

A ÷ C =   _____
Your Magic Number:
Round to nearest whole number.

Mathematical method

This must be done in one sitting, as the yarn will crimp if allowed to stay in the swatch, which will then skew your measurements.

1 **Work a swatch on 20 stitches for at least 8 or 10 rows.** It is important to get away from the cast-on, as your knitting will change as you relax into it. It's always easier to knit on fabric that already exists, rather than onto those first few rows. Crochet can be checked after 4–6 rows.

2 With a locking stitch marker or safety pin, **mark exactly where the working yarn exits the last stitch** by inserting the marker through the plies of the yarn. Now **pull out 1 row**. This is best done by unknitting each stitch, as it is almost impossible to pull out the last stitch of a row without also pulling out the first stitch of the next row. In crochet, simply go very slowly and carefully on the last couple of stitches.

3 Lay this length of yarn onto fabric (as you did for the loops), patting it out as straight as possible but without holding it under tension. Measure from the marker to where the yarn exits the stitch on the needle, and record the measurement. This is how much yarn it took to make 20 stitches. Turn any fractions into decimals. My sample was 19.25". See note about tension (page 30) as this step might have to be performed over both a knit row and a purl row.

4 **Divide this measurement by 20. This is the amount of yarn needed to make 1 stitch.** Record this. My sample was .9625; again, keep the fractions at this point.

To determine your Magic Number Divide the length of the yarn's color repeat (the measurement recorded in Step 5 on (page 25), by the amount of yarn needed to make 1 stitch (Step 4, above). Round to the nearest whole number, as we will now be dealing with stitches. Record it. 52" ÷ .9625 = 54.02597. Now round to the nearest whole number: 54.
This is our Magic Number, the number of stitches needed to make the colors in this yarn stack in the stitch pattern and on the needle or hook size used for the swatch.

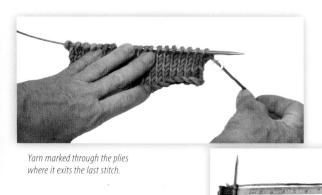

Yarn marked through the plies where it exits the last stitch.

Now un-knit the row. Measure from the marker to where the yarn exits the stitch.

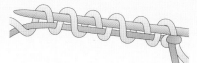

A temporary cast-on

1 Knot working yarn to contrasting waste yarn. Hold needle and knot in right hand. Tension both strands in left hand; separate strands so waste yarn is over index finger, working yarn over thumb. Bring needle between strands and under thumb yarn so working yarn forms a yarn-over in front of waste yarn.

2 Holding both yarns taut, pivot hand toward you, bringing working yarn under and behind waste yarn. Bring needle behind and under working yarn so working yarn forms a yarn-over behind waste yarn.

3 Pivot hand away from you, bringing working yarn under and in front of waste yarn. Bring needle between strands and under working yarn, forming a yarn-over in front of waste yarn. Each yarn-over forms a stitch.

Repeat Steps 2–3 for required number of stitches. For an even number, twist working yarn around waste strand before knitting the first row.

With waste yarn and crochet hook, chain more stitches than you think you need. Cut yarn. With needle and main dyed yarn, pick up and knit 1 stitch in each chain loop to end of repeat.

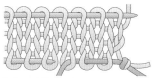

Later, untie knot, remove waste strand of invisible cast-on or unravel chain, and arrange bottom loops on needle.

Note *For either of the next 2 methods, it is very helpful to put a locking stitch marker at the beginning of each color repeat for several repeats (Step 7, page 25). They will alert you that you have begun and then finished a repeat, and make it easier to check the next one. In addition, whenever you begin a new patterned project, whether it is stacked or argyled, having the first few repeats marked will help maintain tension and establish your pattern. Once you have laid out 4–6 loops for measuring, simply place the markers on each loop, rewind the yarn, and begin knitting.*

Counting method

This is a more direct yet equally precise method, but does require concentration.

1 Begin a 20-stitch (or larger) swatch and work 6–8 rows. Now identify a target color and a clean break at the beginning or end of that color. Mark it with a locking stitch marker or safety pin, right through the yarn itself, and mark it again at the end of the repeat. Work to the first marker and begin counting stitches mentally until you arrive at that color again. This number is your Magic Number. The process is most easily done by recording the number of stitches for each row: a partial row as you begin counting, then each full row, then a partial row as you reach the second marker. Trying to count right through as you knit is especially difficult if there are any distractions. Leaving the markers in will let you double check once you are finished.

2 Run through the process once or twice more to make certain you aren't working on an odd strand (one that has been tugged longer or shorter). If you get several close numbers, use the average as a starting point for your Magic Number.

Color-control cast-on method

This method is more visual, but harder to control, and is only recommended if you are comfortable with temporary cast-ons and are a very evenly tensioned knitter (you know who you are).

1 Using any type of temporary cast-on (several are shown here and on page 164), begin to make stitches at the first marker.

2 Cast on until you arrive at that color break once again. Be prepared to pull out and try again or to adjust stitch counts as you swatch, as it can be difficult — but not impossible — to cast on stitches that behave exactly as real stitches will.

3 A simple variation is to use waste yarn to cast on far more stitches than you think you might need. Begin knitting at a marker, and continue to the next marker as above. Now you can simply ignore the remaining waste-yarn stitches, as they will be removed later. Another method is to use the long-tail loop cast-on to cast on more stitches than you think you might need and get rid of the extras later. With this loop cast-on it is also easy to add to the cast-on if you need more stitches.

Note *If you use a temporary cast-on, you will need to remove the waste yarn and bind off the exposed loops.*

Crochet

If you wish to crochet, you can use any of these methods to determine a Magic Number. The easiest way is simply to make a long chain, begin working single crochet at your marked color, and continue until you arrive at that same color break again. The number of single crochets is your Magic Number.

The green on the needle is just slightly to the left of the green two rows below, so this should argyle naturally.

You can see the diagonal movement of the fuchsia.

As knitting continues, the fuchsia reaches the side edge and begins moving to the left.

First trial swatch

1 Cast on half the Magic Number and begin working stockinette stitch. Work more than 7 rows, ending with a WS row when the target color is on the needle. Examine the work. Look 2 rows down for the target color. It should be within a stitch or 2 of aligning with the same color on the needle. But...

If the color on the needle is more than 1 or 2 stitches to the right of the color below, try a smaller needle or decrease stitches (you have used too much yarn).

Or...

If the color on the needle is more than 1 or 2 stitches to the left of the color below, try a larger needle or increase stitches (you have not used enough yarn).

2 If necessary, adjust needle size or stitch count and continue for another 6–8 rows. Check alignment again. Adjust or continue. After about 6", you should be able to walk away from the swatch and see distinct diagonal movement of colors. They may reverse direction as well, beginning an argyle. Or, if you are very precise, the colors may be stacking on top of one another. If you wish to make them argyle, increase or decrease 1 stitch.

3 If you are stacking columns of color, or if you wish a very precise argyle, track the obvious color on every row. If you find that a color has moved a bit too much one way or the other, use a blunt-tipped tapestry needle to ease some yarn in whichever direction the color needs to go.

Fuchsia was lining up too much, so a little extra tension was pulled in the middle of the row and eased to the other end. Now the fuchsia is stepping 2 stitches over.

Stacked patterning

DYED-ACROSS SKEIN

Identify the 2 distinct end colors. Mark the middle of each side with locking stitch markers for several repeats.

DYED-AROUND SKEIN

Decide where the selveges will be and mark the edge with locking stitch markers for several repeats.

FOR BOTH
Cast on with a color-control cast-on, page 27.

If using a temporary cast-on, wind off 2 repeats into a butterfly or onto a bobbin and leave attached to the working yarn—it will be used later for the bind-off.

Attach yarn at one marked side edge and begin working, either ribbing or garter. The first row should end at the next marker or within a stitch or two.

Continue to work, paying particular attention to the target color. Your goal is to make the colors line up from row to row. If the colors are off by only 1 or 2 stitches, use a needle tip to tighten or loosen the last few stitches (see box at left for adjustment). On subsequent rows, keep an eye on where the target color is landing and tighten or loosen tension a bit as needed to keep colors aligned.

* **Otto**: on auto-pilot with no need to check colors once they have been selected and swatched to satisfaction.
Mindful: requires some preparation such as finding a Magic Number, and then some attention to color paths as you knit; perhaps checking every few rows.
Attentive: requires both preparation and constant attention to maintain color paths; must check at end of every row.

Auto-pilot, fondly referred to by me as Otto: the tendency that those of us who knit and crochet have of relaxing into our work so much that the lower brain takes over and we lose mindfulness. Otto is not necessarily our friend. For this reason, I suggest doing intentional patterning work when alert and in good light. As soon as I realize I have had to reposition stitches for several rows, I set the work aside in favor of something less demanding. It's always good to have projects that require different levels of concentration.

DYED-ACROSS SKEIN stacks either when knit flat or in the round.

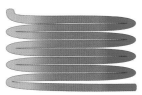 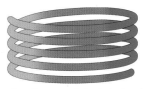

Dyed-across skein, knit flat   *Dyed-across skein, knit circular*

DYED-AROUND skein also stacks either when knit flat or in the round.

When knit flat on Magic Number, colors stack with every-other-row stripes at the sides

When knit in the round, stacks same as dyed-across, but each color appears only once per repeat.

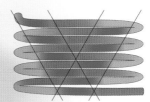 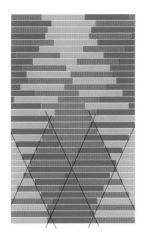

When knit flat on 1 or 2 fewer stitches, all colors move and take turns being solid or striping every-other-row.

Facts about tension

• If your row gauge is bigger (fewer rows per inch than specified), you will use more yarn per stitch, but require fewer rows throughout the project. In general, you will use less yarn. You might find that your garments have less body than desired.

• If your row gauge is smaller (more rows per inch than specified), you will use less yarn per stitch, but require more rows throughout the project. You will use more yarn, and if you are a knitter who is always running out, this is probably why. Your fabric will be firmer.

• Swatch on smaller needles if your rows are loose, or larger needles if your rows are tight. If the stitch gauge changes but the fabric's hand is now more appropriate, simply adjust the stitch count up or down to bring the width to where it should be. It is notable that changing the needle size can often alter row gauge but not stitch gauge, which may stay the same while row gauge tightens or loosens, until eventually the stitch size also changes. In other words, if you immediately get stitch gauge, don't assume that the needle size is correct.

• Look at the purl side of a stockinette swatch. If you see "ditches," then your knit and purl rows are formed under different tensions. Don't try to alter your knitting; simply knit with one size needle and purl with another. This is why a stockinette gauge worked flat often changes when worked circularly: all of the rounds are knit instead of alternating knit rows and purl rows.

Uneven tension results in purl rows being taller than knit rows, with apparent ditches between pairs of rows as a warning sign.

Note about tension
We have all been taught to achieve correct stitch gauge, and rightly so, as this will affect garment size. Yet many have noticed that they are able to match a pattern's stitch gauge but not its row gauge. The biggest difference in tension from knitter to knitter is row gauge. Try as we might, it is very difficult to change our knitting. Instead of struggling and introducing more variables into our work, let's embrace our differences and instead learn how to adjust for them, whatever our knitting project is.

Gauge & size
Before ripping the swatch, take a traditional gauge measurement and record it. While the width of fabric that your Magic Number will produce is hardwired into the skein, knowing the gauge now will let us know what possibilities exist for harnessing this number.

Stitch size can be changed by needle size, but this won't significantly affect the finished width your Magic Number will produce. As stitches get larger, more yarn is used for each stitch, and therefore fewer stitches are required to use the repeat. Conversely, as stitches get smaller, they each use less yarn, but more stitches are needed to use the entire repeat. Changing needle size can make a difference of about an inch of width, but no more. It's best to go for the needle size that produces the nicest fabric and then work from there to find the right stitch count.

By the same token, once a Magic Number is known, we know roughly what stitch count will keep patterning effects from happening. Multiples and even divisions (such as one-half, three-quarters, etc.) of a Magic Number will pattern. While computer-generated charts often show interesting effects at other percentages, those effects show up more cleanly in charts than when knit. It is much harder to control tension and track colors at other percentages.

To avoid patterning, a stitch count should not be near the quarter, half, or whole Magic Number.

Tips for stacking

Few knitters have tension regular enough to stack colors perfectly without some adjustments. While it is possible, and even necessary, to make small adjustments while working, it is critical to get the colors established properly for the first few inches. If the initial row isn't even in tension, you may be trying to force colors into artificial stacks. This can produce some areas of work that are loose and sloppy, and other areas that are too tight. If colors start to drift over several rows, there is no good way to get them back to the correct place. Trying to realign drifted colors can result in the same loose/tight situation. If this begins to happen, rip back to where the color drift began and pay close attention to the next few rows. To assist in setting up the original row correctly, divide the first repeat into quarters, mark each spot with a locking stitch marker through the yarn itself, and make sure that one-quarter of the stitches have been used for each section. While swatching you can record how many stitches are used of each color to assist in distribution.

United we knit

Often, a scarf can be made from 1 skein of yarn; if more skeins are needed, care must be taken when joining a new ball. Intentionally patterned projects also require precise joins. First, make sure that each ball has been wound in the same order (this is most important if working with a dyed-around skein). Next, at the end of the first ball, stop work while there is a full repeat of color remaining. Locate the same color break and order on the new ball — align the old and the new. If the project has seams, move the join to the edge and leave any tails for seaming later. If you are working on a scarf or wrap where ends will be difficult to bury, employ the Fisherman's Knot. This very strong and secure knot allows you to trim the tails as close to the knot as possible, and while it leaves a small bump, there are no pesky tails to hide. The bump disappears into the knitting and can't be detected. Take care to make the knot at a color break to maintain the color repeat as closely as possible. This knot is also great for lace knitting.

Casting on and binding off

If you choose to stack colors, the cast-on becomes critical since you need to begin the first row at a specific place. Whatever type of cast-on you choose, most likely it will use more yarn than a row of stitches, which can throw off carefully planned color placement. For this reason, we can't simply cast on a repeat of color and then begin to work; the cast-on will not have enough stitches to work with the Magic Number. The cast-on which comes closest to actual stitches in yarn usage is the backward-loop cast-on, but it has its own problems with tension, and some knitters find it annoying to work with. I prefer to cast on with waste yarn and then begin at exactly the correct spot. I always leave at least 2 repeat lengths tied in a butterfly at the beginning for use in binding off later, after the scrap yarn is removed. Bound-off edges won't match exactly (if they do, the bind-off is too tight). If the edge is very noticeable, then you can select a decorative bind-off that pulls the colors out of line), or bind off with a coordinating solid (Crème Caramel, page 130). For argyles, it doesn't matter where you begin as each color will move throughout the entire piece, so use any cast-on you prefer. Crocheters: you have it easy—simply chain more stitches than you think you will need and cut off the excess later.

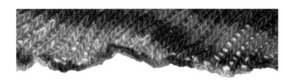

Picot bind-off purposely alters the rate of use on the bound-off edge, allowing a decorative finish that doesn't necessarily match the stacked colors. Firelight cowl, page 156.

Fisherman's knot

Locate joining spot.

1 Overlap ends, aligning in correct color order.

3 Repeat with new yarn around old.

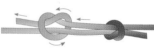

2 Tie old yarn around new with a simple overhand knot (make a loop around new yarn and pull end through) and snug knot as close to joining spot as possible.

4 Pull tightly to set the knot.

5 Trim ends very close—the knot will hold, and although it produces a tiny bump, this can be preferable to ends that pop out.

Take a dip in the pool
Make that Magic Number work for you

I highly recommend a simple scarf as a first intentionally patterned project. It will get you used to tracking colors and adjusting tension to control them. Fisherman's Rib is an easy place to start. A stacked project will require more attention, while an argyle is a bit more forgiving and might therefore be more fun. For any of these approaches, thicker yarns are easiest to learn on as the colors are easier to track and control.

Begin knowing that you may have to start over. From years of experience teaching this technique, I know that in a class of thirty students, three or four will have to drastically alter their Magic Number once they get working. Whether due to inaccuracies in the original calculations or to a change of tension as a stitcher relaxes, adjustments might have to be made. If so, you can change needle size or change the stitch count by casting on or binding off, then continue knitting until the colors work. Once you get a truly accurate stitch count and needle size, you can start over. If everything worked from the beginning, you can simply continue on.

Here are general tips for your first try:

1 Choose a simple stitch pattern. You'll need to concentrate on the colors, and adding the hassle of keeping track of pattern rows can be frustrating.

2 Go through 2 different methods of determining the Magic Number. I suggest using both the mathematical method and the counting method (pages 26-27). They should produce the same results. Doing both is good practice and good insurance—if they are the same, you are good to go; if they are different, try again.

3 Make sure you have identified 1 color to track.

4 Make sure you know what type of dyeing has been done: across the skein or around the skein. It will determine the fabric's appearance and tell you what to expect in tracking the colors.

5 Work a scarf on half the Magic Number as most full numbers are too wide for a scarf.

6 Get used to tracking just 1 color, either the most apparent color if making argyles, or along the edge if stacking. Where 1 color goes, all others follow.

Half Magic scarves

General instructions for knit or crocheted scarves

1 Determine your Magic Number.
2 Using a color-control cast-on (see page 27), cast on half your Magic Number (EXCEPT Surrealist Plaid, where you cast on half minus 1) OR chain half your Magic Number plus 1. **3** Work in stitch pattern. Colors should begin patterning after several rows. **4** If yarn is not patterning, adjust needle size. If scarf uses more than one skein (or if you run into that occasional knot), take care to maintain the color repeat as you join yarns (see Fisherman's Knot, page 31). **5** Work to desired length. **6** Bind off in pattern.

For most scarves you only need half your Magic Number.

A great way to test yarns AND develop your color management skills. Try one or all!

MINDFUL COLOR
EASY KNITTING OR CROCHET

1 See page 164 for abbreviations and techniques. 2 Adjust suggested needle or hook size to make the color repeat work. Gauge is not critical for these scarves.

Argyle Scarf
Colors should line up within a stitch or 2 of the same color 2 rows below. Some variation will occur, with colors reversing direction.

We used 25 stitches (50 was our Magic Number) on a 5mm/H-8 crochet hook and approximately 200 yds in this medium-weight yarn for a 4" x 41" scarf.
Prism Symphony, in color Harvest
DYED-AROUND 64" REPEAT

Crocheted scarves

Crochet also provides a great platform for patterning. Our two Seed Stitch scarves were worked on the same number of stitches, with little attention paid to color alignment in the argyle scarf, and careful attention paid in the stacked scarf. Interestingly enough, the stacked scarf begins with one set of colors stacking in an every-other-row order (since this is a dyed-around skein) and then, just shy of the center back, the colors are allowed to move in a short argyle burst that then realigns the colors for the other end. This was done solely by tightening the stitches ever so slightly through this section, and then resuming the normal gauge for the other side. Seed Stitch is essentially a crochet version of knitted Half Linen Stitch, offering every-other-stitch blending.

Double Crochet also makes patterning easy, and is a nice flexible stitch for a scarf. As always, more attention is needed for stacking, less for an argyle. In either case, crochet can be adjusted simply by pulling a few stitches out and reworking them, with tension a bit tighter or looser as is required for the colors to behave.

We used 25 stitches (50 was our Magic Number) on a 5mm/H-8 crochet hook and approximately 225 yds in this medium-weight yarn for a 4" x 49½" scarf.
Prism Symphony, in color Mohave
DYED-AROUND 64" REPEAT

Stacked Scarf
Attention should be paid to make each stitch line up on top of the same color 2 rows below. You may have to adjust tension slightly as you work to make that happen. In our scarf, we allowed the colors to cross at the halfway point — at the back of neck — so that the other side of the scarf has colors stacking somewhat differently.

CROCHET SEED STITCH
Row 1 Turn and sc in second stitch from hook, (ch 1, skip next stitch, sc in next stitch) 12 times, sc in last stitch — 13 sc stitches; 12 ch-1 spaces.
Row 2 Ch 1, turn; sc in first sc, ch 1, (sc in next ch-1 sp, ch 1), end with sc in last stitch from previous row. Stitch count will remain consistent from row to row.
Repeat Row 2.

Fisherman's Rib scarves

Fisherman's Rib, which is knit in the stitch below, allows either dyed-across or dyed-around skeins to color stack (although somewhat differently). If you are on the correct number of stitches, it doesn't really matter where you start, but you can decide which colors will be on the edge and which in the middle by where you begin the cast-on. You won't really see the colors stacking well for about 4 rows, when you should find that the working-yarn color lines up with the knit-below stitch — but don't pay attention to the purl stitches, as they won't line up; if you get to the working-yarn color too soon, try a smaller needle. If the working-yarn color isn't coming fast enough, go up a needle size. You might have to try a few times to get it right — I suggest you keep going on the original stitches, changing needle size until the repeat patterns, then start over on that needle size.

Spectrum

Kid Slique is a double-dyed yarn, with shiny rayon and kid mohair dyed separately at slightly different repeats. The Magic Numbers are close enough that both strands pattern together with some slight shifting as you work along. Which yarn is more apparent visually is dependent on the particular color, with dominance switching back and forth between the two elements.

Driftwood

This playfully narrow scarf was worked from one skein of dyed-around yarn on a quarter of the Magic Number. Because the number is one quarter instead of one half, the colors stack on every other row of visible knits (really every fourth worked row), yet the patterning is still apparent. Pay attention to colors after a few rows: while there is color gathering and movement, there is also striping within the movement.

We used 27 stitches on 6.5mm/US10½ needles and approximately 250 yds in this bulky-weight yarn for a 8" × 50" scarf.

Prism Kid Slique, in color Harvest
DYED-AROUND DOUBLE-DYE WITH A 68" REPEAT (RAYON) AND 65" REPEAT (KID MOHAIR)

We used 11 stitches on 8mm/US11 needles and approximately 115 yds in this bulky-weight yarn for a 3" × 45" scarf.

Prism Merino 12, in color Playa
DYED-AROUND 52" REPEAT

Rainbow run

With dyed-around yarn and a Half Magic Number, some colors appear on one side, with other colors gathering on the flip side. As they move, they slowly spiral around. Attentively stacked, each side of the scarf would be different, showing only some of the colors.

We used 27 stitches on 6.5mm/US10½ needles and approximately 275 yds in this medium-weight yarn for a 5½" × 50" scarf.
PRISM Indulgence, in color Tahoe
DYED-ACROSS 65" REPEAT

FISHERMAN'S RIB WITH GARTER EDGE
OVER AN ODD NUMBER OF STITCHES
Set-up row [K1, p1] to last stitch, k1.
Row 1 (RS) K1, [**knit 1 in stitch below (k1b), p1**] to last 2 stitches, k1b, k1.
Row 2 (WS) K1, [**p1, k1b**] to last stitch, p1, k1.

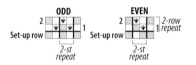

OVER AN EVEN NUMBER OF STITCHES
Set-up row [K1, p1] to last 2 stitches, k2.
Row 1 (RS) K1, [**k1b, p1**] to last stitch, k1.
Row 2 (WS) K1, [**k1b, p1**] to last stitch, k1.

Silver streak

Fisherman's Rib gathers colors in such a way that patterns emerge which might otherwise be lost within the closely weighted colors.

We used 32 stitches on 3.75mm/US5 needles and approximately 425 yds in this fine-weight yarn for a 5" x 63½" scarf.
Prism Saki, in color Denali
DYED-AROUND 48" REPEAT

Columns of color

With a dyed-across yarn, each side of the scarf is the same. If you wish to stack colors, begin at the middle of an end color.

We used 23 stitches on 5.5mm/ US9 needles and approximately 275 yds in this medium-weight yarn for a 5" × 60" scarf.
Schaefer Yarns Miss Priss, in color Irena Sendler
DYED-ACROSS 45" REPEAT

K1, P1 scarves

Ribbing makes fabric that is both flat and condensed, so it is a perfect choice for patterning. A Half Magic Number ribbed scarf is narrower than an equivalent garter scarf, since ribbing pulls in. K1, P1 Rib looks very much like stockinette stitch, allowing color patterns to read well without the added texture of garter ridges.

Autumn argyle

A single skein of dyed-around yarn produces a tidy ascot-style scarf that is a nice width, with easy-to-read argyles. Two skeins would be an extravagant length.

We used 28 stitches on 5.5mm/US9 needles and approximately 170 yds in this bulky-weight yarn for a 3½" × 40" scarf.

Prism Madison, in color Autumn
DYED-AROUND 48" REPEAT

Harvest meanders

Fine yarn and K1, P1 Rib offer a generous scarf with a nice hand. Less-than-careful attention to the color alignment allows the colors to gather and flow in soft meanders: less precise than argyles, but a lovely effect. Ribbing makes a narrower scarf than garter or stockinette, and yet the color reads as cleanly as stockinette would.

We used 54 stitches on 3.25mm/US3 needles and approximately 550 yds in this fine-weight yarn for a 5½" × 73" scarf.

Prism Merino Mia, in color Harvest
DYED-AROUND 60" REPEAT

Syncopation

Simple chevron stitch also allows a scarf to be narrower, which uses less yarn. Since the Half Magic Number is being bent up and down in zigzags, the same number of stitches results in less width. The larger repeat of chevron stitches, however, makes adjusting stitch count to a Magic Number a little trickier. After 6 rows, examine your work for color alignment. Solid colors should be gathering at one side or the other. Isolate one color and track it (where one color goes, all others will follow). If you are off, try a different needle size (see page 28). If you can't make a needle change work, use one of the chevron patterns in a repeat that will most closely match your Magic Number.

We used 39 stitches on 6.5mm/US10½ needles and approximately 350 yds in this medium-weight yarn for a 5" × 68" scarf.

Prism Symphony, in color Portofino *DYED-AROUND, 64" REPEAT*

K1, P1 RIB *OVER AN EVEN NUMBER OF STITCHES*
All rows **[K1, p1]** to end.

K1, P1 RIB *OVER AN ODD NUMBER OF STITCHES*
Row 1 **[K1, p1]** to last stitch, k1.
Row 2 **[P1, k1]** to last stitch, p1.

12-ST CHEVRON *MULTIPLE OF 12 + 3*
Row 1 K1, SSK, **[k9, sl2 tog knitwise-k1-p2sso]** to last 12 stitches, k9, k2tog, k1.
Row 2 K1, **[p1, k4, k1-yo-k1 in next stitch, k4]** to last 2 stitches, p1, k1.

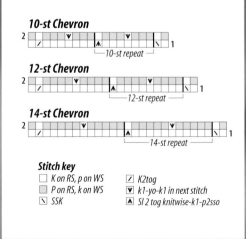

10-st Chevron
└─ 10-st repeat ─┘

12-st Chevron
└─ 12-st repeat ─┘

14-st Chevron
└─ 14-st repeat ─┘

Stitch key
☐ *K on RS, p on WS*
▨ *P on RS, k on WS*
⟍ *SSK*
☑ *K2tog*
▼ *k1-yo-k1 in next stitch*
▲ *Sl 2 tog knitwise-k1-p2sso*

Bias garter scarves

Of course, garter stitch also makes nice flat fabric, but as we have seen, when combined with even a Half Magic Number it can become too wide for a scarf. Another way to narrow the width of a set number of stitches is to work on the bias, simply increasing at one edge and decreasing at the other. Now the row of stitches is pulled onto an angle, so the width of the fabric is smaller.

Surrealist Plaid

One stitch less than a Half Magic Number allows a garter bias scarf to argyle in a most unusual way. Because the stitches are increased at one end and decreased at the other, the dyed-around colors are stretched in one direction and compressed in the other, creating a wacky but intriguing plaid. Check colors after several rows: colors should be roughly stacking but stepping over by 1 or 2 stitches. After 4" or 5", you should be able to see a distinct angular shift.

We used 33 stitches on 3.25mm/US3 needles and approximately 350 yds in this medium-weight yarn for a 5" × 63" scarf.
Prism Symphony, in color Maui
DYED-AROUND 64" REPEAT

Sonnet

Here, dyed-around yarn worked on the bias in garter stitch on a Half Magic Number offers a nicely sized scarf with subtle every-other-row color stacks. Attention was paid to stacking the colors along one edge. Remember, where one color goes, all other colors follow.

We used 54 stitches on 3.25mm/US3 needles and approximately 375 yds in this fine-weight yarn for a 4½" × 70" scarf.
Prism Merino Mia, in color Sagebrush *DYED-AROUND 60" REPEAT*

BIAS GARTER
Row 1 Knit into front and back of first stitch (kf&b), knit to last 2 stitches, k2tog.
Row 2 Knit.

Beyond scarves

If you are intrigued, though, soon you will want to do more than just scarves and wraps. There are lots of options for stunning results designed specifically with Magic Numbers in mind. I have explored many styles that combine rectangles into garments. These garments, while shown in a specific yarn, are easily adapted to other yarns with different Magic Numbers. They tend to be boxy and oversized, allowing you to work an alternate yarn on a different number of stitches and still be successful (and within a few inches of size). These basic shapes translate easily into crochet pieces and readily adapt to different pattern stitches. The oversized approach allows a variety of body shapes and sizes to wear the same garment. Basic shapes have been interpreted in multiple ways, proving that you are only limited by your imagination.

Magic Numbers and size

Magic Numbers and the size they produce are essentially carved in stone. We can change the needle or hook size to change the stitch gauge, but since larger stitches use more yarn and smaller stitches use less yarn, their respective Magic Numbers go down or up accordingly. The end result is a basic size that is hardwired into any given skein. Using partial Magic Numbers can produce interesting results, but so can altering how stitches are used, or designing specifically with a Magic Number and its size in mind. The following projects use basic stockinette or garter stitch, and capture the magic of that number in a variety of ways.

Woodlands flash

Flash knitting is a variation of stacking, and is therefore dependent on a Magic Number. Rather than stacking attentively, normal tension and skein variations cause the colors to flash back and forth in a zigzag. You may increase or decrease a stitch occasionally to reinforce the effect — doing so can manipulate the flash by an inch or so. Fewer stitches will skew the flash to the left in a spiral; more stitches will skew to the right. For larger sizes, work the armhole steek all the way to the bottom, and add side gussets for extended width.

Siren's song

Stacks and argyles unite in a tunic composed of multiple vertical panels. Half Magic Numbers are employed, with 1 fewer stitch causing argyles instead of stacks. Break up the attentive knitting required for stacked panels with more relaxed, mindful argyles. Because the tunic is oversized, many different yarns can be substituted with minimal variations in finished size.

Winter snow

Circular stacks on 3 times the Magic Number of a dyed-around yarn create wavering vertical columns reminiscent of ikat weaving. The circular knitting is then steeked for armholes and front openings. Sandwashed solids echo the hand-dyed multicolors for trim.

Siren's song

INTERMEDIATE KNITTING

ATTENTIVE COLOR

WHAT'S THE MAGIC?

*Stack dyed-across 45"
repeat on Half Magic
Number. Argyle over Half
Magic Number minus 1.*

*1 See page 164 for abbreviations and
techniques AND page 26 for Magic
Number. 2 Use color-control cast-on (see
page 27). 3 Poncho is made up of strips
that are joined together by picking up
stitches, then working 3-needle bind-off.
4 The strips that use half your Magic
Number create a stacked pattern. The
strips that use Half Magic Number minus
1 create an argyle pattern. 5 Start each
strip at the same place in the color repeat.*

***Notes for all strips 1** Use circular
needles and MC.* ***2** Check color stacking
after first 10 rows. Make any necessary
adjustments.* ***3** Start each strip at the
same place in the color repeat.*

DEC 1
At beginning of RS rows K1, k2tog.
At end of RS rows SSK, k1.

---

*SCHAEFER YARNS Miss Priss in color
Tatiana Proskouriakoff (MC); Elaine in
color Tatiana Proskouriakoff (CC)*

---

*Dyed-across yarn creates Half-Magic-Number panels that are either stacked with
mindfulness or reduced by 1 stitch and allowed to argyle. A great detail is the
short-row-enhanced 3-needle bind-off joining the panels. This technique allows the
panels to hang and behave as if they were knitted seamlessly, and adds a touch of
whimsy. Add to the mix a different texture in the same colors, carried from seams to
cowl to sleeve edging. Schaefer Yarns are no longer being produced, so you might
not be able to find this exact yarn. The following pages offer a case study in yarn
substitution; the principles can be applied to any pattern in this book.*

Determine your Magic Number.
Stacked Strips 1, 3, 5, and 8
Cast on half your Magic Number (we cast on 30). Knit 10 rows, then follow diagram until piece
measures 28". Bind off.

Argyle Strips 2 and 4
Cast on half your Magic Number minus 1 (we cast on 29). Continue as for Stacked Strips.

Argyle Strip 6
Work as for Argyle Strips until piece measures 24", end with a WS row.
Shape neck
Color note *Patterning cannot be maintained during neck shaping.*
At beginning of RS rows, bind off 12 once, 3 once, then 2 once. Dec 1 at beginning of every RS row 2
times — 19 stitches decreased. Work even until piece measures 28". Bind off.

Stacked Strip 7
Work as for Stacked Strips until piece measures 24", end with a RS row.
Shape neck
Continue as for Argyle Strip 6 EXCEPT reverse neck shaping. Bind off at beginning of WS rows and
decrease at end of RS rows.

Assembly
Note 1 *Use 4.5mm/US7 circular needle and CC unless otherwise indicated.* ***2** Pick up all
stitches with RS facing.* ***3** Suggested pick-up rate: 2 stitches for every 3 rows along vertical
stockinette edges, 1 stitch for every ridge along vertical garter edges, and 1 stitch in every
bound-off stitch. Embellished row is a multiple of 12 for strips, or 12+6 for shoulders and sides;
work any additional stitches in garter stitch.* ***4** Slip stitches purlwise with yarn at front.*

ONE SIZE
A 52"
B 28"
C 21"

10cm/4"

18 stitches and **26
rows** over stockinette
stitch; **18 stitches** and
36 rows over garter
stitch, using **4.5mm/
US 7 needles**

Medium weight
MC 1300 yds

Bulky weight
CC 400 yds

2 sizes smaller
AND
1 size larger

two **4.5mm/US7** or
size to make color
repeat work AND
second needle for
assembly, 80cm/20"
or longer

stitch markers

Stacked Strips

Cast on ½ your Magic Number and work as follows:

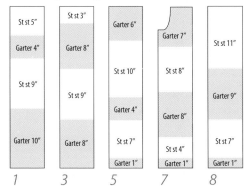

1	**3**	**5**	**7**	**8**
St st 5"	St st 3"	Garter 6"	Garter 7"	St st 11"
Garter 4"	Garter 8"	St st 10"	St st 8"	
St st 9"	St st 9"	Garter 4"	Garter 8"	Garter 9"
Garter 10"	Garter 8"	St st 7"	St st 4"	St st 7"
		Garter 1"	Garter 1"	Garter 1"

Argyle Strips

Cast on ½ your Magic Number minus 1 and work as follows:

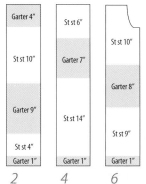

2	**4**	**6**
Garter 4"	St st 6"	St st 10"
St st 10"	Garter 7"	Garter 8"
Garter 9"	St st 14"	Garter 8"
St st 4"		St st 9"
Garter 1"	Garter 1"	Garter 1"

Stitch Key
☐ Stockinette stitch (St st)
▨ Garter

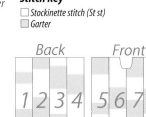

Back — 1 2 3 4 Front — 5 6 7 8

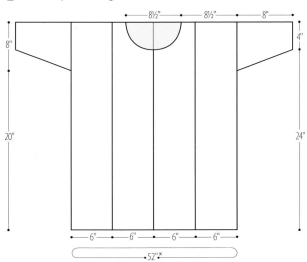

8½" — 8½" — 8"

8"   4"

20"   24"

6" — 6" — 6" — 6"

52".*

*each join adds ½" to circumference
Approximate measurements with piece held upright

Back

Join Strips

Join 1 and 2 Beginning at cast-on edge, pick up and knit (PUK) 120 along side of Strip 1. *Embellishment row* K11, **[turn work; sl 1, k3, turn; p4, k12]** to last stitch, turn; sl 1 wyif, k3, turn; p4, k1. Break yarn and set aside. With second circular needle and beginning at bound-off edge of Strip 2, PUK as for Strip 1. With RS together, join strips using 3-needle bind-off.

Join 2 and 3 PUK as for Strip 1, beginning at cast-on edge of Strip 2. *Embellishment row* K5, **[turn work; sl 1, k3, turn; p4, k12]** to last 7 stitches, turn; sl 1, k3, turn; p4, k7. Break yarn and set aside. With second circular needle and beginning at bound-off edge of Strip 3, PUK as for Strip 1. With RS together, join strips using 3-needle bind-off.

Join 3 and 4 PUK and join as for Strips 1 and 2.

Front

Join Strips PUK and join Strips 5–8 as for Strips 1–4 EXCEPT when joining 6 and 7, begin Strip 7 at beginning of neck shaping.

Finishing

Join left shoulder PUK42 along bound-off edge of left front shoulder.
Embellishment row K9, **[turn; sl 1, k3, turn; p4, k12]** to last 9 stitches, turn; sl 1 wyif, k3, turn; p4, k9. Break yarn.

With second circular needle, PUK124 along bound-off edge of Back. Count front shoulder stitches, then place markers at matching points on back shoulders. With RS together, join shoulders using 3-needle bind-off as follows: Join stitches of first shoulder, break yarn. Place 40 back neck stitches on hold. Place remaining Back shoulder stitches on hold.

Collar With smaller needle and RS facing, knit 40 stitches from back neck holder, PUK60 around front neck — 100 stitches. Do not join. Knit 3 rows. *Next row* Knit, decreasing 4 stitches evenly spaced across each front panel — 92 stitches. Knit 11 rows. Change to larger needle and knit until Collar measures 8". Bind off. Join right shoulder.

Cuffs On each side edge, mark 8" down from shoulder seam on Front and Back. With circular needle, PUK60 between markers. Work in garter and AT SAME TIME, Dec 1 each side every RS row for 8", end with a RS row. Bind off. Repeat for other side.

Join strips 4 and 5 Beginning at cast-on edge of Strip 4, PUK102 to cuff. *Embellishment row* K5, **[turn work; sl 1, k3, turn; p4, k12]** to last stitch, turn; sl 1, k3, turn; p4, k1. Break yarn and set aside. Beginning where cuff starts on Strip 5, PUK as for Strip 4. With RS together, join strips using 3-needle bind-off.

Strips 8 and 1

PUK and join Strips 8 and 1.

Sew Cuff and Collar seams.

Case study

As this book was going to press we learned that long-time hand-dyer Cheryl Schaefer was closing her business. For many other books with knitting patterns, this might be devastating news. For us, it presented an opportunity to show how adaptable the patterns in this book are.

Siren's Song is an oversized poncho-style tunic composed of multiple 6½"-wide panels. Some panels are carefully stacked, while others work on 1 stitch fewer and are allowed to argyle. Most of the work is in stockinette, but areas of garter stitch are interspersed for a visual change of pace, and also to illustrate that patterning is not dependent on pattern stitch, but on Magic Numbers and tension.

Four strips times 6½" gives a total width of about 26", for a 52"-circumference tunic. I swatched 4 other yarns as possible alternatives and each would give a slightly different look and feel to a finished piece.

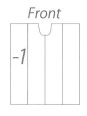

Front

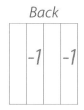

Back

Panels for Siren Song are knit in Half Magic Number (5 panels), or on Half Magic Number minus 1 stitch (3 panels).

Prism Yarns Saki *DYED-AROUND 48" REPEAT with 4 colors:*
clockwise from top left: taupe, gray, gold, and beige.

Saki is a thinner yarn—size 2 instead of 4—so the fabric is thinner and more flexible. A Magic Number of 38 at a gauge of 5.75 stitches per inch (23 stitches over 4") gives us a strip very near in size to the original. The same diagram could be used for similar results. However, because Saki is dyed around instead of across, there are other choices to consider that will affect the visual outcome.

I selected a more somber color combination for a less flashy piece. Where I started in the skein fundamentally altered how the panel will look. In the original, every stacked panel started in the same spot, so each panel was identical except for garter stitch sections or argyles; this alternative could have panels that were consistent or shifted.

One fewer stitch for a half argyle.

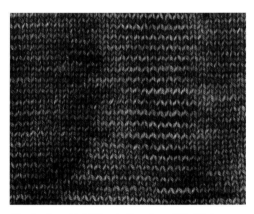

Stacked on Half Magic Number: 38 stitches.
Started in the middle of gold section, so gold stays relatively even at the right edge, while beige and gray alternate rows and taupe is relatively even at the very left edge.

Also on Half Magic Number.
Started at the division between gold and beige, so those 2 colors alternate, then gray and taupe alternate. The darker line in the middle is where the dyed colors overlap. Because the gray/taupe and then the gold/beige are so close in weight to each other, and the optical mixture is so effective, this reads as 3 almost solid colors above. In the swatch at left, there is more weight difference and so we see every-other-row stripes more clearly.

Case study

Prism Yarns Madison *DYED-AROUND 48" REPEAT* with 3 colors:
clockwise from top left: gold, plum, green.

With 3 colors dyed-around, you can select to have 1 color be consistently solid, while the other 2 alternate every other row. I swatched 3 times, each time with a different color as the solid. Here you could pick your favorite, or alternate using all 3. The Half Magic Number of 25 at 4 stitches per inch yields a slightly narrower strip of 6¼". The same strip plan would produce a tunic 50" wide instead of 52" wide. Since Madison is a slightly thicker yarn, a somewhat smaller circumference might not be a bad thing.

Stacked on Half Magic Number: 25 stitches.
Started in the middle of plum, so half of plum was at the beginning and end of every 2 rows. Gold and green alternate every other row, and the left edge is the overlap between 2 colors.

Same number of stitches, started in the middle of gold, so now plum and green alternate.

Same number of stitches, started in the middle of green, so now plum and gold alternate.

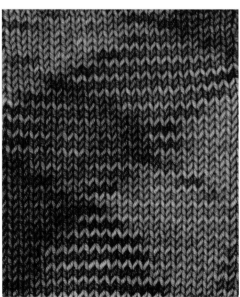

One fewer stitch for a half argyle

Case study

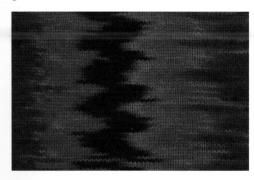

Twisted Sisters Zazu *DYED-ACROSS 54" REPEAT* with 4 colors: deep violet at each end, lighter violet across twice, deep green across two-thirds of the way to the right, lighter turquoise across next to deep green and not consistent.

Case study

Lorna's Laces Haymarket *DYED-ACROSS 50" REPEAT* with 3 colors: subtle blue gray at left end and again across about three-quarters of the way to the right; soft plum at right end and also three-quarters of the way to the left; soft rosy gray across middle. This dyed-across skein is similar in weight to the original. The skein circumference is larger at 50" instead of 45", so a gauge of 4.25 stitches per inch (18 stitches to 4") produces a panel almost 8" wide. Four strips would then become a 31"wide piece; wider, but not too wide. Reducing the number of panels to 3 would give us a more tailored tunic of 23" wide—maybe just right for you.

This much finer yarn stacked on a Half Magic Number of 58 at 7 stitches per inch, producing a panel 8¼" wide. While this would be wider still, the size 2 yarn is much finer and the fabric is very flexible with nice drape. That makes it perfect for a very wide tunic, as the extra fabric would fall nicely around the body. Notice in the skein that the deep green skews at an angle. That angle is accounting for the "flashing" back and forth of green in the swatch. Attempts to force a vertical column resulted in some wonky knitting, so allowing the skein to do what it was designed to do was the best course. It took some getting used to, but you can see that the violet stayed fairly consistent at the sides. When you imagine that the threads are spread back and forth across the skein, it makes sense that the green would wander back and forth similar to the angle that you can see in the skein. This yarn would also argyle well, offering options for duplicating our original look.

Stacked on Half Magic Number of 34. Looks just like the skein, with clear columns of color.

One fewer stitch for a subtle argyle. This was very difficult to see until 6" was completed, and then became much easier to see from across the room, proving that even I have to follow the "walk away and look at it" rule.

For a more custom fit
If, however, you wish garments with a more custom fit, there are multiple approaches.

Change the Magic-Number-to-gauge ratio
This is easier than it sounds. When we were first discovering our Magic Numbers, stitch gauge wasn't so important. Now that we need to make a particular size, it becomes much more so. There are several ways of changing the length that a repeat travels: by shortening it (ribbing), bending it (bias or chevron stitches), or extending it (lace, slip stitches, and Fair Isle).

Here's how
Make a swatch in any intended pattern stitch and work through the necessary steps to determine the Magic Number, using the total number of stitches in the pattern, not just the hand-dyed stitches. That means that if your pattern repeat of 24 has 16 multicolored stitches and 8 solid stitches, you still count the row as 24 stitches for either the counting method or the mathematical method. Also take a traditional gauge measurement. You might be able to change the stitch repeat to bring the Magic Number into a usable format.
For example, working 20 slipped stitches in a body width of 100 stitches might add 2" in width. The slipped stitches could be the same yarn or a contrasting yarn. A contrasting color can be used to outline the patterning colors, allowing the colors to stack and yet making the width much greater, as in the Windowpane Hats.

Add border stitches
Any pattern-stitch repeat that doesn't work out evenly for a color repeat can be extended with simple border stitches. This is particularly useful in large-repeat patterns. For example, if a chevron stitch is a multiple of 12, it is difficult to round up or down to a Magic Number. Instead, use the largest whole repeat you can and then add the remaining stitches to either side as a border. If our Magic Number is 102, for example, we can make 8 repeats of 12 for 96 stitches, and then add 3 stitches in garter to each side. For ease of knitting, place a marker on each end between the border stitches and the pattern itself.

Windowpane
Gently spiraling stacks are worked circularly with solid-color slipped stitches employed to expand the circumference. The solid color adds structure and drama as well as additional width for sizing.

Painted desert
Stacks of 3 dyed-across yarns create interesting columns that switch back and forth between the different colors. Because all are from the same dyer, the repeats are consistent and allow continuity of stacking on the same Half Magic Number. Side gussets are added for additional width.

Twilight
Argyles from a dyed-around, 3-color skein are crisp and clear, even though the colors are closely related in weight. Gussets are added to a modestly sized center panel reliant on the Magic Number and make sizing a snap — simply modify the gusset size for more or less width.

Add gussets

The biggest challenge with intentional patterning is that changing the stitch count interrupts patterning — this is a given, and one that must be dealt with. Remember, I'll never be a singer, and a yarn's Magic Number is set. Minor changes, such as breaking for a neckline, can be ignored. The short distance of interruption is inconsequential and our eyes really don't notice since the pattern has already been established. Even larger areas like the sleeves on our Woodlands Flash (page 104) seem of a piece, especially as they were worked in Half Linen Stitch, which further mixed the colors. What if you want a stacked or argyle piece that reads cleanly, but in a different size? One solution is to use gussets. Gussets allow us to work as much shaping as we need without changing stitch counts and thus interrupting (or causing new) patterns. The gussets can be coordinated solids, worked in a different direction, or use a pattern stitch that randomizes the colors. Remember, the eye will read the most obvious pattern, and will relegate extraneous information to the background. Also, gussets can be a terrific design detail, framing the spectacular effects your patterning will produce.

What now?

Once the Magic Number and gauge are known, the next steps involve going beyond a simple Magic Number. We know the number on which the colors will stack, flash, or argyle: our Magic Number. One-half of the Magic Number will also stack, flash, or argyle, although with different effects. Any multiple of one-half of the whole Magic Number will also be consistent: one and one-half functions the same as one-half, for example. If the intended project requires a stitch count that works with your Magic Number, either to randomize or pattern, then you are good to go.

If, however (and this is far more likely to occur), the intended project requires a stitch count that doesn't work with your Magic Number, you'll have to use other approaches to achieve the results you want. The following strategies change stitch counts to obtain a desired width. In the process, the stitch count may be brought either closer to the Magic Number to encourage patterning, or farther away for randomization. Think of it as caged versus free-range knitting!

One thing I do know: hand-dyed yarns are best suited to approaches that feature the yarn and its colors. Strong design tells one main story instead of encompassing many factors. Rather than simply applying an existing pattern and hoping for the best, make sure you are getting the most from that yarn.

Knitting and crochet, with their endless combinations of stitches, offer a wide variety of options for making fabric. The following sections explore specific strategies that change the pace — fundamentally altering the regular rate of color-repeat consumption that happens with stockinette stitch or simple crochet. Once you have the ability to change stitch counts, you have the ability to control the color repeat and the Magic Number. This control allows you to decide whether you wish to intentionally pattern or to randomize a hand-dyed yarn. Anything that can be patterned can also be randomized. You simply need to know the stitch count that causes colors to gather and pattern and then either select or avoid the full, half, or quarter count. We can employ many strategies to alter the number of stitches needed to obtain a specific size, drawing us closer to or farther from the Magic Number.

Case study: changing stitch count

Malabrigo Silky Merino *DYED-ACROSS 56" REPEAT* with 4 colors:
gold and brown appear once in each repeat, at each end;
plum and orange appear twice in the middle.
Swatches worked in multiple skeins from one dye lot.

A Magic Number of 74 was calculated from the first of 8 skeins. Swatches 3, 4, and 5 show patterning on roughly quarter, half and three-quarter counts. The numbers are not precise due to possible differences in skeins or in my tension from day to day. Always check your color alignment as you begin a new skein and a new session.

Size 4.5mm/US7 needle, gauge in stockinette stitch of 19 sts = 4"

A On randomly selected 50 stitches, some patterning occurs. Note the change halfway through on the same stitch count. Track the orange and you can see that it converges from gentle diagonals to almost stacking in the center. Where one color goes, all other colors follow, and so the brown and plum begin to stack also — they are so close in color weight that they read as one color and hence a stack. The gold is a regularly repeating line. At the very top, orange once again begins to diverge. This stitch count is very close to two-thirds of the Magic Number. Patterns like this show up well in computer-generated charts, but are very difficult to track visually and maintain while knitting.

B On the Magic Number, we can see that with attention, these colors could be stacked; however, less care allows a full argyle to emerge. Notice that gold dominates as the largest diamond and moves symmetrically from the center to each side and then back to the center. Although brown also appears only once, it is a smaller run and so close to plum in weight that they read as the same color, and are about equal in size to orange. Solid colors gather in diamonds at the center.

C Roughly half the Magic Number begins at 34 stitches and then is increased to 36 stitches after 6 rows. Notice that at the very beginning orange, our tracking color, was moving too quickly on a diagonal and so 2 stitches were added. This variance from our Magic Number may have been due to small tension changes or a different skein. Notice the strong half-argyle, with big swaths of gold moving from one side to the other. Solid colors gather along the edge instead of in the middle.

D A three-quarter count of 48 stitches forms 4 double-row gold stripes and is then increased to 49. Compare this to Swatch 1 of 50 stitches.

E These stripes begin with a one-quarter count of 17; increased by one to 18; and then decreased by two to 16 stitches. Again, complex patterns that might read well in computer-generated charts are less easy to maintain and read when actually knit.

Swatching with this skein of Silky Merino continues on page 59.

A Random number of stitches

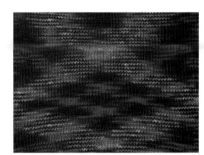

B Magic Number

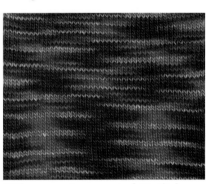

C 34 stitches, then 36 stitches: half Magic Number

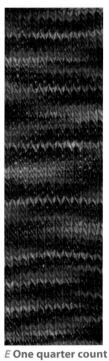

D Three quarters count of 48 stitches

E One quarter count

Change the Pace: Beyond the Magic Number and randomization

Change the repeat-to-gauge ratio: Stitches that expand or contract gauge

A simple way to approach changing the fabric width of a Magic Number is to simply find a stitch that makes the gauge either smaller or larger.

Ribbing contracts

A yarn that is too wide for a garter scarf, even at a half-stack number, might be perfect in ribbing.

One advantage to ribbing is that, if densely worked and left unstretched, it resembles stockinette stitch. This allows you to use more stitches to achieve a desired width, making a nice-sized scarf. Ribbing is ideal for items intended to fit snugly, such as hats.

Ribbing and stockinette both create circular flashes, but ribbing is substantially narrower.

Fruitopia
Hand-painted yarn is already pretty randomized, even though you can detect minor spirals here. The randomized colors mean you can change stitch counts for a shaped crown without worrying about patterning.

Rainbow run
Stacks of color arise in Fisherman's Rib on a Half Magic Number. Usually, dyed-around skeins worked flat produce every-other-row stripes; because Fisherman's Rib is worked into the row below, a stitch is formed into a stitch of the same color, thus producing stacks. Colors not showing on one side have gathered as purl stitches, and show as knit stitches on the reverse.

Harvest meanders
Meandering argyles of color from a dyed-around skein create softly gathered patterns that don't read as crisp argyles, but provide visual organization nonetheless. K 1, P 1 ribbing in a fine yarn contracts and so makes a narrower scarf than one might expect, yet reads as if it were stockinette.

Elongated stitches *formed by double or triple wraps use more yarn per stitch and therefore contract width. This applies to crochet or knitting.*

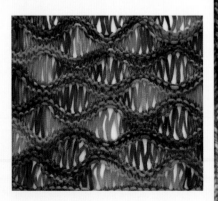

Case study

Lorna's Laces Shepherd Bulky
DYED-ACROSS 62" REPEAT with 4 contrasting colors:
brown at one end, magenta across and at one end;
cream across, and 2 shades of olive across.

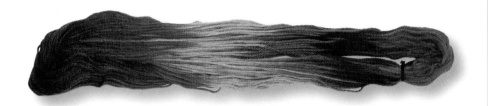

Size 6.5mm/US10½ needle, gauge in stockinette stitch of 13 stitches = 4"

Stockinette stitch would pattern on Magic Number of 56 stitches,
producing a fabric 18" wide.

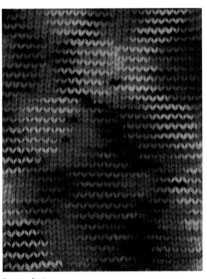

Swatch 1

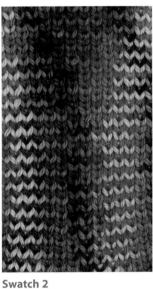

Swatch 2

Swatch 3

Swatch 1 *Half-argyle in stockinette on 28 stitches. Swatch is 9" wide — still quite wide for a scarf.*

Swatch 2 *Half-argyle in K1, P1 Rib on 30 stitches produces fabric 5½" wide — substantially narrower and a good size for a scarf. Colors stack pleasantly in columns, and are slowly beginning to argyle at the top. One stitch more or less, or a needle size change, would encourage argyles.*

Swatch 3 *Fisherman's Rib begins on a one-quarter count of 14 stitches for perfect vertical stacks, then increases to 15 stitches, causing colors to angle.*

Lace expands

Any stitch with many yarn-overs will make fabric wider. Choose a pattern whose stitch count remains the same from row to row if you wish to really control patterning. Intricate lace stitches can compete with highly contrasting colors, so either opt to stack colors (allowing the pattern to form columns that read cleanly) or choose subtle combinations from the same area of the weight scale. Likewise, in crochet, lace stitches that are formed with long runs of chains will expand. Yarn-overs can also be employed for randomizing, since eyelets create patterns that can obscure color patterns, and they also change the rate of color use.

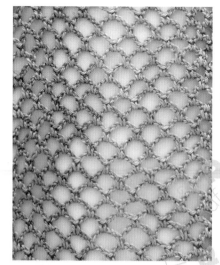

The simplest of crochet stitches can easily control color stacking. Dyed-across skeins provide columns of pure color, while a dyed-around skein stacks with some blended stripes.

Firelight cowl
Stack dyed-across colors in an openwork stitch on twice the Magic Number minus a stitch or 2 for a dramatic spiral. Opposing directions of the stitch and colors adds interest, while a decorative picot edge negates any worry about aligning colors for cast-on and bind-off.

Misty morning duo
Randomized hand-painted colors are given visual structure with vertical columns of eyelets. There is a slight shift in color intensity from one skein to the next that could have been blended had the knitter noticed — a very good reason to carefully inspect all of your skeins, but not a fatal flaw.

Crème caramel

Stacks of color from a dyed-across skein work with a simple lace stitch on twice the Magic Number, expanding the width enough for a nicely sized capelet. When working stacks over a large number of stitches, take care when establishing the stacking that stitches and colors are distributed properly. To do so, count the number of stitches for each color run while researching your Magic Number, and then make sure you are close to the correct count in the first row.

Watercolor

Stacks can happen with dyed-around yarns as well. Depending on the number of colors within the skein, (2 of these 8 yarns are 4-color, the rest are 3-color), the colors stack in various combinations of pure and every-other-row stacks. Especially because the yarn is fine, optical mixture takes over and, from a distance, stack seems to be of one color. In the back, a large mitered square joins the two front legs and is worked in a simpler pattern stitch for both ease of knitting and to eliminate the need for continued color patterning.

Case study

Lorna's Laces Shepherd Sport, in color Camouflage

DYED-ACROSS 64" REPEAT with 3 medium contrasting colors: Brown and olive are on each end and are also repeated across the skein, along with rust. So in 1 repeat, rust appears twice and olive and brown each appear 3 times.

Stockinette gauge of 20 stitches over 4" will pattern on Magic Number of 75 stitches for one full repeat, producing a fabric 15" wide. Lace pattern is Stripe with Twisted Bars (page 160) on 91 stitches for 1 full repeat, producing fabric 19" wide. Notice that the cast-on point was chosen randomly; the colors gather, but in every-other-row patterning that is difficult to control. After a few inches, the colors were realigned to begin at the side edge; colors now stack easily on the same stitch count.

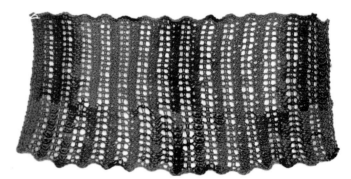

Stripe with Twisted Bars. For instructions for this and other stitches used in Case Studies, see Stitches in Color, page 160.

Change the line: Stitches that interrupt the horizontal

Many stitch patterns employ either slipped stitches (stitches that are not worked but are moved from needle to needle), dipped stitches (the working needle goes not into the next stitch in the row, but down into a previous row), or skipped stitches in crochet (where a space is created in one row that is filled in the next). In each case, the horizontal run of color is broken by intermingling color from another row. This approach is terrific both for randomizing and for patterning. Since slipping uses a different amount of yarn, repeat-to-gauge ratios change, offering possibilities for altering the width.

Half Linen or Fabric Stitch, also known as Tweed Stitch

One of my all-time favorite stitches, the combination of slipping every other stitch with yarn-forward bars across the front is masterful at mixing up colors. With a truly woven appearance, the fabric is relatively flat, and each stitch is outlined as if it is an individual pixel. For randomizing, it can't be beat, and yet when worked on a Magic Number, subtle patterning occurs when colors both stack and intermingle.

Crochet Moss Stitch

Argyles and stacks can easily be created in Crochet Moss Stitch, which resembles Half Linen Stitch in knitting. Colors interplay as stitches intermingle. Attentiveness is required to stack, while mindfulness will argyle almost effortlessly.

Argyle in crochet

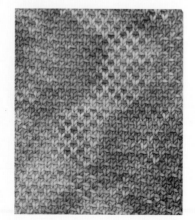

Stacked

Meandering argyles on a Half Magic Number form even within the slip-stitch structure of Half Linen Stitch. Instead of every-other-row stripes, the slipped stitches outline the underlying stitches with a sometimes-contrasting color, creating shifting fields where dominant color alternates with a dominant pattern.

Crochet Moss Stitch page 33

Case study

Prism Merino 12, in color Maui

DYED-AROUND 52" REPEAT with 4 highly contrasting colors, each appearing once: orange, fuchsia, blue, and olive.

Size 6.5mm/US10½ needle, gauge in stockinette stitch of 14 stitches = 4"

Stockinette swatch on 28 stitches is quite striped and beginning to pool (bottom); the switch to Half Linen Stitch changes the amount of yarn used in each row (the slipped rows use less yarn, purled wrong-side rows use more). Colors are gathering more, yet they are also intermingled from slipping.

Merino 12, in color Harvest on 40 stitches, decreasing to 36 stitches and then to 32 stitches. The fairly high contrast in colors produces some distinct stripes and pools, yet those areas are broken by intermingled colors where individual stitches function as pixels. Changing the stitch count does not radically alter how the stitch reads.

Prism Symphony, in color Highlands

DYED-AROUND 64" REPEAT with 5 colors: khaki, olive, melon, rose, blue.

Size 5mm/H-8 crochet hook, 20 stitches = 4"

Moss or Seed Stitch in crochet is similar in appearance to Half Linen Stitch, with a distinctly woven look. Every other stitch is single crochet, with a chain-1 space between stitches. On following rows, the spaces are filled, while another chain is made to bridge the existing stitch. When worked on a Magic Number with attentiveness, clear vertical stacks occur. The same number of stitches, with less attention paid to stacking, produces a meandering argyle, rating this mindful.

Stockinette is patterning while Half Linen changes the pattern fundamentally.

Stitch counts change the look but not substantially, making this a good stitch for a project with shaping.

Moss stitch on Half Magic Number, (bottom); and alternated every 2 rows with solid, (top); the multi-colors still gather, but are disrupted by the solid.

Tweed checks

Randomize highly contrasting colors by isolating each stitch into a pixel. A boxed slip-stitch pattern employs garter stitch to really make colors pop. Multiple swatches show that some color combinations have too much contrast, while others don't have enough. If you are going to do the work, make it count!

Tweed checks   page 118

Case study

Simple slip stitches

Unlike Half Linen Stitch, the working yarn stays at the wrong side of the work. The appearance is less woven, and the work is easier as the yarn stays in place. Those who dislike working ribbing will like this stitch better than Half Linen, whose constant yarn-forward, yarn-back action is similar to ribbing. Colors are still mixed well.

Cartridge-Belt Rib.

Prism Merino 12, in color Highlands
DYED-AROUND 52" REPEAT with 5 colors:
olive, khaki, melon, rose, blue.
Size 6.5mm/US10½ needle; gauge in Cartridge-Belt Rib of 18 stitches = 4".
Here, slipped stitches are worked in vertical ribs with garter stitches placed on either side. The fluted fabric draws in slightly at the same time that it becomes fluffy. Slipped stitches are pulled up into the next row of colors, breaking the rhythm and isolating single stitches. Swatch was begun on 31 stitches, then decreased to 29 stitches and then to 27 stitches. The larger number randomizes the colors, while a Half Magic Number of 27 allows the colors to stack vertically. Although this is a dyed-around yarn, the slipping functions in the same way as knit-in-the-stitch-below: slipped stitches are only worked every other row, thus aligning colors. The vertical columns of color are nicely interspersed with garter texture in between. The fabric is only 6" wide, as compared with 8" wide when worked in Half Linen Stitch—note the difference in gauge between this swatch and the previous one.

Variety of color combinations.

Lorna's Laces Shepherd Worsted, in color Child's Play
DYED-ACROSS 64" REPEAT with 6 colors:
magenta at one end; orange, yellow, green, and blue across; purple at the other end.
Size 5mm/US8 needle, gauge in stockinette stitch of 18 stitches = 4"; gauge in Cartridge-Belt Rib of 23 stitches = 4"
The bright, highly contrasting colors made a great argyle (see page 71), and here the slipped stitches of Cartridge-Belt Rib have

thoroughly randomized them. Although some striping is still present, it is broken up quite nicely. Additionally, the gauge has gotten much tighter (even though the fabric is not dense), allowing a different stitch count than required to pattern in stockinette.

Cartridge-Belt Rib

Case study

Twisted Sisters Jazz, in color Handpaint #61
(discontinued yarn, but principles still hold)
DYED-ACROSS 54" REPEAT with irregular color sections:
5 distinct colors: blue at one end; aqua, dark teal, light magenta
across; dark magenta at the other end. Blue is the most consistent
in color and size; aqua to teal is different from 1 side of the skein
to the other, and light magenta to dark magenta is also somewhat
inconsistent. This produces interesting effects when patterned.
Size 4.5mm/US7 needle, gauge in stockinette stitch of 17 stitches = 4"

A This swatch of randomly selected 50 stitches shows graphic
splotching, pooling, and striping from these highly contrasting colors.

B An intentionally patterned swatch was begun on 64 stitches and
increased to 66 stitches after 6 rows, producing fabric 15" wide.
Despite the intentional irregularities in dyeing, a strong argyle
emerges and becomes more complex, with darker bits of color
coming and going.

C Simple slipped stitches begin on 50 stitches with the same size
needle, reducing the gauge to 21 stitches = 4". The number is very
close to a Half Magic Number for the new gauge, as can be seen
where the colors skew on a diagonal at the beginning. The fabric is
9½" wide, larger than half the stockinette fabric of 15", so we have
gained substantial width by slipping every third stitch. As the stitch
count increases to 54 and then to 58, the colors become more and
more randomized.

D Alternate a solid color every 2 rows in a slightly more complicated
pattern stitch, French Weave Plain, and the results become very
interesting. The black provides visual structure, outlining the lightest
stitches and accentuating gathering colors as they stack and shift. The
effect is decidedly stained glass in appearance. Worked on 47 stitches.

A Random selection of 50-stitch
stripes and splotches.

B Full Magic Number
plus 2 stitches.

C 50 stitches with slip-stitch patterns,
becomes increasingly randomized
as the stitch count increases.

D The addition of black and a slip-stitch pattern gives
structure and interest as the colors gather and stack.

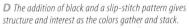

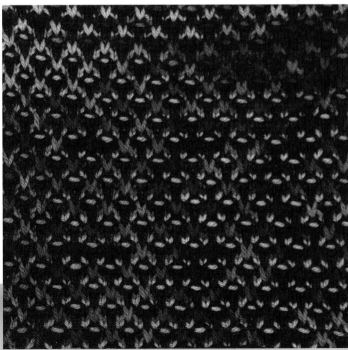

Right-side floats

Stitches that employ long strands floated across the public face are abundant. The floats may be left in their original horizontal line, or picked up in a subsequent row, pulling the line on the diagonal. These stitches often have a quilted or woven look to them, and they are particularly effective at imposing visual order onto a melee of colors.

Herringbone Jacket page 113
Sampler Jacket page 88

Herringbone weave
Randomize bold colors of any hand-dye by floating long strands across the surface. A float uses yarn at a different rate than a stitch, resulting in an interruption of pooling. Although some gathering occurs, it is also broken up by other colors.

Sampler jacket
Randomize and control a large group of hand-dyed and sandwashed colors by mixing bands of textured and slipped stitches. Each individual pattern stitch was chosen for its ability to randomize colors or impose visual order. Thin dividing lines of solid colors provide punctuation. Although there are some accent colors, most are in the same general weight range.

Case study: right-side floats

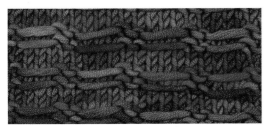

Swag stitch.

Jacquard Stitch.

Prism Merino 12, in color Highlands *DYED-AROUND 52" REPEAT* with 5 colors: olive, khaki, melon, rose, blue.

Size 6.5mm/US10½ needle; gauge in Swag Stitch of 14 stitches = 4"
Swag Stitch Right-side lines of color span 3 stitches and nicely overshadow any striping or pooling that occurs in the stockinette-stitch background. The bulky yarn creates assertive lines and casts textural shadows that make the floats even more important. The yarn's particular twist causes the floats to take on a slight diagonal cast, adding to the mystery.

Size 6.5mm/US10½ needle; gauge in Jacquard Stitch of 15 stitches =4"
Jacquard Stitch The same yarn is here worked in a more tightly woven stitch, where floats travel over 2 stitches and step over every row in a subtle zigzag. The gauge is a little firmer, and the colors gather in subtle drifts, but the regular diagonal weaving is apparent.

Woven Diagonal Herringbone.

Little Butterfly Stitch.

Lorna's Laces Bullfrogs & Butterflies, in color Turtle Rodeo
DYED-ACROSS 61" REPEAT with 4 colors:
rust at one end and again across the skein (3 times); teal at one end and again across the skein (3 times); gray and green.

Size 5.5mm/US9 needle, gauge in Woven Diagonal Herringbone of 17 stitches = 4"

Woven Diagonal Herringbone Several playful things happen here: wide diagonal columns of thread-thin lines march to the left as they move up the swatch, while the colors are loosely gathering in shallow columns that move to the right. Any pooling is regularly interrupted, resulting in nicely randomized colors.

Malabrigo Silky Merino
Swatching continues with the skein used on page 49.

Size 4.5mm/US7 needle, gauge in Little Butterfly Stitch of 19 stitches =4"

Three subsequent RS rows contain floats that span 3 stitches and are separated by plain purl rows. On the sixth row, the floats are gathered under the working needle as the middle stitch is worked, pulling those lines into little butterflies of color. In a highly contrasting yarn such as this, there are places where light strands are outlined on a dark ground; in other places dark strands are outlined on a light ground; in still other places the pattern tends to disappear. Our big brains, however, read the pattern as all-over, filling in missing information as needed. Where colors might pool undesirably, they are often broken by pleasantly contrasting diagonal lines; altogether, a successful randomization of these strong colors.

See Color in Stitches, page 160, for stitch instructions.

Knit-in-the-stitch below.

As a stitch is drawn up from a row below, the horizontal line of color is broken. Fisherman's Rib in particular has interesting properties, as yarns that are dyed around the skein can be made to stack when worked flat. Since every knit stitch is worked into the row below, the working yarn is creating a stitch into the same color, producing stacks or flashes. The purl stitches disappear into the other side, lending an interesting shadow play to the surface. A dyed-across skein will also stack easily, no matter where in the skein you begin. For this reason, a Fisherman's Rib scarf is an ideal beginner's project for intentional patterning.

Case study: knit-in-the-stitch below

Fisherman's Rib can be worked on either even or odd stitches. Knit the first and last stitch of every row to keep selvedges tidy. At right, Fisherman's Rib on 27 stitches looks random and very slightly striped. An increase to 30 stitches allows the colors to begin stacking, although at an angle. Another increase to 31 stitches (very near our Half Magic Number) allows them to stack well, with some movement, most likely caused by slight tension differences as well as the varying stitch counts for each color as you move through the skein.

At far right, Fisherman's Rib on 18 stitches produces an every-other-row gathering of colors on a shallow angle to the right. A decrease of 1 stitch to 17 stitches (very close to a quarter Magic Number) steepens the angle.

Fisherman's Rib patterns in an interesting way at a one-quarter count.

Fisherman's Rib, dyed-across skein. Stitch count begins random and moves towards a Half Magic Number. Amazing what a large visual difference occurs from a small stitch-count change — remember the butterfly effect?

Lorna's Laces Bullfrogs & Butterflies, in color Turtle Rodeo
DYED-ACROSS 61" REPEAT with 4 colors:
rust at one end and again across the skein (3 times); teal at one end and again across the skein (3 times); gray and green.
Size 6mm/US8 needle, gauge in Rambler Pattern of 10 stitches = 4"
Knit-in-the-stitch-below combined with right-side purl texture nicely randomizes these regularly repeating colors. This yarn would normally work at 18 stitches over 4" in stockinette; here, the gauge is greatly expanded.
To see how this yarn works in other stitches, see page 59.

Rambler Pattern.

Sunset   page 94
Peaks & Waves   page 127

Sunset
Three elements (1 contrasting dyed-around, 1 tonal dyed-across and 1 sandwashed solid) combine in single row stripes worked in Fisherman's Rib. Thin stripes assist in breaking patterns, as does the soft fabric that spreads enough to reveal mysterious purl valleys alternating with knit columns. When a stripe wants to form across a row, the differently colored purl stitch creates a visual stop.

Case study: crochet in the row below

Spike Stitches in crochet are the perfect vehicle for breaking a horizontal. Any Spike Stitch is worked down into a row below the current row, and may go as far as 5 rows down. There are many variations that use Spike Stitches as their basis. They work in similar ways yet provide different effects. In knitting, dip stitches that reach down into stitches below those on the needle are similar.

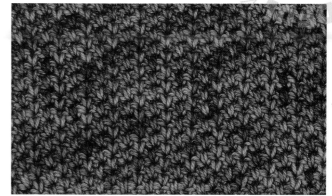

Interlocking Block Stitch worked with 1 multicolored yarn. Notice that colors are forced into repetitive blocks of color.

Prism Symphony, color Orchard
DYED-AROUND 64" REPEAT with 4 colors: gold, rust, magenta, olive.
Size 5mm/H-8 crochet hook, 20 stitches = 4"

Prism Symphony, color Denali
DYED-AROUND 64" REPEAT with 4 colors: grey, taupe, beige, camel.
Size 5mm/H-8 crochet hook, 17 stitches = 4"

INTERLOCKING BLOCK STITCH
MULTIPLE OF 6 + 3 (ADD 2 FOR BASE CHAIN)
Special abbreviation: Sdc (Spike double crochet):
Work dc over ch-sp by inserting hook into top of next row below (or base chain).
Row 1 Skip 3 stitches (count as 1 dc), 1 dc into each of next 2 stitches, (ch 3, skip 3 stitches, 1 dc into each of next 3 stitches) to end, turn.
Row 2 (Ch 3, skip 3 stitches, Sdc 1 over each of next 3 stitches) to last 3 stitches, ch 2, skip 2 stitches, sl st into top of turning chain, turn.
Row 3 Ch 3 (count as 1 Sdc), skip 1 stitch, Sdc 1 over next 2 stitches, (ch 3, skip 3 stitches, Sdc 1 over each of next 3 stitches) to end, turn.
Repeat Rows 2 and 3.

Alternating Spike Stitch (Boardroom, page 144).

Peaks & waves
Randomize and control a large group of hand-dyed and layered colors with crocheted Spike Stitch. While this stitch would randomize any single hand-dyed yarn nicely, changing to a different color weight for the spike row nicely outlines the changing stitch size, creating an interesting and playful structure.

For many hand-dyed yarns, even a half Magic Number produces a very wide scarf, so here we make it narrower by working our patterning number on the bias. Bias shaping can be worked on whatever stitch count is needed for your yarn to pattern or stack.

Change direction:
Stitches that break the horizontal line

Rather than bringing new colors into a run of color, these next stitches actually change the direction of the horizontal line. One way to make a given number of stitches into narrower fabric is to make them bend up and down, as in a chevron. Hand-dyed yarns with clean color breaks often produce magical stripes in entrelac, creating rectangles with alternating bias direction. Small modules can also harness stripes. Large modules, however, will have stitch counts that change so much as the module is built that a section of patterning will almost always occur.

Bias knitting or crochet allows us to achieve a desired width with more

stitches. By simply decreasing at one end and increasing at the other, the same number of stitches produces narrower fabric as the width is pulled onto the diagonal.

Surrealist Plaid
Argyle worked on the bias compresses stripes in one direction and stretches them out in the other for a truly mysterious plaid.

Case study: bias knitting

Prism Symphony in color Mohave

DYED-AROUND 64" REPEAT with 4 colors:
khaki, olive, melon, aqua
Size 6mm/US8 needle, gauge of 18 stitches = 4"
Symphony patterns on a half count of 42 stitches, producing a fabric about 9½" wide. Garter stitch worked on the bias by increasing at the beginning and decreasing at the end of every other row makes a fabric about 5¼" wide—far more suitable for most scarves. Decreasing at one side and increasing at the other side **every** row makes it narrower still—a lithe 3¾" wide! As seen in our pair of scarves, if attention is paid to stacking colors in columns, a similar appearance is maintained whether worked with no shaping or on the bias. Allow the colors to travel, however, and an intricately moving plaid appears, where some color runs are elongated and others are compressed.

Sonnet
Stacks of dyed-around colors worked on the bias form interesting diagonal shimmers, and produce a scarf of more modest proportions.

Piece begins with increases and decreases worked every other row, then becomes narrower when shaping is worked every row.

Chevron Stitch both changes the stitch count needed to achieve a given width and imposes a regular pattern onto multicolors. An easy stitch to manipulate, chevron stitches can be wide or narrow, changing the stitch count between increases and decreases as needed to achieve a desired total width.

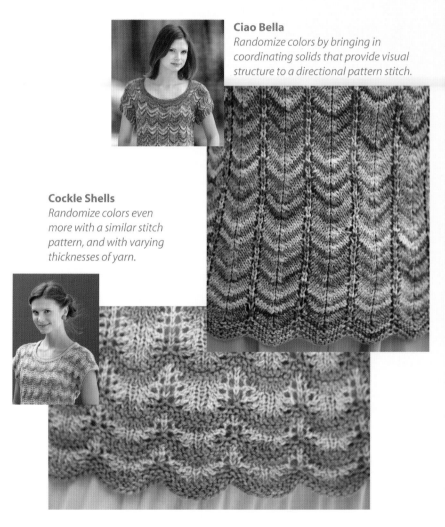

Ciao Bella
Randomize colors by bringing in coordinating solids that provide visual structure to a directional pattern stitch.

Cockle Shells
Randomize colors even more with a similar stitch pattern, and with varying thicknesses of yarn.

A variety of color combinations.

Case study: chevron stitch

Prism Symphony, in Portofino
DYED-AROUND 64" REPEAT with 4 colors:
gold, peach, rose, blue.

Size 4mm/US6 needle, gauge of 39 stitches = 4½".
Size 5.5mm/US9 needle, gauge of 39 stitches = 5¼".
Both in Chevron Stitch, multiple of 12 plus 3.

At the tighter gauge, the colors are randomized into stripes and dramatic zigzags impose visual order. The larger gauge is on a Half Magic Number, and so colors gather and travel in soft paths. The scarf was knit by my 84-year-old mom, who per my instructions was not mindful of color stacking, proving that the right stitch count and gauge can easily produce spectacular results.

 Syncopation
*Work the same stitch on a Magic Number,
and the colors gather in soft groups.*

Modular mitered diamonds
Small modules such as triangles and mitered squares utilize natural striping to great advantage. The modular shapes impose an overriding visual order.

Boogie Woogie Bag

Stripes become more appealing when worked at a stitch count that standardizes them. Here, entrelac squares use just the right number of stitches to produce visually consistent stripes. It is easy to vary the squares to use an appropriate amount of yarn--simply swatch a few different sizes until you like the effect.

Entrelac also exploits stripes to achieve great results. Stripes that might be too random in larger stitch counts become regular and visually dynamic as the small interlaced rectangles change direction. Popcorns, nupps, and other stitches which stop in the middle of the row and then go back and forth or increase and decrease rapidly can also concentrate colors into small sections.

Bloomin' Bag

Felting hand-dyed yarn softens colors and blurs stripes. This bag is punctuated by both a self-bobbled yarn that changes its colors throughout and knitted bobbles in a sparkly yarn. Neither of the novelty yarns felt, highlighting the textural difference in a playful way.

Felted entrelac.

Case study: popcorns

Here, one color, gold, was selected for the popcorns. Every time gold was reached, a popcorn large enough to use the entire color was formed. On a random number of stitches, the popcorns are scattered across the surface. When the stitches are increased and near a Half Magic Number, the background colors begin to pattern and the popcorns align in the same diagonals.

Popcorns worked on a solid ground isolate the hand-dyed colors into individual shapes.

String of Purls stitch isn't really a popcorn, but it does stop in the middle of the row and work back and forth, concentrating color into larger ovals on a solid surface.

Take charge of the color combination
We can control unruly colors by introducing additional hues. Because it is difficult for dyers to control exactly how much of a color goes into a skein, an accent color might take over visually. The strategies here all give you ultimate control over how much of each color is present.

Alternating 2 rows A and 2 rows B allows a color to be diluted at the same time that randomizing occurs. This is particularly effective in simple pattern stitches.

In Linen or Half Linen, stripes are broken into dashes of color. The addition of a semisolid can give an overall theme to the piece, allowing stronger multicolors to become accents.

Trader's bag
Randomize a highly contrasting hand-dye (and reduce the amount of bright colors) by working Linen Stitch alternating with a more subdued solid color.

Tropical Garden
Use optical mixture to blend already randomized hand-painted colors by alternating two rows and two rows as you move through a group of colors that have been arranged through a progression of hue and weight. A lace stitch provides visual structure and interest, and yet is simple enough to not compete for attention.

Sonata
Optical mixture and blending control a widely varying group of colors. Careful arrangement from light to heavy, coupled with sections of alternating rows to move from one color to another, provides a painterly canvas.

Weighing in on color choice Whenever you add colors to an existing hand-dyed yarn, you must decide if you want a color story or a pattern story. Remember our axioms:

Highly contrasting colors produce fabric with more splotching, pooling, and striping.

Closely weight-related colors appear more harmonious, and read as one surface, particularly from a distance.

Therefore:

To make a pattern story, choose colors of contrasting weight.

To make a color story, choose colors of similar weight.

Now is when you must put that into practice. Different tactics serve different goals. If you wish harmonious color stories, select colors that are similar in visual weight and then use simple techniques such as 1-row stripes (with or without Half Linen Stitch), or combining strands together. If you wish to feature a pattern stitch, then select contrasting color weights and hues that will make the pattern show while also enhancing the hand-dyed yarn.

Single-row stripes worked in 3 colors are a favorite tactic of mine. One-row stripes possess a great advantage visually, as they don't assert themselves strongly as stripes. Normally working a single row can cause logistical difficulty, but with 3 yarns it is easy: Cast on with A; drop A, attach B and work across with B; drop B, attach C and work across with C; A is waiting at the end of the row. As long as you take care not to go on autopilot and work 2 rows with one yarn, you can't get lost, even if you are working back and forth on circular needles. Always start where there are 2 strands, and don't use the one you've just finished. This method imparts ultimate control over color and fabric. For example, if 1 of 4 colors in a hand-dyed yarn is really bright and takes over, well…it is 25% of the surface, so no wonder. Now add 2 more strands of yarn, whether they are other multicolors or solids, and that one-quarter has been reduced to one-twelfth — a very big difference indeed. It has gone from being a boisterous loudmouth to a welcome accent. Additionally, you can successfully use yarn of different gauges since no yarn goes on for more than 1 row at a time. Different thicknesses are evened out over the expanse of the fabric. A thicker yarn will be somewhat more obvious, and very thin yarns might tend to disappear, but the whole cloth will be quite consistent. This is also a great way to make a stiff yarn soft, or add body to a limp yarn.

As a bonus, A, B, C stripes can be used with any pattern stitch. Half Linen Stitch in particular is a great choice, as the slipped stitches will intermingle colors even further. One-row stripes can also be easily worked in crochet.

Geisha

A, B, C stripes can randomize and control a large group of colors. Here we have used 3 different textures: matte merino, silky Tencel® and a metallic rayon, all dyed in different and somewhat contrasting colorways. The thin stripes are further blended by using a modified Half Linen Stitch, working slip stitches on every 4th row.

Three yarns: one highly contrasting, one with tonally related colors, one sandwashed solid.

Tip To keep the 3 yarns from snarling as you work, place 1 ball on either side of you and 1 between your legs. When you turn the work, hold it up and look at where the strands lie. Turning in one direction twists them, the other does not. Occasionally you will need to pass a strand over or under to keep them straight.

Case study: multiple strands

Prism Merino Mia, in color Spice
DYED-AROUND 55" REPEAT with 4 colors:
soft gold, rust, rose, blue.

Prism Saki, in color Portofino
DYED-AROUND 44" REPEAT with 4 colors:
gold, peach, rose, blue.

Prism Gossamer, in color Fog
DYED-AROUND 60" REPEAT with 4 colors:
soft tonal shades of grey, taupe, plum and slate;
very close weights

Another approach involved pairing 2 sock-weight yarns whose colors were similar but whose repeats were different. Now any attempt by one set of colors to pattern is interrupted by the other yarn.

Merino Mia and Gossamer, in color Fog
Here, there is no question that the lace-weight kid mohair softens the colors, but once a shaped piece was begun, the Merino Mia had enough visual presence to begin patterning as the stitch count changed. A doubling of the Gossamer would make it as important visually as the Merino Mia, minimizing any patterning.

Merino Mia and Saki: As 2 strands of different repeats are held together, decreased, and then increased, the patterning that might occur is hidden by the differently repeated second strand.

One strand of each held together.

Multiple strands

Multiple strands offer a great avenue for optical mixture. Combining strands not only breaks up splotching, but offers another way to control colors, either by adding additional colors or simply by emphasizing one or several. The watch point here is that the fabric will be thicker. Thin yarns such as lace-weight wool or even sock-weight yarns can successfully be combined to make mid-weight garments. Kid mohair in any weight is a great equalizer, as the soft halo mutes and blends sharper colors from plied strands.

Sun shadows
Optical mixture prevails in this tour-de-force of blending. Each panel is worked in 3 strands of lace-weight wool, moving from one color to another by gradually adding and removing strands. A large group of varying colors is arranged to show contrast without jarring shifts, and is tied together with accent lines to join the panels.

Three strands of lace-weight held together.

Two-color knitting

Fair Isle

Two-color knitting such as Fair Isle and mosaic stitches can produce spectacular results. Keep the charts simple and the motifs small, and it will look as if you painstakingly chose a color for each stitch. Make sure there is enough contrast between the hand-dyed yarn and the ground colors, or it will be a lot of work for little return. You want to be able to "read" the pattern easily, even from some distance. This is a great time to make sure you look at the work from across the room before proceeding. If there is some commonality between hand-dyed and ground colors, there will be areas where figures might blend into the background. As long as there is enough contrast to read the pattern for most of the area, our brains will fill in the rest.

Mosaic Stitches

Have much the same effect as Fair Isle stitches — magical fabric with intriguing designs. Select simple mosaic stitches with good graphic detail. I like them worked in stockinette rather than the traditional mix of stockinette and garter stitches, as I find flat stitches read better when emphasizing color — texture just seems to get in the way. Any mosaic can be worked in stockinette by simply purling the wrong-side stitches even if they are written to be knit.

Highlands

Randomized colors can still lend visual structure to your fabric with simple Fair Isle motifs in highly multicolored hand-dyes paired with subtle layered semisolids. In some areas the colors begin to stack and spiral within the motifs, adding to the mystery.

Case study: two-color knitting

Randomize and structure hand-dyed colors by imposing a strong geometric mosaic pattern. Colors can be totally random or worked to a Magic Number as ours has been — you can detect some pooling and gathering of colors, but the real story is in the geometry.

Simple Fair Isle motifs.

Three different solid/multicolor combinations in Maze Pattern, worked on a Half Magic Number.

Two different multicolors in Maze Pattern, both yarns at Half Magic Number.

Case study: slip stitches with multiple yarns

Two- and three-color slip stitches offer a great resource for controlling color amount and imposing pattern. Any good stitch dictionary will be filled with variations. Since only 1 strand at a time is worked, you can work with numerous multicolors and/or solids and not lose your place.

Prism Symphony
DYED-AROUND 64" REPEAT

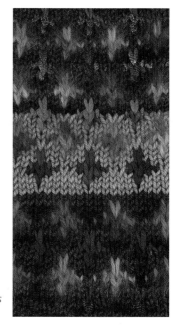

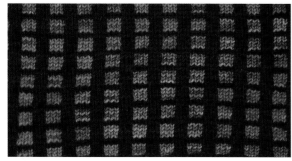

Solid and hand-dyed, worked on a Half Magic Number to pattern within the boxes.

Three colors in Dice Check.

Bottom: pattern color is very close to visual weight of background, and pattern is lost. Why bother?
Middle: contrast is too harsh and colors are not enhanced.
Top: a brighter, lighter color choice enlivens the original background and second color.

Dice checks
Randomize 2 hand-dyed yarns with an intermingled slip stitch pattern and a sandwashed solid. The hand-dyed colors are broken nicely into little boxes, creating their own unique pattern.

Dice Checks page 120

Case study

Twisted Sisters Jazz, in color Handpaint 58

Let's look back at our hypothetical example of a multicolor where one of 4 colors really stands out: add 1 additional strand, and you have reduced that color from one-quarter to one-eighth; add another strand and it is reduced to one-twelfth. If the added colors are solid, we have now imposed visual organization onto the hand-dyed colors. These types of stitches will often result in stained-glass effects.

Twisted Sisters Jazz, in color Handpaint #58
DYED-ACROSS 50" REPEAT with 3 colors:
orange at one end; 2 shades of blue in middle; olive at the other end; slight olive from overlap of orange and blue; slightly darker patches of scarlet on orange.
Size 4.5mm/US7 needle, gauge in stockinette stitch of 18 stitches = 4"

A Randomly selected 50 stitches in stockinette produces fairly regular stripes of orange and green, with blue interrupting periodically, almost in argyles. Orange is dominant color.

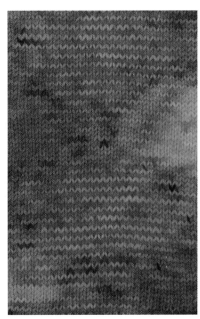

A Random 50 stitches.

B Half-argyle was worked on 30 stitches for 6 rows, then increased to 32 stitches as the orange was moving too drastically. On the larger number, orange marches in perfect order from side to side on a diagonal, with green and blue following suit. Darker splashes of scarlet and blue become nice accents to a regularly defined pattern. While orange appears in the same quantity as in the first swatch, the other colors are given a chance to compete for attention by virtue of gathering together. There is strength in numbers, after all!

B Half Magic Number.

C Two-tone Lattice Stitch.

C A coordinating semisolid aqua was added to reduce and tame the orange. Two-tone Lattice Stitch uses this solid aqua for 50% of the rows, but it has become more than 50% of the color showing, as some stitches are slipped for 3 rows (hiding some hand-dyed stitches). This has now reduced the orange from roughly 30% of the surface to perhaps 15%; it has gone from demanding total attention to functioning as lively accent.

Adding shape Not everyone wants to wear boxy, unshaped garments, but adding shape presents challenges with hand-dyed yarns, as shape requires changing stitch counts. Now is the time to consider everything we have learned, and select those strategies that will allow us ultimate control. It might even be more than one strategy combined, such as multiple strands with a pattern stitch.

London fog
Randomize a crisply-dyed multi-color by adding 2 strands of kid mohair. The mohair's soft halo blurs and blends colors, disguising patterns that otherwise would show. Employ that crisp dyeing in a narrow bias band of syncopated stripes for a classic couture trim

Geisha
Randomize 3 different repeats by working A, B, C 1-row stripes.

Boardroom
Randomize colors with a simple Spike Stitch that allows for lots of stitch-count changes without dangerous patterning. Two different weights of yarn yield a structured jacket and a sleek skirt.

Portofino spice
Randomize 2 different repeats by pairing 2 thin strands together. When a changing stitch count brings 1 strand near its Magic Number, the other 1 helps to break the patterning.

Short rows are a great randomizer, as they have constantly changing stitch counts. Even when a patterning count is reached, the count isn't maintained long enough to establish a pattern. Add in contrasting colors, and short rows are tailor-made for hand-dyed yarns.

Color waves
Randomize and structure colors with short-row wedges that create a playful ruffled scarf. Punctuation is added to each wedge with a contrasting outline.

Nautilus
Randomize and structure colors with short-row wedges. Subtle dyed colors of similar weight make a quiet statement, while more highly contrasting colors are never allowed to pool or pattern as the stitch counts constantly change.

Carnivale
Argyle panels of a strongly-contrasting hand-dye and then contour them with solid colors and short rows. Sideways-knit sections allow you to size the panels as needed, and provide a nice visual break from a striking, busy pattern.

Solids and Layers One last style of hand dyeing deserves its own mention. Hand dyers rarely produce truly solid colors, and why should they? Hand dyeing can't really compete with the efficiencies of factory dyeing. The semisolid, sandwashed and layered colors that hand dyers make are truly beautiful in their own right. Subtle shifting of tones and shading add mystery and depth to these very special colors. While we have used this style of dyeing throughout the book as complements to hand-dyed multicolors, here are 2 projects intended to showcase layered colors all on their own. Since many hand-dyers dye their color range across a number of yarns, you can contrast different textures dyed the same color, as we did in Aegean Dream. Be warned that colors will not be an exact match, however, as different fiber types take the dyes slightly differently.

Windowpanes
Layered colors make a quiet statement of soft boxes. There is a nice interplay of undertones that shift harmoniously from one color to the other.

Aegean dream
Contrasting textures tell the story here, where a thin kid mohair and a wide metallic ribbon both have been dyed in a layered color of blue and green. Different fibers take dye with some variation, so more green shows in the ribbon than in the mohair. Shoot the ribbon through at random, then finish with a luxurious fringe.

Unification theory: Finishing techniques

Seams

Devoted followers of seamless knitting have always existed. I am not one of them. Perhaps harkening back to my dressmaking days, I find seams lend visual and virtual structure to garments, and I don't mind them even when they are obvious. Unless you choose to use a decorative seam, I prefer mattress stitch for vertical seams and slip-stitch crochet, for shoulders and sleeve insertions. It continues to be a point of controversy every time I state my preference for bound-off and slip-stitched shoulder seams over 3-needle bind-off, but I do have my reasons. If sleeves are attached, it is very difficult to get a 3-needle bind-off that is firm enough to keep shoulders seams from stretching and thus sleeve tops from drooping down the upper arm. Firmly bound-off shoulders that are then placed right sides together and slip-stitched (underneath the bound-off edge, not through it) have three firm edges holding the seam in place: each bound-off piece and the slip-stitch chain.

A shoulder seam should not have any elasticity in it at all. If your carefully measured sleeves are constantly too long, it quite likely is the shoulder seam stretching rather than the sleeve itself. Not only does this lead to sleeve-cap droop, but it imparts an overall sloppiness to the garment. Neatly fitted shoulders and sleeve tops, whether set-in or modified-drop, are essential to a good-looking garment.

That being said, there are great uses for 3-needle bind-off, and I have used it many times for projects in this book. Anywhere that you want to join pieces and have them behave as the knitting itself will, 3-needle is the go-to technique. Because pieces are knit together and the tension of the bind-off itself can be controlled with needle size, they will behave as if the knitting was seamless. When worked on the public side, these seams become a decorative accent that frames each panel rather than trying to disguise the join. Contrasts in color or texture add another design element, such as in our Made in the Shade (page 82) or Siren's Song (page 40).

Another decorative option is to place wrong sides together and crochet through both layers. A single-crochet row followed by reverse single crochet (also known as crab stitch) produces a distinct raised seam with a slightly scalloped edge that I love. The single-crochet row can be eliminated, working reverse single crochet directly, which makes a flatter yet still decorative join, as in our Painted Desert Vest (page 100). In all of these cases, hand-dyed yarns behave in a magical way: because a single row becomes the focal point, the colors change through their paces in the same run as seen in the dye skein — no unwanted pooling or patterning here!

Applied I-cord and bias bands

Both of these techniques are particularly appropriate for Chanel-style jackets, providing a visual frame for the entire piece. Since I-cord is made with very few stitches, almost all hand-dyed yarns will create delightful little dashes of color. If the body of the garment is multicolored, set the I-cord apart with a few rows of garter stitch in a coordinating solid color, as in our Woven Herringbone Jacket (page 113).

Another trick learned from dressmaking is an applied bias band. Like I-cord, it produces regular stripes, but here the stripes are distinctly on the diagonal. Simply knit a bias strip (increasing at one end and decreasing at the other end) long enough to cover the desired edge. I like to finish the long edges of the bias band with a row of reverse single crochet. This provides a ditch into which you can invisibly top stitch the band, as well as a nice edge. Fold the band to the inside and stitch invisibly again. It's a little more work than applied I-cord, but worth the effort.

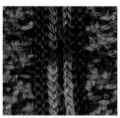 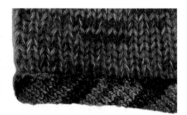

I-cord applied to the edges is set off with rows of solid garter stitch.

Plied, classic wool is paired with kid mohair for a soft, hazy look in the body. The wool worked alone as a bias band nicely echoes the intensified colors from the body.

Framing

Almost all hand dyers offer solids or semisolids that are dyed to coordinate with their multicolors. A big advantage to using these coordinated yarns is that yarn weight and behavior will be consistent, but even more so, the color aesthetic contains the same DNA. Whether you have chosen to randomize a hand-dyed yarn, use additional colors in pattern stitches, or intentionally pattern, realize that front bands, cuffs, bottom bands and collars will most likely be done on a stitch count or pattern that is not consistent with the main portion of the sweater. Think it through before beginning, so you can start with a framing yarn to begin with. Or begin with a temporary cast-on, and release this later to complete the edges after you have seen the total effect.

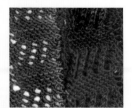

Reverse single crochet join.

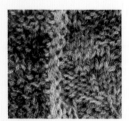

3-needle join.

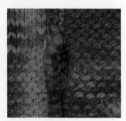

3-needle join with short-row detail.

No matter what approach you have taken in your hand-dyed project, finishing can provide couture touches that will make or break the final product. Many great resources exist for fine finishing techniques, but I'd like to cover some basics that are specifically useful with hand-dyed yarns.

Ravelry Pooled Knits

The online knitting community Ravelry (http://www.ravelry.com) includes a group devoted to intentional patterning with multicolored yarns. It is a lively group with lots of informative posts and pictures of pooled knitting and crochet. New members are always welcome, and you can find specific information there about many different yarns and effects, as well as gain inspiration from what others have done.

Karla Stuebing, David Chudzicki, and the Magic Chart Generator

One of the moderators of the Pooled Knits Ravelry group is Karla Stuebing, a knitter and research psychologist/statistician (her Ravelry id is Statnerd). She has focused her scientific skills on answering knitting questions using statistical software. One of the fruits of her inquiries is a pattern generator for hand-dyed yarns. She can select colors and the number of stitches for each color and quickly create graphic representations of different stitch counts. Independently, but spurred on by Karla's original idea, David Chudzicki, a mathematician working in predictive analytics, also developed a pattern generator that he has made available on the web for all to use, and he and Karla are collaborating on future features. It can be found at *www.plannedpooling.com* or search for "pooled knit generator" on Ravelry. I find it interesting that two such scientifically oriented and skilled people have turned their attention to knitting, with such lovely results. Using the generator can cut down on a lot of swatching, but I have found that some of the more subtle patterns that read well in charts are a bit lost when actually knit. You'll need to know the colors in the skein and the stitch counts for each color. Once you have narrowed your selection, you'll still want to swatch on that number to ensure that you are getting good results. The more complex a pattern is, the more difficult it will be to make tension adjustments and stay with the pattern.

Moving forward

Now you understand how hand-dyed yarns are created, and how they behave when knit or crocheted. In the following sections we will go beyond simply stitched fabric (stockinette, garter stitch, single crochet) to alter the appearance using pattern stitches — not for the beauty and interest of the stitch itself, but as a means to alter how the colors interact. Each approach is illustrated with swatches and sample projects. Each project is marked as either patterned or randomized. Most of the projects, while obviously rendered in a specific yarn, are very adaptable to other yarns. Anything marked randomized will most likely work with little consideration for repeats. If you wish to intentionally pattern to the same dimensions as the pictured project, however, you will have to find a yarn whose repeat matches the repeat used. To that end, the materials specification will detail not only yardage and yarn size but also the color repeat, so that you may more successfully duplicate our results.

Big, bold color

Twilight tunic

EASY + KNITTING

MINDFUL COLOR

WHAT'S THE MAGIC?

*Argyle dyed-around 64"
repeat on Magic Number.*

Color note *Even though we want the
colors to travel, we begin with a Magic
Number since pure stacking requires
full attention. Most of us will argyle on
a Magic Number. Adjust as needed.*

Notes 1 *See page 164 for abbreviations
and techniques AND page 26 for
Magic Number.* **2** *Use color-control
cast-on (page 27).* **3** *The Back and
Front are worked separately, then the
shoulder seams are joined. Stitches
are picked up along the sides to work
gussets and cuffs from side to side.*
4 *To custom size the garment, work
fewer or more rows in the gussets.*

DEC 1
At beginning of RS rows K1, k2tog.
At end of RS rows SSK, k1.

K1, P1 RIB
OVER AN EVEN NUMBER OF STITCHES
All rows or rounds [K1, p1] to end.

---

*(Previous page) Size 2: PRISM YARNS
Symphony in color Twilight*

---

*A 3-color dyed-around skein produces crisp, clean argyles that are relatively
easy to maintain (little attention was paid during the knitting process for this
piece). Even though the center front panel breaks stitch count at the neckline,
our eyes focus on the patterns. Side gussets turn the modest 18" center panel
into a generous 24" to 32" width for a joyous, playful piece that can easily be
sized up or down. Circular knitting at the neckline produces a deep turtleneck
of spirals.*

Back panel

Determine your Magic Number or a needle size to work with our number of 92.
With smaller needles, cast on your Magic Number (we cast on 92). Knit 12 rows — 6 garter
ridges — allowing colors to travel slightly. If needed, increase or decrease by 1 or 2 stitches to force
argyle. Change to stockinette stitch and work until piece measures 26" from beginning when held
upright to allow for downward stretch. Bind off firmly.

Front panel

Work as for Back until piece measures 22" when held upright. End with a WS row.
Shape neck
Next row (RS) Mark center 20 stitches for neck (21 if your Magic Number is odd). Knit to first marker,
attach second ball of yarn and bind off to marker; work to end. Working both sides at the same time
with separate balls of yarn, at each neck edge bind off 3 once, then 2 once. Dec 1 at each neck edge
every RS row 3 times — 8 stitches decreased each side. Work even until piece measures same length as
Back. Bind off firmly. Sew shoulder seams.

Side gussets

Mark each side edge of Front and Back, 6½" down from shoulder seam. With RS facing and smaller
needles, pick up and knit (PUK) along one side edge, from cast-on edge to shoulder seam to cast-on
edge, at a rate of 2 stitches for every 3 rows, making sure to have the same number of stitches from
cast-on edge to marker on each half. Work in garter stitch (knit every row) for **3** (**5**, **7**)".
Shape cuffs
Next 2 rows [**Work to first marker, place stitches just worked on hold, work to end**] twice.
Work K1, P1 Rib across remaining stitches for 3½". Bind off in pattern.
Repeat on other side edge.

Finishing

Place stitches on hold back onto needles.
With RS facing, join sides using 3-needle bind-off. Sew cuff seams.

10cm/4"

OVERSIZED FIT
Size **1** (**2**, **3**)
A **49** (**57**, **65**)"
B 26"
C **16** (**18**, **20**)"

20 stitches and
30 rows over
stockinette stitch,
using **smaller
needles**

Medium weight
1250 (**1500, 1750**) yds

4.5mm/US7,
or size to
make color
repeat work

4.5mm/US7
AND 2 sizes larger,
40cm (16") long

stitch markers

Collar

With RS facing, smaller circular needle, and starting at left shoulder seam, PUK along neck edge at the following rates: 2 stitches for every 3 rows along vertical edges and 1 stitch in every bound-off stitch. Place marker and join to work in the round. Work K1, P1 Rib for 4", adjusting total stitch count to a multiple of 2 on first round if necessary. Change to larger circular needle and continue in rib until piece measures 9½". Bind off loosely in pattern.

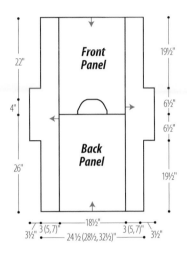

1,2 Work Back and Front Panels over your Magic Number.

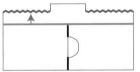

3 Seam shoulders. Pick up stitches along one side of panels and work side gusset to add width to the panels. Finish with ribbed cuff.

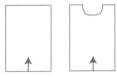

4 Pick up stitches along other side of panels and work side gusset and cuff.

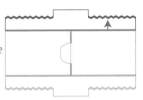

5 Close sides with 3-needle bind-off.

— Seam
— Picked-up stitches
〜〜 Stitches on hold
→ Direction of knitting

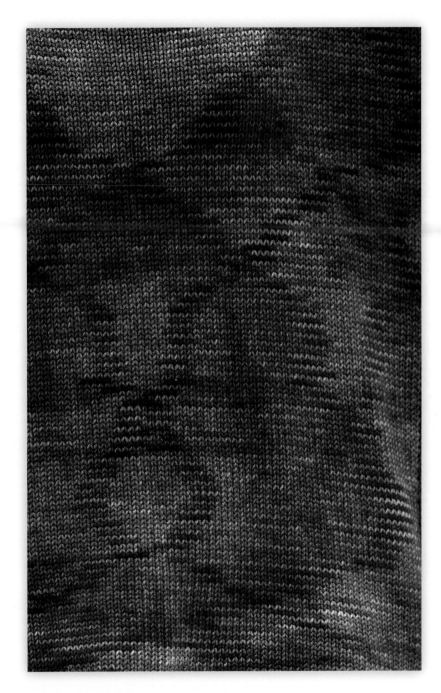

Sonata

EASY KNITTING

OTTO COLOR

WHAT'S THE MAGIC?

Randomize and optically mix 60" repeat with Half Linen Stitch.

Color note *Colors are blended by working a transition section alternating 2 rows of the old color with 2 rows of the new color. Start all color changes on a RS row. This approach will handle a broad range of color weight. Be sure to select individual yarns with little weight contrast within the yarn, but skeins that go through a larger range. Then, rank the skeins lightest to heaviest; decide whether you want the jacket center to be light or heavy, and go from there.*

Knitting notes 1 *See page 164 for abbreviations and techniques.* **2** *To "set" stitches, periodically grasp cast-on edge and fabric at needle and pull very hard, then tug gently width-wise to bring knitting back into shape. Stitches will lie more neatly and become more defined.* **3** *Fronts and Back are worked side to side. Sleeves are worked bottom up.* **4** *While alternating colors, carry colors not in use loosely along side edge.* **5** *Jacket can be made longer by casting on more stitches for Fronts and Back.* **6** *Measure for length with piece held up; measure for Stripe Sequences with piece lying flat.*

Half Linen Stitch assists in this softly blended jacket that shades through 8 different hand-dyed colors, ranging from light to heavy and back again. Each color works on its own for some time, then alternates every 2 rows with the next color. Changes from one color to another occur rather stealthily, with no apparent break. More painting with yarn!

Back

With smaller needle and C, cast on **154** (160, **170**). Work Half Linen Stitch in Stripe Sequence for Back and Fronts. During alternating color sections, alternate 2 rows of first color and 2 rows of second color for indicated length. Piece measures approximately **24** (27, **30**)". Bind off.

Fronts *MAKE 2*

Work as for Back until piece measures **10** (11, **12½**)", end with a RS color F row. *Next row* (WS) Work across row, catching waste yarn on WS to mark placement for attaching front band facing. Place stitches on hold.

Sleeves

With smaller needle and A, cast on **64** (70, **76**). Change to larger needle and work Linen Stitch for 13 rows. Change to smaller needle and, beginning with Row 2, work Half Linen Stitch in Stripe Sequence for Sleeve and AT SAME TIME, **[work 7 rows; Inc 1 each side on next row]** 17 times, working new stitches into pattern — **98** (104, **110**) stitches. Piece measures approximately **15** (14, **14**)", or continue to desired length. Bind off.

LINEN STITCH

Row 1 (RS) [K1, sl 1] to end.
Row 2 (WS) [P1, sl 1] to end.

2-st repeat

HALF LINEN STITCH

Row 1 (RS) [K1, sl 1] to end.
Rows 2 and 4 (WS) Purl.
Row 3 [Sl 1, k1] to end.

2-st repeat

Note Slip stitches purlwise with yarn at RS of work.

INC 1

At beginning of RS rows K1, M1.
At end of RS rows M1, k1.

DEC 1

At beginning of RS rows K1, k2tog.
At end of RS rows SSK, k1.

Stitch key

☐ Knit on RS, purl on WS
☑ Sl1 with yarn at RS

OVERSIZED FIT
Size 1 (2, **3**)
A 46 (52, **58**)" narrows slightly when worn
B 23½ (24½, **26**)"
C 27 (27½, **29**)"

10cm/4"

26 stitches and **48 rows** over Half Linen Stitch, using **smaller needles**

Fine weight
A, H
165 (175, **225**) yds each
B, C, D, E, F, G
350 (375, **450**) yds each

3.75mm/US5
AND
2 sizes larger,
60cm (24") or longer

stitch marker
contrasting waste yarn

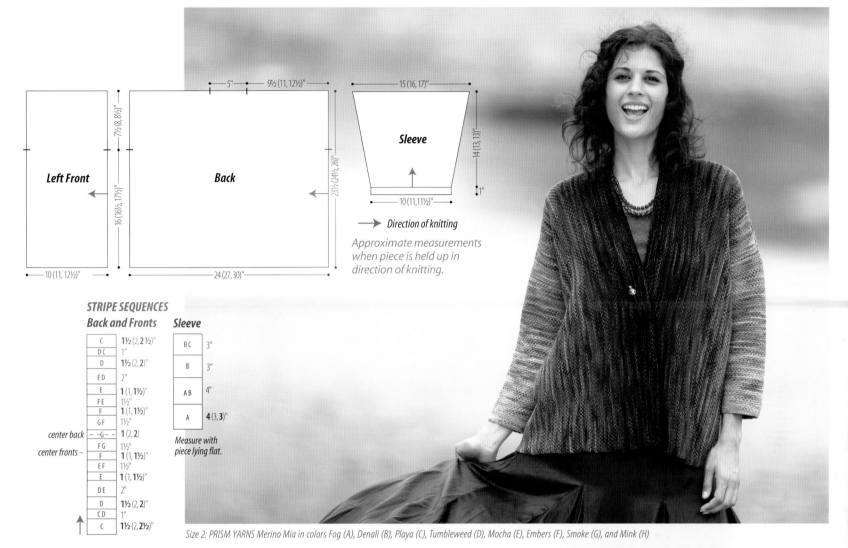

Left Front

7½ (8, 8½)"

16 (16½, 17½)"

10 (11, 12½)"

Back

5" 9½ (11, 12½)"

23½ (24½, 26)"

24 (27, 30)"

15 (16, 17)"

Sleeve

14 (13, 13)"

1"

10 (11, 11½)"

→ *Direction of knitting*

Approximate measurements when piece is held up in direction of knitting.

STRIPE SEQUENCES

Back and Fronts

C	1½ (2, 2½)"
DC	1"
D	1½ (2, 2)"
ED	2"
E	1 (1, 1½)"
FE	1½"
F	1 (1, 1½)"
GF	1½"
center back — –G– –	1 (2, 2)
center fronts – FG	1½"
F	1 (1, 1½)"
EF	1½"
E	1 (1, 1½)"
DE	2"
D	1½ (2, 2)"
CD	1"
↑ C	1½ (2, 2½)"

Sleeve

BC	3"
B	3"
AB	4"
A	4 (3, 3)"

Measure with piece lying flat.

Size 2: PRISM YARNS Merino Mia in colors Fog (A), Denali (B), Playa (C), Tumbleweed (D), Mocha (E), Embers (F), Smoke (G), and Mink (H)

Finishing

Sew shoulder seams firmly.

Front and Neck band Place right front stitches onto smaller needle, ready to work a RS row. With F, work in pattern across Right Front to shoulder seam. Pick up and k24 across back neck. Place left front stitches onto a needle, ready to work a RS row. Work in pattern across Left Front to end — **332** (344, **364**) stitches. Continue in pattern, alternating F and G for 1", then G only for 1". Change to H and, on next WS row, knit (turning row). Continue with H in pattern for 2", end with a WS row.

Attach facing [Pick up stitch above marked row and slip to left needle (PU), SSK picked-up stitch with next stitch on left needle] twice, pass first stitch over second stitch — 1 stitch bound off and facing attached. **[PU next stitch, SSK, pass first stitch over second stitch]** to end.
On each side edge, mark **7½** (8, **8½**)" down from shoulder seam on Fronts and Back. Sew sleeves between markers. Sew side and sleeve seams.

Alternate colorways, from top to bottom: Autumn, Jewels, Landscape, Neutrals

Sun shadows

OTTO COLOR

EASY + KNITTING

WHAT'S THE MAGIC?

Randomize and optically mix 49" repeat with 3 strands and pattern stitches.

Notes 1 *See page 164 for abbreviations and techniques.* **2** *Entire jacket is composed of 5 (5½, 6)" wide panels that are joined with 3-needle bind-off.* **3** *Work with 3 strands of yarn held together throughout. Each panel gradates from 1 color to another following Stitch and Color Sequence.* **4** *When adding a new strand, work 4 stitches before cutting the strand of the previous color.* **5** *Measure for length with piece held upright.*

Alternate colorways, from top to bottom: Autumn, Landscape, Neutrals Go ahead and mix light and heavy colors in this piece. Be sure that each panel shades between like-weighted colors for the most effective optical mixture.

Oh, the joys of thin yarn! Here, 3 strands of lace-weight wool are knit together throughout an oversized panel coat that is an ever-changing celebration of color. Each panel is constructed of 2 colors: it begins with 3 strands of A, changes to 2 A and 1 B, then 1 A and 2 B, finishing with 3 strands of B. The gradual shift allows each panel to move through changes in both hue and color weight. The panels are then arranged in a complex dance of color shadings. Contrasting colors selected from the palette outline each panel with an external 3-needle bind-off.

Notes for panels *Follow diagrams for Stitch and Color Sequence. For ease of assembly, each body panel and each sleeve panel should have the same number of rows.*
Selvedge stitches *For body panels and center sleeve panel, slip first stitch and work last stitch in stockinette (knit on RS, purl on WS).*

Body panels MAKE 9

Cast on **26** (30, **34**) for Pat 1 and 2 panels — **3** (3½, **4**) repeats of pattern + 2 selvedge stitches.
Cast on **25** (29, **33**) for Pat 3 panels — **5** (6, **7**) repeats of pattern + 3 + 2 selvedge stitches.
Work colors and pattern stitches according to Stitch and Color Sequence, working each color combination for 7", to a total of 28". Bind off *firmly*.

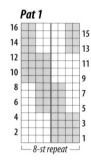
Pat 1

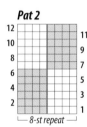
Pat 2

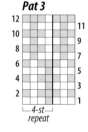
Pat 3

Red line indicates end of RS rows and beginning of WS rows for Size 2.

Stitch key
☐ Knit on RS, purl on WS
▨ Purl on RS, knit on WS

For In Other Words for these charts, see page 160.

OVERSIZED FIT
Size **1** (2, **3**)
A **51** (55½, **60**)"
B **28**"
C **29**"

10cm/4"

22 stitches and **28 rows** over all stitch patterns with 3 strands held together

Superfine weight
6 colors 1025 (1075, **1125**) yds each

5.5mm/US9

3.75mm/F-5

Spare needle for 3-needle bind-off

STITCH AND COLOR SEQUENCE

Back

5 (5½, 6)"

3D	3C	3E	3F	3A
1E 2D	1A 2C	1F 2E	1D 2F	1C 2A
2E 1D	2A 1C	2F 1E	2D 1F	2C 1A
3E	3A	3F	3D	3C

28"

7"

25 (27½, 30)"

Left Front

3C	3A
1B 2C	1D 2A
2B 1C	2D 1A
3B	3D

Right Front

3E	3B
1F 2E	1A 2B
2F 1E	2A 1B
3F	3A

10 (11, 12)"

Stitch pattern key

Pat 1 Broken diagonal rib
Cast on **26** (**30**, **34**)

Pat 2 Checkerboard
Cast on **26** (**30**, **34**)

Pat 3 Seeded rib check
Cast on **25** (**29**, **33**)

Color key

A Periwinkles
B Highlands
C Tumbleweed
D Tahoe
E Plum Dandy
F Woodlands

Diagrams show stitch pattern and color blends for each panel.
For example, far left back panel is worked in Pat 1: cast on **26** (**30**, **34**)
with 3 strands of E (**3 E**); work 7". Add 1 strand of D, knit 4 stitches,
cut 1 strand of E (**2 E 1 D**); work 7". Add second D, k4, cut second E
(**1 E 2 D**); work 7". Add third D, k4, cut third E (**3 D**); work 7".
For sleeve panels shown on next page, work each color combination
for **4** (**3¾**, **3½**)".

*Size 3: PRISM YARNS Lace Wool in colors Periwinkles (A), Highlands
(B), Tumbleweed (C), Tahoe (D), Plum Dandy (E), and Woodlands (F)*

Center Sleeve panels *MAKE 2*

Work colors and pattern stitches according to diagram as for body, but work each combination for **4** (3¾, **3½**)" only to a total of **16** (15, **14**)". Bind off loosely in pattern.

Right-side Sleeve panels *MAKE 2*

Work increased stitches into pattern.
Cast on 17. Work selvedge stitch at end of RS and beginning of WS rows only, and increase 1 at beginning of RS every 6 rows 14 times. Work even until piece measures **16** (15, **14**)". Bind off *loosely* in pattern.

Left-side Sleeve panels *MAKE 2*

Work as for Right-side sleeve panel EXCEPT reverse shaping. Work selvedge stitch at beginning of RS and end of WS rows only, and increase 1 at end of RS every 6 rows.

Finishing

Collarband Cast on 33. Work Pat 3, shading through colors and using any remaining yarn as you wish; collar can go through more than one color sequence. Work 194 rows (or length of your Body panel) for Right Front, **40** (44, **48**) rows for back neck and 194 rows for Left Front.

Join Panels Lay out the panels and double check that you like the color flow. Choose a contrasting color for each seam. With 3 strands held together, pick up and knit (PUK) 1 stitch in each slipped stitch along the long edge of first panel. PUK the same number of stitches along adjacent edge of next panel. With WS together, work 3-needle bind-off *loosely*. Repeat for each set of panels of back, fronts, and sleeves. Join shoulder seams with 3-needle bind-off worked *firmly*.

With 3-needle bind-off, join sleeve top to armhole edge and join side seams.

Turn jacket inside out and with 3 strands of any color and crochet hook, slip-stitch crochet firmly along shoulder seams and back neck edge, drawing total shoulder seam in to measurement of approximately **25** (27½, **30**)", with no stretch allowed. Lace-weight wool is delicate and stretchy and requires a firm shoulder seam.

Attach Collarband With 3 strands of a contrasting color, prepare Right Front and right half of back neck: PUK in each slipped stitch of Right Front and **10** (11, **12**) along back neck to center. Mark center of Collarband and PUK in each slipped stitch. Join with 3-needle bind-off. Repeat with second color for Left Front, left back neck, and second half of Collarband.

With RS facing, PUK in each slipped stitch of remaining long edge of collar. Fold collar to inside and attach collar facing: beginning at lower Right Front, **[slip 1 stitch, insert right needle into first stitch where collar joins body; knit through both picked-up and slipped stitches]** twice, then pass first stitch over second stitch: 1 stitch bound off and collar facing attached. Continue, working each stitch on needle together with a picked-up stitch from body, to end.

Winter snow

Dyed-around yarn is worked on triple the Magic Number, creating stacks whose jagged edges are reminiscent of ikat. The entire piece is worked circularly and then steeked for armholes and front opening. Solid cream sleeves and sandwashed taupe and beige complement the stacks with an intarsia-box trim.

Winter snow

ATTENTIVE COLOR

INTERMEDIATE KNITTING

WHAT'S THE MAGIC?

Stack dyed-around 64" repeat worked circularly, on 3 times Magic Number.

Color notes

1 Check your gauge and color stacking carefully both prior to beginning and after every row.
2 If changing needle size does not achieve our Magic Number of 94, you will need to do a little math. Your MN × 3 =____. Divide the difference between your MN and ours by 4 = D. Add (or subtract) 1 × D to each Front and 2 × D to Back. That's it!
3 During finishing, you will cut the center front steek up the vertical area of A, and avoid cutting into B or C. If the colors start to move too far, manipulate tension or change needle size to make certain that colors are stacking relatively vertically. (It is quite possible that from day to day you might need a different size needle — this teaches you more about your knitting than you ever thought you would know!)

Knitting notes 1 *See page 164 for abbreviations and techniques AND page 26 for Magic Number.* **2** *Use color-control cast-on (page 27).* **3** *Body is worked circularly with steeks and then cut open for front and armholes. Stitches are picked up along armholes after cutting steeks, then sleeves are worked circularly from the top down.* **4** *Fronts are narrower than Back to allow for front bands, so placement of armhole bind-off is not centered.* **5** *Sleeve bands and bottom band are worked in stranded color work. Carry colors not in use loosely along side edge.* **6** *Measure for length with piece held up to allow for downward stretch.*

PRISM YARNS Symphony in colors Dune (MC), Crème (A), Beige (B), and Taupe (C)

Determine your Magic Number or a needle size to work with our number of 94.

Body

With larger 24" needle, MC, a temporary cast-on, and beginning in the center of a section of A, cast on 282 or triple your Magic Number (see Color Note 2). Join to work in the round, being careful not to twist stitches. K2, k1 tbl, place marker (pm) for end of steek, work to last 3 stitches, pm for beginning of steek, k1 tbl, k2. Work in stockinette, stacking colors and knitting first and last steek stitches tbl, until piece measures 18", end at center of steek.

Armhole Steek K60 for Right Front, k8 and place on hold, for armhole, knit until there are 146 on needle for Back after bind-off, k8 and place on hold for armhole, knit to end for Left Front. ***Next round*** **[Work to held stitches, pm, cast on 8 for steek using backward-loop method, pm]** twice. Continue in stockinette, knitting first and last steek stitches tbl, until piece measures 8" from steek cast-on. Bind off. With RS facing, crochet hook, and MC, finish crochet-and-cut steeks along armholes and center front. Sew shoulder seams.

Sleeves

Change to dpn when necessary.

Place held armhole stitches on larger 16" needle. With RS facing and A, pick up and knit (PUK) at a rate of 2 stitches for every 3 rows along vertical edges (picking up through both layers of body and steek facing), and work across 4 armhole stitches; pm for beginning of round. Work 3" even. **[Knit 3 rounds; SSK, knit to last 2 stitches, k2tog on next round]** 20 times — 48 stitches decreased. Work even until piece measures 14½" from pick-up. Work 12 rounds of Sleeve Band chart. Bind off.

Finishing

Bottom Band Remove waste yarn from cast-on edge and place all stitches except steek stitches onto larger 24" needle — 276 stitches. Work 12 rows of Bottom Band chart. Bind off.

  10cm/4"

ONE SIZE
A 60"
B 26"
C 30"

20 stitches and **30 rows** over stockinette stitch, using **larger needle**

Medium weight
MC 1050 yds
A 700 yds
B 100 yds
C 175 yds

4mm/US6, or size to make color repeat work, 40cm (16") AND 60cm (24") or longer AND 1 size smaller, 60cm (24") or longer

4mm/US6

4mm/G-6

stitch markers waste yarn

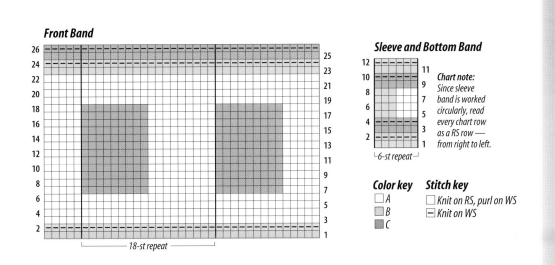

Front Band

Sleeve and Bottom Band

Chart note:
Since sleeve band is worked circularly, read every chart row as a RS row — from right to left.

└ 6-st repeat ┘

└ 18-st repeat ┘

Color key
☐ A
▨ B
▨ C

Stitch key
☐ Knit on RS, purl on WS
⊟ Knit on WS

Front Band

Notes 1 *When picking up stitches, leave approximately a 3-yrd tail, winding it into a butterfly.* ***2*** *Pick up along back neck in the first full stitch below the bind-off, even though it leaves a ridge on the inside.* ***3*** *Rows 7–18 are worked in intarsia. Cut 17 pieces each of A and C, 3½ yds long, and wind into butterflies. When changing color in a row, twist A and C on the WS to prevent holes. First color A block is worked with yarn from previous row.* ***4*** *Front steeks are hidden inside front band when facing is attached to pick-up row.*

With RS facing, larger 24" needle, and C, starting at lower right front corner, PUK along front and neck edges at the following rates: 2 stitches for every 3 rows along vertical edge (picking up through one layer only, leaving steek facing free), and 1 stitch for every bound-off stitch. Count stitches and adjust to a multiple of 18 + 1 on next row if necessary. Knit 1 row. Cut C.

Work 26 rows of Front Band chart. Last row is turning row for facing. With smaller 24" needle and A, work stockinette stitch until facing is same width as Front Band, end with a WS row.

Attach facing [Pick up stitch immediately next to pick-up row and slip to left needle (PU), SSK picked-up stitch with next stitch] twice, pass first stitch over second stitch — 1 stitch bound off and facing attached. **[PU next stitch, SSK, pass first stitch over second stitch]** to end.

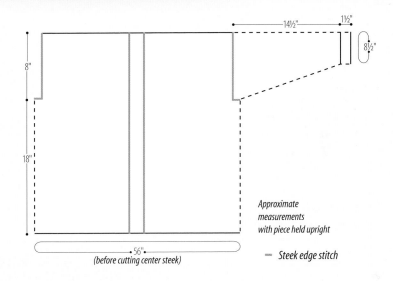

Approximate measurements with piece held upright

— *Steek edge stitch*

14½"   1½"

8½"

8"

18"

56"
(before cutting center steek)

SIZING OPTIONS

Model garment has a narrow sleeve. For a wider sleeve, begin the armhole steek at 17 (16)" — 9 (10)" below shoulder seam. For sleeve, PUK more stitches as necessary and decrease an additional 2 (4) times.

Jacket may be made on double your Magic Number for a more traditional fit.

Sampler jacket

EASY KNITTING

OTTO COLOR

WHAT'S THE MAGIC?

Randomize 64" repeat with pattern stitches and solid colors.

Notes 1 *See page 164 for abbreviations and techniques.* **2** *Use 3 sizes of needles: the size used for garter-stitch gauge AND 2 sizes larger AND 3 sizes smaller to get consistent gauge over pattern stitches.* **3** *Sleeve shaping is made according to measurement, not row count.* **4** *While pattern sections are roughly equal in size, patterns should end on rows indicated, so may be slightly over or under measurement as long as final size is reached.* **5** *Measure for length with piece held up; measure for pattern bands with piece lying flat.*

INC 1

At beginning of row K1, M1.
At end of row M1, k1.

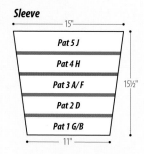

Sleeve
— 15" —

Pat 5 J
Pat 4 H
Pat 3 A/F
Pat 2 D
Pat 1 G/B

15½"

— 11" —

PRISM YARNS Symphony in colors 105 (A), Highlands (B), 111 (C), Autumn (D), 112 (E), Yosemite (F), 201 (G), Mozambique (H), 801 (I), Embers (J), and Cabernet (L)

This jacket was inspired by one that Beryl and Lindy at Tricoter in Seattle made, who in turn were inspired by a kimono designed by Carol Lapin, CC Conway, and Nadine Shapiro, that was featured in Simply Knit 3. The Tricoter version was the first jacket that I observed on many different bodies, looking great on all of them! Here I have taken the basic shape and concept and added a sampler of textured and slipped stitches to the mix. The stitches serve to randomize a variety of coordinating hand-dyed multicolors, which are further enhanced with judiciously selected sandwashed solids. Oh, the possibilities!

Sleeves

With **smaller needles** and **A**, cast on 56. Knit 8 rows.

Band 1
With **gauge needles** and **G**, knit 1 row. Work **Pat 1** for 2½", end with Row 4 or 8. Purl 1 row.
With **C**, knit 4 rows, Inc 1 each end of first and third row — 60 stitches.

Band 2
With **smaller needles** and **D**, Inc 1, knit to end — 61 stitches. Work **Pat 2** for 2½", end with Row 8 or 16. Purl 1 row.
With **gauge needles** and **E**, knit 4 rows, Inc 1 at end of first row — 62 stitches.

Band 3
With **larger needles** and **A**, knit 2 rows. Work **Pat 3** for 2½", end with Row 4 or 8.
With **gauge needles** and **G**, knit 4 rows, Inc 1 each end of first row and last 2 rows — 68 stitches.

Band 4
With **H**, knit 1 row. Work **Pat 4** for 2½", end with a RS row. Purl 1 row.
With **I**, knit 4 rows, Inc 1 each end of first row and M1 in middle of first row — 71 stitches.

Band 5
With **larger needles** and **J**, work **Pat 5** for 2½", Inc 1 each end of row after 1" and again after 2", working additional stitches in garter stitch and ending with Row 2 or 6 — 75 stitches.
With **gauge needles** and **A**, knit 2 rows. Bind off.

SIZING OPTIONS

To adjust the size, work each pattern stitch for more or fewer inches. For example, by working 2" of each pattern, Back will measure 25" and each Front will measure 10" for a circumference of approximately 51". Since the Body is narrower, you will want to add length to the Sleeve, working each pattern for 3".

 10cm/4"

ONE SIZE
A 27"
B 27"
C 31", approximate measurements, as worn

20 stitches over Pat 1 using **gauge needles**
Row gauge varies depending on pattern.

Medium weight
A, D 500 yds
B, F, J, L 175 yds each
C, E, I 25 yds each
G 125 yds
H 300 yds

5mm/US8
or size to obtain gauge
AND
2 sizes larger
AND
3 sizes smaller

3.75mm/F-5   2 spare needles

Pat 1

6-st repeat

Pat 2

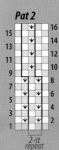

2-st repeat

Pat 3

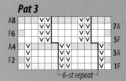

6-st repeat

Pat 4

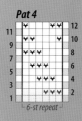

6-st repeat

Pat 5

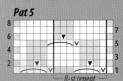

8-st repeat

Stitch key

☐ K on RS, p on WS
☐ P on RS, k on WS
▼ Sl 1 purlwise with yarn at RS of work
∨ Sl 1 purlwise with yarn at WS of work
k K2tog below
↓ K in the row below
⌢ Pass slipped stitch over 4
▼ K1 under running thread between stitch just worked and next stitch

For In Other Words for these charts, see page 160.

Sampler jacket

Whew! Now, the body is worked in 4 pieces, then the Back is joined with 3-needle bind-off at the center.

DEC 1

At beginning of row K1, k2tog.
At end of row SSK, k1.

Left Front

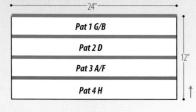

Back

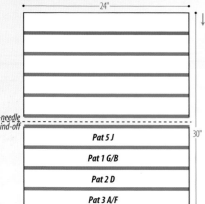

Right Front

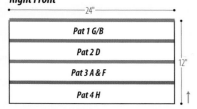

Approximate measurements when piece is held up in direction of knitting.

Color key
A   105
B   *Highlands*
D   *Autumn*
F   *Yosemite*
G   *201*
H   *Mozambique*

Right Front

With **gauge needles** and **A**, cast on 122. Knit 2 rows.
Band 1
With **H**, knit 1 row. Work **Pat 4** for 2½". Purl 1 row.
With **G**, knit 4 rows.
Band 2
With **larger needles** and **A**, knit 2 rows. Work **Pat 3**, knitting 2 stitches at beginning and end of every row, for 2½", end with Row 4 or 8.
With **gauge needles** and **E**, knit 4 rows, Dec 1 at end of last row — 121 stitches.
Band 3
With **smaller needles** and **D**, work **Pat 2** to 9" from cast-on, end with Row 8 or 16. Purl 1 row.
With **gauge needles** and **C**, knit 4 rows.
Band 4
With **G**, knit 1 row, Inc 1 at end of row — 122 stitches. Work **Pat 1** for 2½". Purl 1 row.
With **I**, knit 2 rows. Place stitches on hold.
Repeat for Left Front.

Right Back

Work as for Right Front EXCEPT do not place stitches on hold. With **I**, knit 2 more rows, Dec 1 at each end of first row and end of second row — 119 stitches.
With **larger needles** and **J**, work **Pat 5** until piece measures 14½" from cast-on.
With **gauge needles** and **E**, knit 2 rows. Place stitches on hold.

Left Back

Work as for Right Back. With RS together and **E**, join Backs with 3-needle bind-off.

Finishing

Sew shoulder seams firmly. (Place WS together and slip stitch through selvedge with crochet hook. It is important that there not be any stretch in the shoulder seams.)
Place front stitches on **gauge needles** (you may need 2 circular needles). Beginning at right front bottom edge with **I**, knit all stitches to back neck, pick up and knit (PUK) 30 along back neck edge, knit all stitches of Left Front — 270 stitches. Knit 1 row. With **L**, work 8 rows in stockinette stitch.

Intarsia blocks

Note *Wind 13 bobbins of A and 14 bobbins of L. Use a separate bobbin for each block of color. When changing color in a row, twist yarns on the WS to prevent holes.*
With **gauge needle**, k11 **L**, [k8 **A**, k12 **L**] to last 19 stitches, k8 **A**, k11 **L**. Continue in stockinette stitch, working 11 more rows as established. Cut **A**. With **L**, work 8 rows. With **A**, work 3 rows, then knit WS turn row. Work 28 rows in stockinette. Turn jacket inside out and fold collar band to inside.
Attach front facing/collar
Insert right needle into first **L** stitch of body (where **L** joins **I**), and then into first stitch on left needle, and knit these 2 stitches together. **[Insert right needle into next L stitch of body and first stitch on left needle, and knit these 2 stitches together, then pass first stitch over]** to end (you are both joining facing and binding off at the same time).
With **gauge needles** and **A**, pick up 300 stitches around bottom edge. Knit 4 rows, then bind off loosely.

Moonlight

EASY KNITTING

ATTENTIVE COLOR

WHAT'S THE MAGIC?

Stack double-dyed repeat of 58" on Magic Number.

Color note *The vest is patterned over a full Magic Number. If our Magic Number of 73 does not pattern, even with a needle-size change, the 2-stitch repeat and simple shape make it easy to adjust the pattern to your number.*

Notes 1 *See page 164 for abbreviations and techniques AND page 26 for Magic Number.*
2 *Use color-control cast-on (see page 27).*
3 *Vest is worked in one piece from lower back to shoulders, then back neck stitches are bound off and fronts are worked separately.*
4 *Information is color-coded as follows:* Moonlight, *Sunset,* All versions.

Moonlight PRISM YARNS Kid Slique in color Playa

A soft yarn such as Kid Slique allows loosely worked Fisherman's Rib to spread and adjust to a body's contours without any shaping. Colors on the rayon portion were intentionally patterned, while the solid kid mohair strand softens transitions. Subtle colors and poor light for nighttime knitting resulted in meandering color rivers—not an unpleasant effect at all!

Determine your Magic Number or a needle size to work with our number of 73.

Back and Fronts

With larger needles, cast on 73. Work Fisherman's Rib, beginning with Set-up Row for 20".
Shape neck
Work across 25 stitches and leave on hold for Right Front, bind off until 25 stitches remain for Left Front, work to end. Continue on 25 stitches of Left Front (check to make certain that colors are still stacking) for 20". Bind off. Rejoin yarn at neck edge and work Right Front.

Finishing

Sew side seams for 11". Mark Fronts for 1 large button approximately 12"–13" from bottom. With smaller crochet hook, work 1 row sc around front and neck edges, working 1 sc in every 2 rows along Fronts and each stitch across back neck, drawing back neck in slightly to stabilize. Work 1 row reverse sc, working 1 stitch in each stitch and working an 8-chain button loop at right front marker. Work Armhole border as for Sunset (page 94).

SIZING OPTIONS *For a larger vest, add a gusset.*

Fisherman's Rib

Stitch key
☐ Knit on RS, purl on WS
▨ Purl on RS, knit on WS
▾ Knit1 below (k1b)

FISHERMAN'S RIB
Set-up row (WS) [K1, p1] to last stitch, k1.
Row 1 (RS) K1, [knit 1 in stitch below (k1b), p1] to last 2 stitches, k1b, k1.
Row 2 K1, [p1, k1b] to last 2 stitches, p1, k1.

P1, K1 RIB
Row 1 (WS) [P1, k1] to last stitch, p1.
Row 2 (RS) [K1, p1] to last stitch, k1.

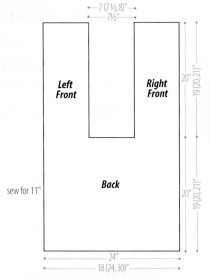

7 (7½, 8)"
7½"

Left Front

Right Front

Back

19 (20, 21)"
20 (20, 21)"

20 (20, 21)"
19 (20, 21)"

sew for 11"

24"
18 (24, 30)"

Approximate measurements, slightly stretched.

OVERSIZED FIT
A 48"
B 20"
Sizes 1 (2, 3)
A 36 (48, 60)"
B 19 (20, 21)"

10cm/4"

12 stitches and 25 rows
12 stitches and 22 rows
over Fisherman's Rib,
slightly stretched, using
larger needles

4
Medium weight
600 yds

B 250 (300, **525**) yds

5
Bulky weight
A 175 (225, **400**) yds

C 175 (225, **400**) yds

6.5mm/US10½
or size to make color
repeat work
AND
2 sizes smaller

4mm/G-6
5.5mm/I-9

38mm (1½") button

Sunset

EASY KNITTING

OTTO COLOR

WHAT'S THE MAGIC?

Randomize repeat of 52" and 62" with a solid by alternating 1-row A, B, C stripes.

Color notes 1 *With 3 different wools worked in 1-row A, B, C stripes, there is no specific attention paid to stacking. Two of the colors are softly variegated, while the third has 5 distinctly different colors and wants to pattern. The 2 tonal colors spread the highly variegated colors out, minimizing A's random pooling.* **2** *To work A, B, C, stripes: Cast on with A, drop A and join B; work Set-up Row, drop B and join C; work Row 1. A is waiting at the beginning of Row 2. In this manner, alternate 1 row of each of the 3 colors over the 2 rows of Fisherman's Rib pattern. You can't lose your place, even on circular needles, as you always begin where there are 2 colors, and you never use the color just finished.* **3** *To keep yarns from tangling, place 1 ball on each side of you and 1 ball in front. When you turn, lift the work up and look at how the strands lie — in 1 direction they twist, in the other they stay separate. You will occasionally need to move a strand over or under a needle to keep the order.*

Sunset Size 2: PRISM YARNS Merino 12 in color Harvest (A); BLUE MOON Gaea in color Copperline (B); and LORNA'S LACES Shepherd Worsted in color Intrigue (C)

*For **Notes**, **Size**, **Gauge**, **Needles** and **Note** see page 92.*

The same shape worked with different yarns results in a much different style. Firmer wool yarns, while the same gauge, do not have the same soft drape. This fun and perky vest is a great accent piece, however. A strongly colored multi color is toned down in A, B, C stripes with a tonal rust strand and a monochromatic gold/green combo. You can see that the gold is following a path and trying to pattern, but the stripes break the unwanted strong patterning. Our vest was worked on 73 stitches; on different stitch counts and with different yarns, patterning may or may not occur.

Back and Fronts

With larger needles, cast on **55** (**73**, **91**). Work Fisherman's Rib with 1-row A, B, C stripes (see Color note 2), beginning with Set-up Row for **19** (**20**, **21**)".

Shape neck

Work across **17** (**25**, **33**) and leave on hold for Right Front, bind off until **17** (**25**, **33**) stitches remain for Left Front, work to end. Continue on **17** (**25**, **33**) stitches of Left Front for **19** (**20**, **21**)". Bind off. Rejoin yarn at neck edge and work Right Front.

Finishing

Sew side seams for 11".

Armhole border With smaller crochet hook and B, work 1 sc in every 2 rows around armhole edge. With larger crochet hook and A, slip stitch through the back loop of each sc.

Front and neck borders With smaller needles, B, and beginning at Right Front, pick up and knit (PUK) 1 stitch for every 2 rows to back neck, 1 stitch in each stitch across back neck (underneath the bound-off edge and directly into the stitch), and 1 stitch for every 2 rows to bottom. Turn and work P1, K1 Rib. Continue working P1, K1 Rib as follows: 1 row C, 1 row A, 1 row B; repeat once, then work 1 row C. Bind off in pattern with A to 9" from beginning (or desired placement for button loop).

Work button loop

With yarn forward, slip next C stitch, with yarn back, slip next C stitch and pass first C stitch over (leave A stitch on needle). Continue to bind off C stitches to desired size (we bound off 4 stitches for a 1½" button). Return to A and yarn over, pass A stitch over (chain stitch made). Repeat for desired length of chain (we made 6 chains). Bind off in pattern to end. Do not cut A. With larger crochet hook, work 1 row slip stitch along bottom edge, through the bottom loop of every stitch (nothing should show except A; the edge will look like the bound-off edge of Front). Sew button to Left Front.

Tropical garden

OTTO COLOR

INTERMEDIATE KNITTING

WHAT'S THE MAGIC?

Structure a randomized hand-paint with lace stitch.

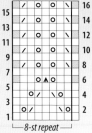

A true hand-painted yarn with little tendency to pattern becomes the perfect vehicle for painting with yarn. Simply alternate repeats of 1 color (A) with repeats of 2 colors (2 rows A, 2 rows B). Move into a repeat of B alone, and continue to progress through a range of colors.

Blended legs

Arrange 9 colors in a pleasing order. Assign colors A, B, C, D, E, F, G, H, I.
With A, loosely cast on 89. Following Blended Legs diagram, work 1 repeat of Arrow Lace in designated color(s). When 2 colors (A B) are shown, alternate 2 rows A with 2 rows B.
Place stitches on hold and work second leg.

Join for mitered square

With I, work across both legs, placing marker in middle — 178 stitches. Turn and knit back.
Note For the rest of the square, alternate 2 rows H with 2 rows I until H is used up, then work remaining rows in I alone.
Rows 1, 5, 7, 11 Knit to 2 stitches before marker, k2tog; slip marker (sm), SSK, knit to end — 2 stitches decreased. **Rows 2, 4, 8, 10** Purl. **Row 3** K1, **[yo, SSK]** to 3 stitches before marker, k1, k2tog; sm, SSK, k1, **[yo, k2tog]** to last stitch, k1 — 174 stitches. **Row 9** K1, **[yo, SSK]** to 2 stitches before marker, k2tog; sm, SSK, **[yo, k2tog]** to last stitch, k1 — 168 stitches. **Rows 6 and 12** Knit. Repeat Rows 1–12 for mitered square, decreasing stitch count by 2 every RS row, until 8 stitches remain. Continue to decrease at markers and discontinue eyelets until 2 stitches remain. **Next row** K2tog and fasten off. Pin to desired dimensions and steam. Allow to dry before unpinning.

Arrow Lace

Stitch key
- ☐ Knit on RS, purl on WS
- ☐ Purl on RS
- ☑ K2tog
- ◣ SSK
- ▲ SK2P
- ⊙ Yarn over (yo)

ARROW LACE *MULTIPLE OF 8 + 1*

Row 1 and all WS rows Purl. **Row 2** K1, [yo, SSK, k3, k2tog, yo, k1] to end. **Row 4** K2, [yo, SSK, k1, k2tog, yo, k3], end last repeat k2. **Row 6** P1, [k2, yo, sl 1-k 2 tog-psso (SK2P), yo, k2, p1] to end. **Rows 8, 10, 12, 14, 16** P1, [SSK, (k1, yo) twice, k1, k2tog, p1] to end.

Notes 1 See page 164 for abbreviations and techniques. **2** Both long legs of wrap are worked, then mitered square is worked across their stitches to complete wrap.

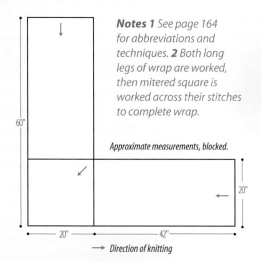

Approximate measurements, blocked.

Blended Legs   Miter

Join legs with mitered square. Alternate 2 rows I, 2 rows H until H is used up. End with I.

⟶ *Direction of knitting*

Make 2

☐ 16-row repeat of Arrow Lace in colors shown.
A B Alternate 2 rows A, 2 rows B; etc.

Tropical garden (left): KOIGU YARNS KPPPM in colors P105L (A), P628 (B), P221 (C), P205 (D), P471 (E), P470B (F), P518 (G), P741 (H), and P882B (I)

Watercolor (right, and on following spread): PRISM YARNS Merino Mia in colors Terra Cotta (A), Coral Reef (B), Sierra (C), Blue Lagoon (D), Tumbleweed (E), Nevada (F), Thunderclap (G), Woodlands (H), and Night Music (I)

10cm/4"

ONE SIZE
Each leg approximately
20" × 42" after blocking

25 stitches = 5" and
32 rows = 4" over Arrow
pattern, blocked

Fine weight
A, B, C, D, E, F, G, H 170 yds each
I 340 yds

4.5mm/US7 or size to obtain gauge.

Watercolor

ATTENTIVE COLOR

INTERMEDIATE KNITTING

WHAT'S THE MAGIC?

Stack dyed-around 60" repeat on Magic Number.

Lace expands, increasing the width achievable with Magic Number

Color notes 1 *Because of the larger stitch repeat, adjust needle size or, if your Magic Number (page 26) is different and not divisible by the repeat, make as many full repeats as possible and then add garter stitches to the sides as a border, bringing the total to your Magic Number.*

2 Dyed-around skeins can stack, as shown in this lacy wrap. Depending on the number of colors within the skein (2 of these 8 colors are 4-color combinations, the rest are 3-color), the colors stack in pure or every-other-row columns. Especially because the yarn is fine, optical mixture takes over and the every-other-row stacks appear as pure color from a distance.

3 Careful attention was paid to aligning like colors when new skeins were added. For example, blue in the center as shown at right. In the back, a large mitered square joining the fronts is worked intarsia-style using a different, simpler pattern stitch for ease of knitting as stitch counts change, and also to eliminate the need for continued color patterning.

ONE SIZE
For **Size, Gauge, Needle**s and **Note**
see page 96.

Fine weight
9 colors 175 yds each

Stacked legs

Arrange 9 colors in a pleasing order. Assign colors A, B, C, D, E, F, G, H, I. Determine your Magic Number or a needle size to work with our number of 97. With A and using color-control cast-on (page 27), cast on 97 (or your Magic Number, see Color Note 1). Work 6 repeats of Arrow Lace, then change to B. Following Stacked Legs diagram, work 6 repeats of B and C, end with 3 repeats of D. Place stitches on hold. Work second leg, following diagram. Do not bind off.

Join for mitered square

Square alternates 2 rows of color E with 2 rows of colors D and F, which are worked for half of their respective rows only. Twist colors D and F around each other at color change to avoid holes.

With E, work across D stitches from one leg, place marker, work across F stitches from other leg — 194 stitches. Turn and knit back.
Row 1 With D, knit to 2 stitches before marker, k2tog; slip marker (sm), drop D, add F, SSK, knit to end — 192 stitches. *Row 2* With F, purl to marker; with D, purl to end. *Row 3* With E, k1, **[yo, SSK]** to 3 stitches before marker, k1, k2tog; sm, SSK, k1, **[yo, k2tog]** to last stitch, k1 — 190 stitches. *Row 4* With E, purl. *Row 5* With D and F, repeat Row 1 — 188 stitches. *Row 6* With F and D, knit. *Row 7* With E, repeat Row 1 — 186 stitches. *Row 8* With E, purl. *Row 9* With D, k1, **[yo, SSK]** to 2 stitches before marker, k2tog; sm, with F, SSK, **[yo, k2tog]** to last stitch, k1 — 184 stitches. *Row 10* With F and D, purl. *Row 11* With E, repeat Row 1 — 182 stitches. *Row 12* With E, knit. Repeat Rows 1–12 for mitered square, decreasing stitch count by 2 every RS row, until 8 stitches remain. Continue to decrease at marker and discontinue eyelets until 2 stitches remain. *Next row* K2tog and fasten off. Pin to desired dimensions and steam. Allow to dry before unpinning.

Stacked Legs

F 3×	D 3×
G 6×	C 6×
H 6×	B 6×
I 6×	A 6×

6×, 3× Number of repeats of Arrow Lace worked in designated color

Color key
A *Terra Cotta*
B *Coral Reef*
C *Sierra*
D *Blue Lagoon*
E *Tumbleweed*
F *Nevada*
G *Thunderclap*
H *Woodlands*
I *Night Music*

Miter

Join legs with mitered square. Alternate 2 rows E, 2 rows D/F, changing color at the miter.

Painted desert

EASY+ KNITTING

ATTENTIVE COLOR

WHAT'S THE MAGIC?

Stack dyed-across 51" repeat on Half Magic Number.

Color notes 1 *The vest is designed so colors will stack on top of one another in each panel, creating vertical columns of color. Before winding, identify the dye pattern (page 24). For a dyed-across skein, mark the center of the end colors. Cast on, then begin the first row of garter edging at one of the markers. The next marker should appear at the next edge. If you reach the marker before the row's end, try a smaller needle. If you reach row's end before the marker, try a larger needle.*
2 *If half your Magic Number does not work with our 49-stitch panels even with a needle-size change, OR if you wish to use a different yarn, determine the stitch count needed to pattern, then fit in the lace repeat, working any extra stitches as garter-stitch borders on each panel.*
3 *Vest is worked in 3 patterned panels and 2 unpatterned side gussets. When adding yarn, remember to begin at a selvedge edge at the middle of an end color.*
4 *Begin with side gussets, which are not color stacked, to familiarize yourself with the pattern stitch.*

Knitting notes 1 *See page 164 for abbreviations and techniques AND page 26 for Magic Number.* ***2*** *Use color-control cast-on (page 27).*

BLUE MOON Socks That Rock Mediumweight in colors Coppertree (A) and Corvid Fledge (B); Socks That Rock Lightweight in color Jabberwocky (C)

Three different dyed-across skeins are worked into panels that stack. Since all 3 yarns are from the same dyer, they have the same repeat and segue from one to another with the same stitch count. The panels are joined with reverse single crochet, which also finishes the edges. Smaller side gussets add desired width without concern for color stacking.

Determine your Half Magic Number or a needle size to work with ours (49).

Side gussets *MAKE 2*
With C, cast on 17. Knit 2 rows, then work Tilting Blocks for 4 repeats (64 rows). Bind off.

Stacked Left, Center, and Front panels
Following Color Sequence, cast on 49, knit 2 rows, work Tilting Blocks for the number of 16-row repeats shown in each color. Bind off.

Finishing
Lay pieces out according to schematic. With WS together, C, and crochet hook, join pieces, working 1 row reverse single crochet through both layers.
Edging Work 1 round single crochet around front and bottom edges, then 1 round reverse single crochet. Repeat around each armhole.

TILTING BLOCKS *MULTIPLE OF 16 + 1*
Rows 1, 3, 5, 7 (RS) **[(SSK, yo) 4 times, k8]**, to last stitch, k1.
Rows 2, 4, 6, 8 (WS) **[k9, p7]**, to last stitch, k1.
Rows 9, 11, 13, 15 K1, **[k8, (yo, k2tog) 4 times]** to end.
Rows 10, 12, 14,16 K1, **[p7, k9]** to end.

Stitch key
☐ *Knit on RS, purl on WS*
▨ *Purl on RS, knit on WS*
☑ *K2tog*
▧ *SSK*
⊡ *Yarn over (yo)*

Tilting Blocks

16-st repeat

ONE SIZE
Designed to overlap as desired at the center fronts and to dip at the sides.
A 53"
B 53"

10cm/4"
32 stitches and **32 rows** over Tilting Blocks measures 6¼" wide and 3¾" high.

Fine weight
3 colors 375 yds each

3.75mm/US5, or size to make color repeat work

3.25mm/D-3

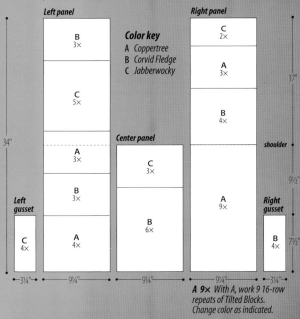

COLOR SEQUENCE

Left panel

B
3×

C
5×

A
3×

B
3×

Color key
A Coppertree
B Corvid Fledge
C Jabberwocky

Center panel

C
3×

B
6×

Left
gusset

C
4×

A
4×

Right panel

C
2×

A
3×

B
4×

A
9×

Right
gusset

B
4×

34"

shoulder

17"

9½"

7½"

3¼"   9¼"   9¼"   9¼"   3¼"

A 9× With A, work 9 16-row
repeats of Tilted Blocks.
Change color as indicated.

SIZING OPTIONS

*You could eliminate the side gussets and seam
Left and Right panels together OR work a
narrower Center panel that does not pattern.*

Highlands

OTTO COLOR

INTERMEDIATE + KNITTING

Talk about a bare canvas! Here is a tour de force of Fair Isle knitting, taking full advantage of 2 different multicolored, dyed-around skeins that are coordinated with a group of layered semisolids. Simple Fair Isle motifs allow the individual colors to shine. Worked circularly and then steeked, there are areas where the colors begin to stack and spiral, adding to the mystery.

WHAT'S THE MAGIC?

Randomize dyed-around 60" repeat with Fair Isle stitches and coordinating solids.

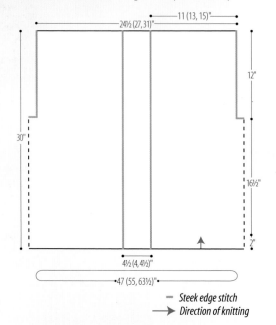

Notes *1 See page 164 for abbreviations and techniques. 2 Vest is worked in the round and steeked at center front and armholes. 3 Charts are worked in stranded color work. Carry color not in use loosely along WS of work, weaving in carries that are longer than 3 stitches. 4 Use backward-loop method to cast on steek stitches. 5 Measure length with piece held up.*

Body

With smaller needle and D, cast on **306** (360, **414**). Work K2, P2 Rib as follows: 6 rows D, 2 rows C, 6 rows D.

Change to stockinette stitch and, with B and F, work Row 1 of Chart 1; do not turn work. ***Next row*** With B, place marker (pm), using backward-loop method cast on 8 for center steek, pm and join to work in the round. Continue in stockinette stitch, following Chart and Color Sequence for **306** (360, **414**) body stitches and Steek Chart for 8 steek stitches, through second Chart 3 stripe. ***Next round: Begin armhole steeks:*** Work Chart 4 with D and B and AT SAME TIME, work **70** (84, **97**), bind off 8; work **150** (176, **204**), maintaining pattern either side of steeks, bind off 8; work remaining stitches in pattern. ***Next round*** Work **70** (84, **97**), pm, cast on 8 for armhole steek, pm, work **150** (176, **204**), pm, cast on 8 for armhole steek, pm, work remaining stitches in pattern.

Continue, working steek stitches in alternating stripes of multi color and solid and knitting first and last steek stitches tbl, and working remaining stitches in chart patterns.

After completing Chart and Color Sequence, piece measures approximately 30" when held upright. Beginning at center of front steek, bind off 4 steek stitches, **[work to marker, bind off 8 armhole steek stitches]** twice, work to marker, bind off remaining steek stitches. Place stitches on hold.

Finishing

With RS facing, crochet hook, and yarn, finish crochet-and-cut steeks along center front and armholes. With RS facing, place Fronts and Back together and join shoulders using 3-needle bind-off as follows: join **70** (84, **97**) stitches of first shoulder, bind off back neck stitches until **70** (84, **97**) stitches remain, join second shoulder.

Armbands With RS facing, smaller circular needle, D, and beginning at center of armhole, pick up and knit (PUK) at the rate of 4 stitches for every 5 rows along crochet fold line. Place marker (pm) and join to work in the round, adjusting stitch count to a multiple of 4 on first round if necessary. Work K2, P2 Rib as follows: 6 rounds D, 2 rounds C, 6 rounds D. Bind off in pattern.

Front and neckband PUK along crochet fold line of Right Front, 1 in each bound-off stitch across back neck, and along crochet fold line of Left Front. Work as for armbands EXCEPT work back and forth in rows, AND adjust total stitch count to a multiple of 4 + 2 on first row if necessary.

Schematic measurements:
11 (13, 15)"
24½ (27, 31)"
12"
30"
16½"
2"
4½ (4, 4½)"
47 (55, 63½)"

— Steek edge stitch
→ Direction of knitting

Approximate measurements when piece is held up in direction of knitting.

10cm/4"

OVERSIZED FIT
Size 1 (2, **3**)
A 50 (58, **66**)",
B 30", approximate size as worn
C 15 (17, **19**)"

26 stitches and **30 rows** in stockinette over charts using **larger needle**

Fine weight
A 500 (550, **600**) yds
B, D, and **F 400** (425, **475**) yds each
C and **E 300** (335, **360**) yds each
G 225 (250, **275**) yds

3.75mm/US5
AND
1 size smaller,
60cm (24") or longer

3.75mm/F-5

stitch marker

Chart and Color Sequence

Chart 1

6
5
4
3
2
1
6-st repeat

Chart 2

4
3
2
1
6-st repeat

Chart 3

6
5
4
3
2
1
6-st repeat

Chart 4

6
5
4
3
2
1
6-st repeat

Chart 5

6
5
4
3
2
1
6-st repeat

Chart 6

6
5
4
3
2
1
6-st repeat

B	D	Chart 3 4× or to 30"
A	C	Chart 2 2×
A	G	Chart 1 3×
A	E	Chart 6 3×
B	E	Chart 5 1×
B	D	Chart 4 4×
		Begin armhole steek
A	C	Chart 3 3×
A	E	Chart 2 4×
B	F	Chart 1 2×
B	G	Chart 6 2×
A	D	Chart 5 1×
A	E	Chart 4 2×
A	C	Chart 3 4×
B	G	Chart 2 2×
B	F	Chart 1 3×

Work Charts 1–6 for designated number of 6- or 4-row repeats and colors shown.

Stitch key
- ☐ Knit
- ☐ Purl
- ☑ Ktbl

Color key
- ☐ Semisolid or layered C, D, E, F, or G
- ☐ Multicolor A or B

All charts are a multiple of 6 stitches.

Steek Chart

☑ ☐ ☐ ☐ ☐ ☐ ☑   all rounds
8-stitches

Size 2: PRISM YARNS Merino Mia in colors Ginger (A), Highlands (B), Plumberry (C), Olivine (D), Lapis (E), Slate (F), and Sapphire (G)

Classic color

Woodlands flash

INTERMEDIATE KNITTING

ATTENTIVE COLOR

WHAT'S THE MAGIC?

*Flash/stack dyed–around 67"
repeat, worked circularly on
double the Magic Number.*

Notes 1 *See page 164 for abbreviations and techniques
AND page 26 for Magic Number.* **2** *Size can be altered
by cutting steeks at the underarm either to make
smaller, or to add gussets and make larger. The flash
pattern will not work if the size is altered by changing
the number of working stitches.* **3** *Wind Big Kid into as
large a ball as possible for the body. If a ball winder is
available, begin on the ball winder, then finish winding
by hand once the ball is too large for the winder.
About one-third of the skein can be wound separately
for sleeves and collar. If by chance you need to piece,
find where the colors match and join in color order
using the fisherman's knot as described on page 31.*

INC 1

At beginning of RS rows K1, M1.
At end of RS rows M1, k1.

DEC 1

At beginning of RS rows K1, k2tog.
At end of RS rows SSK, k1.

K1, P1 RIB

All rows or rounds [K1, p1].

HALF LINEN STITCH

*Slip stitches purlwise with
yarn at RS of work.*
Row 1 (RS) Sl 1, [sl 1, k1] to
last stitch, k1.
Rows 2, 4 Sl 1, purl to end.
Row 3 Sl 1, [k1, sl 1] to last
stitch, k1.

Half Linen

*2-st
repeat*

Stitch key

☐ *Knit on RS, purl on WS*
☑ *Slip1 with yarn at RS*

*Flash knitting is dependent on color repeat, size of skein, and gauge. A
sweater can be pushed slightly smaller or larger than written, but not by
much or the flash will be interrupted. Fewer stitches will make the flash
skew to the left in a spiral; more stitches will make it skew to the right.
Armholes are formed with steeks, allowing the flash to continue to the
neckline. If a different size is desired, one option is to steek the sides all
the way down and add underarm gussets to enlarge the sweater's girth.
The gussets won't match the body, but also won't interfere with the
appearance of the flash, as we can see with the Half-Linen-Stitch sleeves.
Here we have occasionally increased or decreased a stitch or two to keep
the flash moving back and forth. You have ultimate control!*

Body

Determine your Magic Number or a needle size to work with ours (60).
With larger needle, cast on twice your Magic Number, minus 7 or 8 (it needs to be
an even number, we cast on 112). Change to smaller needle and work 1 row in K1,
P1 Rib. Place marker (pm) and join to work in the round, being careful not to twist
stitches. Work 1 row in K1, P1 Rib for 1½". Change to larger needle and stockinette
stitch. **Next round** Knit, increasing 8 stitches evenly spaced — 120 stitches or twice
your Magic Number. Continue in stockinette stitch, checking for color alignment as
you work, until piece measures 15".

Armhole steek

Decide which portion of flash will become center front. Removing beginning-of-
round marker, pm at side seams, including the same number of stitches between
markers for Front and Back; assign one marker as your new beginning of round. If the
total number of stitches is odd, place the extra stitch in the Front. **Next round [Work
to 4 stitches before side marker, bind off 8 for underarm]** twice. **Next round
[Work to bound-off stitches, pm, cast on 8 for steek using backward loop
method, pm]** twice. Continue in stockinette, knitting first and last steek stitches tbl,
until piece measures 6" from steek cast-on.
Shape neck
Mark 10 center Front stitches for neck (11 if your number of Front stitches is odd). Knit
to first neck marker, bind off marked neck stitches, work to end. Working back and
forth on all stitches, bind off 3 at each neck edge once, then 2 once. Dec 1 at each
neck edge on next RS row. Work even until piece measures 9" from steek cast-on.
Bind off firmly.

ONE SIZE
A 40"
B 24"
C 30"

10cm/4"

12 stitches and
15 rows over
stockinette stitch,
using **larger
needles**

Medium weight
650 yds

6.5mm/US10½, 60cm
(24") or longer
5.5mm/US9, 40cm (16")
larger needle for collar
bind-off (12.75mm/US17)

6.5mm/K-10½

stitch markers

Sleeves

With larger needle, cast on 26. Do not join. Change to smaller needle and work K1, P1 Rib for 2". Change to larger needle and Half Linen Stitch. **[Work 3 rows even; Inc 1 each side on next row]** 14 times, working new stitches into pattern — 54 stitches. Work even until piece measures 18", or 3" less than desired length to shoulder.

Shape cap

At beginning of every row, bind off 3 stitches 12 times. Bind off remaining 18 stitches.

PRISM YARNS Big Kid in color Woodlands

Finishing

With RS facing, crochet hook, and yarn, finish crochet-and-cut steeks along armholes. Sew shoulder seams, folding the 4-stitch steek flap to inside along armhole edge. Sew sleeve seam to 1" less than underarm, leaving sewing yarn attached. Set sleeve into armhole edge, along the crochet fold-line and between underarm stitches. Tack remaining sleeve seam to bound-off underarm stitches.

Collar

With larger needle, beginning at right shoulder seam, pick up and knit (PUK) along neck edge at the following rates: 3 stitches for every 4 rows along vertical edges and 1 stitch in every bound-off stitch, adjusting to an even number on next round if necessary. Place marker (pm) and join to work in the round. Work K1, P1 Rib for 8". Collar should flash like Body. Bind off very loosely. The collar edge should be able to spread around the neck as it folds over.

Color notes 1 Brushed and inelastic yarns such as Big Kid can result in big gauge differences in knitters. Also, if the gauge swatch is worked flat, your gauge may change when you work circularly. Please check your gauge and color alignment carefully, both prior to beginning and a few inches into the garment. 2 Increasing or decreasing a stitch or two randomly spaced in a round will help control how the flash looks and will not significantly affect finished size. 3 Steeking continues the flash at the armhole steek, the fabric will be cut for sleeve insertion.

SIZING OPTIONS

Gussets If you wish to size your sweater differently from ours, cast on twice the Magic Number and mark the side seams immediately. Knit to within 3 stitches of marker, knit next stitch tbl, knit 4, knit 1 tbl, and repeat at other side seam. Continue to knit these stitches tbl for entire Body tube. Make armhole steeks as instructed.

Cut each body steek as for armhole steek to the bottom of the sweater. With larger needle and RS facing, PUK64 from cast-on edge to armhole steek, picking up into twisted stitches and folding steek facing to inside. Work Half Linen Stitch for half of desired additional width (for example, if you want a 44" sweater, that is a 4" additional (2" on each side). With second needle, PUK64 on other side and join, with RS together using a 3-needle bind-off. Repeat for other side. If you have made your sweater body longer, you will have to adjust the number of picked up stitches.

Sleeve sizing If you are making the body wider, leave enough of the sleeve seam unsewn to accomodate the sleeve insertion into the gusset. You may also wish to add 2, 4 or 6 stitches to the sleeve circumference for larger sizes.

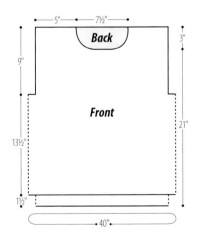

Cockle shells

EASY KNITTING

OTTO COLOR

WHAT'S THE MAGIC?

*Randomize 62"
repeat with solid
colors and directional
pattern stitch.*

Notes 1 *See page 164 for abbreviations
and techniques.* **2** *Yarn C is held double
throughout.* **3** *Carry colors not in use loosely
up the side of the work.* **4** *For stripes to match,
sleeve bands and neckband are worked back
and forth in rows.* **5** *Pick up all stitches with
RS facing.* **6** *Measure lengths when piece is
held up to allow for downward stretch.*

CREST OF THE WAVE multiple of 12 + 1
RS rows K1, [k2tog twice, (yo, k1) 3
times, yo, SSK twice, k1] to end.

WS rows Purl.

Chart

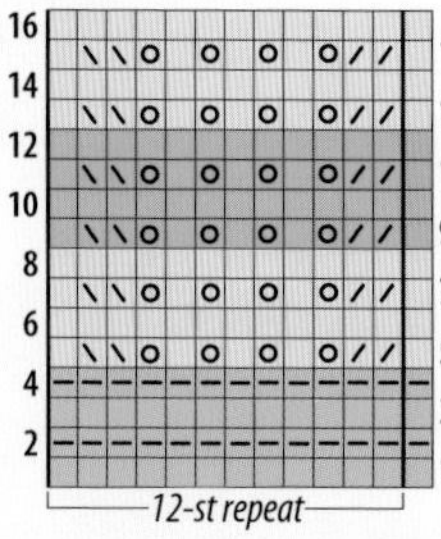

(chart grid, rows numbered 1–16, columns 1–15)

12-st repeat

Stitch key
☐ *Knit on RS, purl on WS*
⊟ *Purl on RS*
☑ *K2tog*
☒ *SSK*
⊙ *Yarn over (yo)*

Color key
▨ *A*
☐ *B*
▩ *C*

*Small: BLUE MOON Marine Silk Worsted in
color Mossay (A); Socks that Rock Lightweight
in color Chawton Cottage (B); and Marine
Silk Lace in color China Rose (C).*

---

*Here, 3 different weights of yarn are used together successfully: tonal fine silk that
is doubled, tonal heavy silk worked singly, and multicolored sock wool worked
singly. The 2 mostly solid colors and the softly scalloped pattern stitch lend
structure that allows the soft hand-dyed colors to join in perfect harmony. Thinner
silk yarns also lend a nice drape to a piece which acquires shape from its wearer.*

Back

With larger needles and A, cast on **85** (97, **109**, 121, **133**). Knit 4 rows. **[Work Crest of the Wave
in 2 rows B, 2 rows C, 2 rows B; with A, knit 4 rows]** twice. Work Crest of the Wave in 2 rows B,
4 rows C, 2 rows B. Work 16 rows of Chart **4** (4, **4**, 5, **5**) times. Piece measures approximately **13** (13,
13, 15, **15**)".

Shape sleeves

Next 2 rows **[Cast on 12, work across in pattern]** twice — **109** (121, **133**, 145, **157**) stitches.
Continue in pattern until piece measures approximately 9" from sleeve cast-on, end with a WS row.
Place stitches on hold.

Front

Work as for Back until piece measures approximately 4" from sleeve cast-on, end with a WS row.

Shape neck

Work **37** (43, **49**, 55, **61**), join a second ball of yarn and bind off center 35, work to end. Working
both sides at the same time with separate balls of yarn, work even until piece measures same length
as Back, end with same Chart row.

With RS together, join shoulders using 3-needle bind-off as follows: join **37** (43, **49**, 55, **61**)
stitches of first shoulder; bind off Back neck stitches until **37** (43, **49**, 55, **61**) stitches remain; join
second shoulder.

Finishing

Sleeve bands

With smaller needles and 2 strands C, pick up and knit (PUK) along sleeve edge at the following
rates: 2 stitches for every 3 rows along vertical edges and 1 stitch in every bound-off stitch. Knit 3
rows. Change to A and knit 1 row. Bind off.

Neckband

With smaller needles and 2 strands C, beginning at right shoulder, PUK along neck edge. Do not
join. Knit 3 rows. Change to B and knit, decreasing 26 evenly spaced around. Knit 1 row. Change to 2
strands C and knit 4 rows. Change to A and knit 1 row. Bind off. Sew neckband seam. Sew side and
sleeve seams. Block.

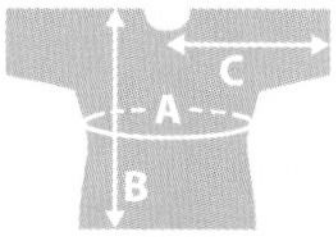

STANDARD FIT
XS (S, M, L, **1X**)
A 31 (35, **40**, 44, **48**)"
B 22 (22, **22**, 24, **24**)"
C 10½ (11½, **12½**,
13½, **14½**)"

10cm/4"

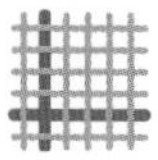

28½ stitches and **32 rows** over
Chart, unblocked
AND
22 stitches and **32 rows** blocked,
using **larger needles**

Light weight
A 260 (300, **345**,
410, **445**) yds

Fine weight
B 310 (345, **405**,
480, **525**) yds

Superfine weight
C 355 (400, **465**, 570,
605) yds, held double
throughout

4.5mm/US7 or size
to obtain gauge
AND
2 sizes smaller

Back

Front

6½ (8, 9, 10, 11)"

6½"

5"

9"

13 (13, 13, 15, 15)"

17 (17, 17, 19, 19)"

2"

15½ (17½, 20, 22, 24)"

Approximate measurements when
blocked piece is held upright

109

Ciao bella

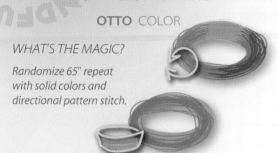

EASY KNITTING

OTTO COLOR

WHAT'S THE MAGIC?

*Randomize 65" repeat
with solid colors and
directional pattern stitch.*

Notes 1 See page 164 for abbreviations and
techniques. **2** Carry colors not in use loosely along side
edge. **3** Measure for length with piece help upright.

CHEVRON *MULTIPLE OF 13 + 2*
Row 1 (RS) K1, **[SSK, k4, yo, k1, yo,
k4, k2tog]** to last stitch, k1.
Row 2 (WS) Knit for Garter Chevron;
purl for Stockinette Chevron..

Chevron

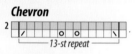

13-st repeat

Stitch key
☐ Knit
▨ Knit for garter,
   purl for stockinette
☑ K2tog
☒ SSK
⊡ Yarn over (yo)

Stripe Sequence

(rows numbered 2–18 on left, 1–17 on right)

Color key
▨ A
▨ B
▨ C
▨ D

*Look out Missoni, here we come! Our tee is worked in 3 coordinating solids
and 1 multicolor. A lot of swatching went into developing the right color
balance for the first sample: some combinations had too much contrast
while others didn't have enough. Yarn choice is important here: the yarn
should have inherent drape, or the tee will be boxy instead of fitted.*

Back
With smaller needles and B, cast on **106** (119, **132**, 145, **158**). Work Garter Chevron in Stripe
Sequence for 8 rows. Change to larger needles. Work Stockinette Chevron in Stripe Sequence
until piece measures **14** (14½, **15**, 15½, **16**)", end with a WS row.
Shape sleeves
Next row Cast on 13, work across in pattern. **Next row** Cast on 13, purl to last 7 stitches,
k7 — **132** (145, **158**, 171, **184**) stitches. **Next row** K1, **[SSK, k4, yo, k1, yo, k4, k2tog]** to last
stitch, k1. **Next row** K7, purl to last 7 stitches, k7. Repeat last 2 rows until piece measures **8** (8,
8½, 8½, **9**)" from sleeve cast-on. Bind off.

Front
Work as for Back until piece measures approximately **4** (4, **4½**, 4½, **5**)" from sleeve cast-on, end
with a WS row.
Shape neck
Work across **41** (47, **54**, 60, **67**), place next **50** (51, **50**, 51, **50**) on hold, join a second ball of yarn
and work to end. Working both sides at the same time with separate balls of yarn, work even
until piece measures same length as Back. Bind off.

Finishing
Neckband
Sew right shoulder seam. With RS facing, smaller needles, and B, pick up and knit (PUK) **18** (17,
18, 17, **18**) along left front neck, k**50** (51, **50**, 51, **50**) from hold, PUK**18** (17, **18**, 17, **18**) along
right front neck, PUK**50** (51, **50**, 51, **50**) from back neck — 136 stitches. **Next row** *[K3, k2tog]
10 times, k18; repeat from * once — 116 stitches. Knit 2 rows A, 2 rows B, 2 rows A. **Next row**
With B, *k18, **[k8, k2tog]** 4 times; repeat from * once — 108 stitches. Bind off.
Sew shoulder and neckband seam. Sew side seams.

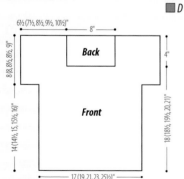

6½ (7½, 8½, 9½, 10½)"   8"

Back   4"

8 (8, 8½, 8½, 9)"

14 (14½, 15, 15½, 16)"

Front

18 (18½, 19½, 20, 21)"

17 (19, 21, 23, 25½)"

*Approximate measurements when piece
is held up in direction of knitting.*

CLOSE FIT
S (M, **L**, 1X, **2X**)
A 34 (38, **42**, 46, **51**)"
B 22 (22½, **23½**, 24, **25**)"
C 10½ (11½, **12½**, 13½, **14½**)"

10cm/4"

25 stitches and **28 rows**
over Stockinette Chevron,
using **larger needles**

Light weight
A **300** (350, **400**, 450, **500**) yds
B **and** D **225** (250, **300**, 325, **375**)
yds each
C **100** (115, **135**, 150, **176**) yds

5mm/US8 or size
to obtain gauge
AND
2 sizes smaller

Ciao bella

(Previous page) Small: PRISM YARNS Tencel® Tape in colors Denali (A), 701 Gray (B), 104 Brown (C), and 405 Tan (D)

Small: PRISM YARNS Tencel® Tape in colors Highlands (A), Aegean (B), Plumberry (C), and 307 (D)

Medium: PRISM YARNS Tencel® Tape in colors Parrot (A); 203 Red (B), 208 Turquoise (C), and Hibiscus (D)

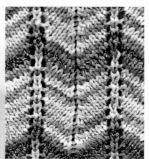

Small: PRISM YARNS Tencel® Tape in colors Fog (A), 901 (B), 211 (D) and Elise in color Shadow (C)

SIZING OPTIONS

Ciao Bella is easy to adjust in size by using a larger needle and thus a slightly looser gauge. The pattern repeat is rather large, which limits sizing to large jumps. Slightly shifting the gauge allows for more fine-tuning of measurements, and also a broader range of yarn selection. Our Parrot version (larger photo) was worked on a size larger needles and used the stitch counts for a size Small to achieve a Medium.

Herringbone weave

A woven slip-stitch pattern randomizes the strong colors of this bulky yarn. Thick yarns make bolder stripes and pools, so they require strong measures to overcome patterning tendencies. Some slight pooling occurs, especially on the upper arms, but is lessened by the long floats of opposing color. A coordinating sandwashed solid provides a frame around all pieces, which are joined with an external 3-needle bind-off. Edge that frame with a 2-stitch I-cord bind-off, and enjoy the syncopation of hand-dyed colors marching around!

Herringbone Weave

INTERMEDIATE KNITTING

OTTO COLOR

WHAT'S THE MAGIC?

Randomize 62" repeat with long right-side floats.

Notes 1 *See page 164 for abbreviations and techniques.* **2** *The long slips tend to draw the fabric in, necessitating a larger needle than recommended for the yarn.*

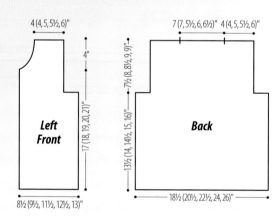

Left Front

4 (4, 5, 5½, 6)"

4"

17 (18, 19, 20, 21)"

8½ (9½, 11½, 12½, 13)"

Back

7 (7, 5½, 6, 6½)" 4 (4, 5, 5½, 6)"

7½ (8, 8½, 9, 9)"

13½ (14, 14½, 15, 16)"

18½ (20½, 22½, 24, 26)"

Sleeve

14 (15, 16, 17, 17½)"

4"

17 (17, 18, 18, 19)"

7½ (8½, 8½, 9½, 10½)"

Back

With temporary cast-on, smaller needle, and A, cast on **82** (90, **98**, 106, **114**). Change to larger needle. Work Woven Transverse Herringbone chart until piece measures **13½** (14, **14½**, 15, **16**)", end with a WS row.

Shape armhole At beginning of next 2 rows, bind off **8** (12, **16**, 16, **16**) — **66** (66, **66**, 74, **82**) stitches. Work even until armhole measures **7½** (8, **8½**, 9, **9**)", end with a WS row. Bind off firmly.

Left Front

With temporary cast-on, smaller needle, and A, cast on **38** (42, **50**, 54, **58**). Work as for Back until piece measures same length as Back to armhole.

Shape armhole Shape armhole at beginning of RS row as for Back — **30** (30, **34**, 38, **42**) stitches.

Shape neck At beginning of every WS row, bind off **5** (5, **6**, 7, **8**) once, 3 once, then 2 once. Dec 1 at end of every RS row twice — **18** (18, **21**, 24, **27**) stitches. Work even until piece measures same length as Back to shoulder, end with a WS row. Bind off firmly.

Right Front

Work as for Left Front EXCEPT reverse shaping. Bind off armhole at beginning of WS row. Shape neck at beginning of RS rows.

Sleeves

With temporary cast-on, smaller needle, and A, cast on **34** (38, **38**, 42, **46**)". Change to larger needle and Woven Transverse Herringbone chart. Work 6 rows. **[Inc 1 each side on next RS row; work 5 rows even]** **14** (14, **16**, 16, **16**) times, working new stitches into pattern — **62** (66, **70**, 74, **78**) stitches. Work even until piece measures **17** (17, **18**, 18, **19**)", end with a WS row.

Shape cap *Rows 1 and 2* Work to last 2 stitches, wrap & turn (W&T). *Next row* **[Work to 2 stitches before wrap, W&T]** 22 times — **14** (18, **22**, 26, **30**) stitches in center between wrapped stitches. Cut A and slip wrapped stitches from left needle to right needle. *Next row* (RS) With smaller needle and B, knit across all stitches, picking up wraps with point of right needle and knitting them together with the stitch that they wrap. Place on hold.

Finishing

Sleeve edging Remove waste yarn from cast-on edge and place stitches onto smaller needle, ready to work a RS row. *Next row* With B, knit, decreasing 4 evenly spaced — **30** (34, **34**, 38, **42**) stitches. Knit 3 rows even. Cut B. Join A and cast 2 onto left needle. *Next row* **[K1, SSK last stitch of I-cord with 1 stitch of sleeve, sl 2 back to left needle]** until all sleeve stitches are worked. Bind off 2 I-cord stitches.

STANDARD FIT
S (M, L, 1X, **2X**)
A 37 (41, **45**, 48, **52**)"
B 21 (22, **23**, 24, **25**)"
C 28½ (28½, **30**, 30½, **32½**)"

22 stitches to 12.5cm/5" and 24 rows to 9.5cm/3¾" over Woven Transverse Herringbone, using **larger needles**

Bulky weight
A 750 (840, **1000**, 1100, **1225**) yds
B 125 (135, **160**, 180, **200**) yds

8mm/US11,
AND
Two 4 sizes smaller
60cm (24") or longer

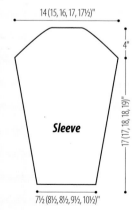

Medium: LORNA'S LACES Shepherd Bulky in colors Rockwell (A) and Kerfuffle (B)

Notes 1 Pick up shoulder and back neck stitches in the first full stitch below the bind-off. Joining the shoulders with a 3-needle bind-off on the RS gives a visual seam, while the bound-off edge provides the stability of a shoulder seam. **2** Pick up stitches at the following rates: 1 stitch for each bound-off stitch and 1 stitch for every 2 rows along vertical edges. **3** Pick up and purl (PUP) all stitches with WS facing, smaller needle, and B.

Join shoulders PUP across right front shoulder. Cut B. With second smaller needle, PUP the same number of stitches across right back shoulder. Do not cut B. With WS together and B, join shoulders using 3-needle bind-off. Repeat for left shoulder.

Join Sleeves PUP along armhole edge of body, leaving bound-off edges free. Do not cut B. With WS of sleeve and body together, join using 3-needle bind-off. Repeat for second sleeve. Invisibly sew side of sleeve to armhole bind-off.

Join sides and sleeves Beginning at bottom of sleeve, PUP along sleeve and side edge. Cut B. With second smaller needle, PUP along the other side and sleeve edge. Do not cut B. With WS together, join using 3-needle bind-off. Repeat for other side and sleeve. **Bottom edging** Remove waste yarn from cast-on edges and place stitches onto smaller needle, ready to work a RS row. **Next Row** With B, knit, decreasing 8 evenly spaced across Left Front to side seam, 16 across Back, and 8 across Right Front. Continue as for sleeve edging, but do not bind off I-cord stitches at the end. Place on hold. Do not cut yarn.

Front and neck edging With RS facing, smaller needle, and B, pick up and knit (PUK) along right front edge to neck, PUK1 in corner, place marker (pm) PUK2 in corner, PUK along neck edge to other corner, PUK1 in corner, pm, PUK2 in corner, PUK along left front. Knit 1 row. **Next row** (RS) Knit to 1 stitch before marker, knit in front and back (kf&b) of next stitch, slip marker (sm), kf&b of next stitch, decrease 3 evenly spaced to shoulder seam; decrease 6 evenly spaced across back neck; decrease 3 evenly spaced to 1 stitch before marker, kf&b in next stitch, sm, kf&b in next stitch, knit to end. Knit 1 row even. Cut yarn.

Place 2 I-cord stitches onto left needle and, with A, work corner as follows:
[k2, sl 2 back to left needle] once to ease corner. Work I-cord along front and neck, attaching it as for sleeve, and working marked corners as for first corner. Work corner at bottom edge. Graft I-cord ends together.

Chart

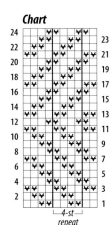

24 · · · 23
22 · · · · 21
20 · · · 19
18 · · · 17
16 · · · · 15
14 · · · 13
12 · · · 11
10 · · · 9
8 · · · · 7
6 · · · 5
4 · · · 3
2 · · · · 1

└─ 4-st ─┘
repeat

INC 1
At beginning of RS rows K1, M1.
At end of RS rows M1, k1.

DEC 1
At beginning of RS rows K1, k2tog.
At end of RS rows SSK, k1.

Stitch key
☐ *Knit on RS, purl on WS*
⛝ *Sl1 with yarn at RS*

WOVEN TRANSVERSE HERRINGBONE
MULTIPLE OF 4 + 2
Slip stitches purlwise with yarn at RS of work.
Row 1 (RS) K2, [sl 2, k2] to end.
Row 2 P1, [sl 2, p2] to last stitch, p1.
Row 3 Sl 2, [k2, sl 2] to end.
Row 4 P3, [sl 2, p2] to last 3 stitches, sl 2, p1.
Rows 5–12 Repeat Rows 1–4 twice more.
Row 13 Repeat Row 3.
Row 14 Repeat Row 2.
Row 15 Repeat Row 1.
Row 16 Repeat Row 4.
Rows 17–24 Repeat Rows 13–16 twice more.

Mosaic

OTTO COLOR

INTERMEDIATE KNITTING

Simple mosaic stitches, whether worked on a Magic Number or not, are extremely effective with hand-dyed yarns. Here, an easy geometric motif stretches the Magic Number enough to pattern on a size Small. A hand-dyed yarn with high contrast will show patterning even more. Select a layered or solid color with some weight contrast, either heavier or lighter, to make sure the pattern shows. To maintain patterning for larger sizes, one option is to work center panels on your Magic Number, then add gussets at the sides to achieve the desired width. Or, toss your fate to the wind and make larger sizes per the pattern numbers. You might not get pools, but you will get mosaic magic!

WHAT'S THE MAGIC?

Randomize 64" repeat with solid color and mosaic stitch.

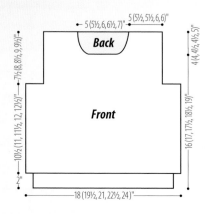

Notes 1 *See page 164 for abbreviations and techniques.* **2** *Carry colors not in use loosely along side edge.* **3** *When working shaping, if a slip stitch falls at the edge, work the stitch in stockinette stitch instead.*

Back

With A and smaller needles, cast on **82** (88, **94**, 100, **106**). Work K1, P1 Rib for 12 rows. Change to larger needles. *Next row* (WS) Purl, increasing **7** (9, **11**, 13, **15**) evenly spaced — **89** (97, **105**, 113, **121**) stitches. Work Caesar's Check until piece measures **12½** (13, **13½**, 14, **14½**)", end with a WS row.
Shape armholes At beginning of next 2 rows, bind off **8** (8, **10**, 10, **12**) — **73** (81, **85**, 93, **97**) stitches. Work even until armhole measures **7½** (8, **8½**, 9, **9½**)", end with a WS row. Bind off firmly.

Front

Work as for Back until armhole measures **3½** (4, **4**, 4½, **4½**)", end with a WS row.
Shape neck Work **31** (34, **36**, 39, **41**), join a second ball of yarn and bind off center **11** (13, **13**, 15, **15**), work to end. Working both sides at the same time with separate balls of yarn, bind off at each neck edge 3 once, then 2 once. Dec 1 at each neck edge every RS row **2** (2, **3**, 4, **5**) times — **24** (27, **28**, 30, **31**) stitches remain on each side. Work even until piece measures same length as Back. Bind off firmly.

Sleeves

With smaller needles and A, cast on **34** (34, **36**, 38, **42**). Work K1, P1 Rib for 12 rows. Change to larger needles and stockinette stitch. *Next row* (WS) Purl, increasing 4 evenly spaced — **38** (38, **40**, 42, **46**) stitches. **[Work 5 rows even; Inc 1 each side on next row] 13** (15, **16**, 17, **17**) times — **64** (68, **72**, 76, **80**) stitches. Work even until piece measures **17½** (18, **18½**, 19, **20**)", or **3½** (3½, **3½**, 4, **4½**)" less than desired length to shoulder.
Shape cap At beginning of every row, bind off 2 stitches **14** (16, **16**, 18, **20**) times, then 4 stitches 6 times. Bind off remaining **12** (12, **16**, 16, **16**) stitches.

Finishing

Sew shoulder seams. Set in sleeves. Sew side and sleeve seams.
Neckband With RS facing, circular needle, and A, pick up and knit around neck edge at the following rates: 2 stitches for every 3 rows along vertical edges and 1 stitch for every bound-off stitch. Count stitches and adjust to an even number on next round if necessary. Place marker and join to work in the round. Work K1, P1 Rib for 8 rounds. Bind off loosely in pattern.

Back / Front schematic

5 (5½, 6, 6½, 7)" • 5 (5½, 5½, 6, 6)"
Back
4 (4, 4½, 4½, 5)"
7½ (8, 8½, 9, 9½)"
10½ (11, 11½, 12, 12½)"
Front
16 (17, 17½, 18½, 19)"
2"
18 (19½, 21, 22½, 24)"

Sleeve schematic

14 (15, 16, 17, 18)"
3½ (3½, 3½, 4, 4½)"
Sleeve
15½ (16, 16½, 17, 18)"
2"
8½ (8½, 9, 9½, 10)"

STANDARD FIT
S (**M**, **L**, 1X, **2X**)
A 36 (**39**, **42**, 45, **58**)"
B 20 (**21**, **22**, 23, **24**)"
C 28½ (**30**, **30½**, 32½, **34**)"

10cm/4"
20 stitches and 35 rows over Caesar's Check
AND
18 stitches and 24 rows over stockinette stitch using **larger needles**

Medium weight
A 525 (**575**, **650**, 725, **675**) yds
B 325 (**350**, **400**, 450, **500**) yds

5mm/US8, or size to obtain gauge
AND
2 sizes smaller

2 sizes smaller
40cm (16") long

stitch marker

Caesar's Check

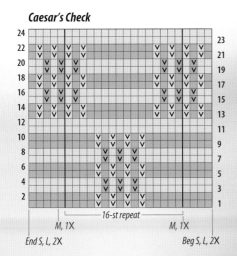

16-st repeat

M, 1X   M, 1X

End S, L, 2X   Beg S, L, 2X

Stitch key
☐ Knit on RS, purl on WS
☑ Sl 1 with yarn at WS

Color key
☐ A
▨ B

INC 1
At beginning of RS rows K1, M1.
At end of RS rows M1, k1.

DEC 1
At beginning of RS rows K1, k2tog.
At end of RS rows SSK, k1.

K1, P1 RIB
OVER AN EVEN NUMBER OF STITCHES
All rows or rounds [K1, p1].

CAESAR'S CHECK *MULTIPLE OF 16 + 1*
Slip stitches purlwise with yarn at WS of work.
Row 1 (RS) With B, **[k5, (sl 1, k1) 3 times, sl 1, k4]** to last stitch, k1. ***Row 2 and all WS rows*** Purl all stitches worked on previous row with same color; slip all slipped stitches. ***Row 3*** With A, **[k6, (sl 1, k1) 3 times, k4]** to last stitch, k1. ***Rows 5–10*** Repeat Rows 1–4 once, then repeat Rows 1 and 2 once more. ***Row 11*** With A, knit. ***Row 13*** With B, **[(k1, sl 1) 2 times, k9, sl 1, k1, sl 1)]** to last stitch, k1. ***Row 15*** With A, **[sl 1, k1, sl 1, k11, sl 1, k1]** to last stitch, k1. ***Rows 17–22*** Repeat Rows 13–16 once, then repeat Rows 13 and 14 once more. ***Row 23*** With A, knit. ***Row 24*** With A, purl.

Medium: PRISM YARNS Symphony in colors Plumberry (A) and Arroyo (B)

Tweed checks

OTTO COLOR

INTERMEDIATE KNITTING

WHAT'S THE MAGIC?

Randomize 64" repeat with solid color and slip-stitch pattern.

Notes 1 *See page 164 for abbreviations and techniques.* **2** *When working shaping, if a slip stitch falls at the edge, work the stitch in stockinette stitch instead.* **3** *Carry colors not in use loosely along side edge.*

INC 1
At beginning of RS rows K1, M1.
At end of RS rows M1, k1.

DEC 1
At beginning of RS rows K1, k2tog.
At end of RS rows SSK, k1.

K1, P1 RIB
OVER AN EVEN NUMBER OF STITCHES
All rows or rounds [K1, p1] to end.

TWEED CHECKS *MULTIPLE OF 10 + 3*
Slip stitches purlwise with yarn at WS of work.
Rows 1–4 With A, knit on RS, purl on WS.
Rows 5, 6 With B, k1, sl 2, [(k1, sl 1) 3 times, k1, sl 3] to last 10 stitches, [k1, sl 1] 3 times, k1, sl 2, k1.
Rows 7, 8 Work as Rows 1, 2.
Rows 9–16 Repeat Rows 5–8 twice.
Rows 17–18 Repeat Rows 5–6 once.

Large: PRISM YARNS Symphony in colors Slate (A) and Yosemite (B)

A simple slip stitch lends architecture to a unisex style that becomes a handsome tailored sweater. Lots of swatching was done to get just the right color contrasts: some have too much, others not enough (see photos page 56). This is a great canvas for rich, lush wool. The colors gather slightly in drifts, but the strong box pattern and reduction of multi-colors into little dots help to randomize those drifts.

Back

With smaller needles and A, cast on **102** (112, **122**, 132, **142**). Work K1, P1 Rib for 2". Change to larger needles. ***Begin Chart: Row 1*** Inc 1 at beginning of row, knit to end—**103** (113, **123**, 133, **143**) stitches. Continue working even in Chart until piece measures **15** (16½, **16**, 17, **17**)", end with a WS color A row.

Shape armholes
At beginning of next 2 rows, bind off 10—**83** (93, **103**, 113, **123**) stitches. Work even until armhole measures **8** (8½, **9**, 10, **10**)", end with a WS color A row. Bind off firmly.

Front

Work as for Back until armhole measures **6** (6½, **7**, 8, **7½**)", end with a WS color A row.

Shape neck
Next row (RS) K**37** (41, **45**, 49, **53**), join a second ball of yarn and bind off center **9** (11, **13**, 15, **17**), knit to end. Working both sides at the same time with separate balls of yarn, at each neck edge bind off 5 once then 2 once. Dec 1 each neck edge every RS row **4** (4, **5**, 6, **7**) times—**26** (30, **33**, 36, **39**) stitches remain each side. Work even until piece measures same length as Back. Bind off firmly.

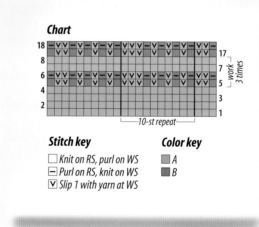

Chart

—10-st repeat—

work 3 times

Stitch key
☐ Knit on RS, purl on WS
— Purl on RS, knit on WS
Ⅴ Slip 1 with yarn at WS

Color key
▨ A
▨ B

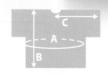

10cm/4"

STANDARD FIT
S (M, **L**, 1X, **2X**)
A 37 (41, **45**, 48, **52**)"
B 23 (25, **25**, 27, **27**)"
C 27½ (30½, **31½**, 34½, **35**)"

22 stitches and 34 rows over chart, using larger needles

Medium weight
A 1065 (1260, **1375**, 1610, **1710**) yds
B 460 (540, **575**, 690, **735**) yds

4.5mm/US7
AND
1 size smaller

4.5mm/US7, 40cm (16") long

118

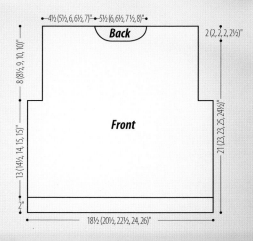

4½ (5½, 6, 6½, 7)" — 5½ (6, 6½, 7½, 8)"

Back

2 (2, 2, 2, 2½)"

8 (8½, 9, 10, 10)"

13 (14½, 14, 15, 15)"

21 (23, 23, 25, 24½)"

Front

2"

18½ (20½, 22½, 24, 26)"

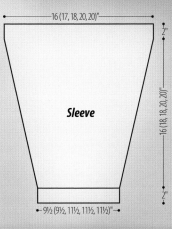

16 (17, 18, 20, 20)"

Sleeve

16 (18, 18, 20, 20)"

2"

2"

9½ (9½, 11½, 11½, 11½)"

Sleeves

With smaller needles and A, cast on **49** (49, **59**, 59, **59**). Work K1, P1 Rib for 2". Change to larger needles. *Begin Chart: Row 1* Knit, increasing 4 evenly spaced — **53** (53, **63**, 63, **63**) stitches. **[Work 5 rows even, Inc 1 each side on next row]** 18 (20, **18**, 24, **24**) times, working new stitches into pattern — **89** (93, **99**, 111, **111**) stitches. Work even until piece measures **18** (20, **20**, 22, **22**)". Mark each side of last row for sleeve cap.

Shape cap

Work even for 2", end with a WS color A row. Bind off.

Finishing

Block lightly. Sew shoulder seams.

Neckband

With RS facing, circular needle, and A, pick up and knit (PUK) along neck edge at the following rates: 2 stitches for every 3 rows along vertical edges and 1 stitch in every bound-off stitch, adjusting to an even number on next round, if necessary. Place marker and join to work in the round. Work K1, P1 Rib for 8 rounds. Bind off loosely in pattern.

Set in sleeves, matching markers to beginning of armhole bind-off. Sew side and sleeve seams.

Dice checks

INTERMEDIATE KNITTING

OTTO COLOR

WHAT'S THE MAGIC?

Randomize two 64" repeats with third, solid color and slip-stitch pattern.

Color note *Select colors that are similar in overall weight, although this is a case where a few highlights and lowlights add interest. We are not as concerned with seeing the pattern clearly as we are with using the pattern stitch to mix up colors and break stripes and pools.*

Notes 1 *See page 164 for abbreviations and techniques.* **2** *When working shaping, if a slip stitch falls at the edge, work the stitch in stockinette stitch instead.* **3** *Carry colors not in use loosely along side edge.*

This interesting pattern uses A, B, C colors differently. A is worked for a single row in 2 places; B and C begin their paired rows from opposite ends. The variation mixes 2 hand-dyed colors beautifully, breaking stripes into individual blocks of color. One solid yarn ties everything together, offering both a main color and a visual relief to frame the hand-dyes.

Back

With smaller needles and A, cast on **76** (84, **96**, 108, **116**) stitches. Work K1, P1 Rib for 2". Change to larger needles. **Begin Dice Check: Row 1** (WS) Purl, increasing 10 evenly spaced across row — **86** (94, **106**, 118, **126**) stitches. Continue working even in pattern until piece measures **13½** (13, **13½**, 14, **14½**)", end with a WS row.

Shape armhole

At beginning of next 2 rows, bind off **10** (10, **12**, 15, **17**) — **66** (74, **82**, 88, **92**) stitches. Work even until armhole measures **7½** (8, **8½**, 9, **9½**)". Bind off firmly.

Dice Check

5
3
1

6
4
2

└─4-st repeat─┘

Stitch key
☐ Knit on RS, purl on WS
☑ Sl1 with yarn at RS

Color key
☐ A
☐ B
☐ C

DICE CHECK *MULTIPLE OF 4 + 2*
Slip stitches purlwise with yarn at WS of work.
Row 1 (WS) With A, purl.
Row 2 With B, k1, sl 1, **[k2, sl 2]** to last 4 stitches, k2, sl 1, k1.
Row 3 With B, p1, sl 1, **[p2, sl 2]** to last 4 stitches, p2, sl 1, k1.
Row 4 With A, knit.
Row 5 With C, p2, **[sl 2, p2]** to end.
Row 6 With C, k2, **[sl 2, k2]** to end.

K1, P1 RIB *OVER AN EVEN NUMBER OF STITCHES*
All rows or rounds [K1, p1] to end.

INC 1
At beginning of RS rows K1, M1.
At end of RS rows M1, k1.

DEC 1
At beginning of RS rows K1, k2tog.
At end of RS rows SSK, k1.

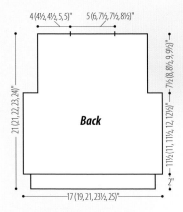

4 (4½, 4½, 5, 5)"   5 (6, 7½, 7½, 8½)"

21 (21, 22, 23, 24)"

Back

7½ (8, 8½, 9, 9½)"

11½ (11, 11½, 12, 12½)"

2"

17 (19, 21, 23½, 25)"

Medium: PRISM YARNS Symphony in colors 106 (A), Harvest (B), and Thunderclap (C)

10cm/4"

STANDARD FIT	20 stitches and 36 rows over Dice Check using **larger needles**	Medium weight	5mm/US8 AND 2 sizes smaller	7 25mm (1")
S (**M, L,** 1X, **2X**) A 34 (37, 41, 46½, **50**)" B 21 (21, **22**, 23, **24**)" C 27½ (29½, **31**, 32½, **34**)"		A 620 (700, **780**, 875, **970**) yds B and C 335 (375, **420**, 475, **525**) yds each		

Dice checks

Left Front

With smaller needles and A, cast on **36** (40, **44**, 52, **56**). Work as for Back to armhole EXCEPT increase 6 evenly spaced on first pattern row — **42** (46, **50**, 58, **62**) stitches.

Shape armhole

Bind off **10** (10, **12**, 15, **17**) at beginning of RS row — **32** (36, **38**, 43, **45**) stitches. Work even until armhole measures 4½ (5, **5½**, 6, **6½**)", end with a RS row.

Shape neck

At beginning of WS rows, bind off **5** (7, **9**, 11, **13**) once, **3** once, then **2** once. Dec 1 at end of every RS row twice — **20** (22, **22**, 25, **25**) stitches. Work even until piece measures same length as Back. Bind off firmly.

Right Front

Work as for Left Front EXCEPT reverse shaping. Bind off armhole at beginning of WS row. Shape neck at beginning of RS rows.

Sleeves

With smaller needles and A, cast on **36** (36, **38**, 42, **44**). Work K1, P1 Rib for 2". Change to larger needles. **Begin Dice Check: Row 1** (WS) Purl, increasing **6** (6, **8**, 4, **6**) evenly spaced across row — **42** (42, **46**, 46, **50**) stitches. Work 8 rows even. **[Inc 1 each side on next row; work 9 rows even]** 12 (14, **14**, 16, **15**) times, working new stitches into pattern — **66** (70, **74**, 78, **80**) stitches. Work even until piece measures **18** (19, **19½**, 20, **21**)" or desired length to shoulder minus **3** (3, **3**, 3½, **3½**)".

Shape cap

At beginning of every row, bind off **2** stitches **28** (28, **28**, 30, **30**) times. Bind off remaining **10** (14, **18**, 18, **20**) stitches.

Finishing

Note 1 *Pick up stitches and knit (PUK) with RS facing, smaller needles, and A.* **2** *Pick up at the following rates: 1 stitch for every 2 rows along vertical edges, and 1 stitch in every bound-off stitch.*

Sew shoulder seams. Set in sleeves. Sew side and sleeve seams.

Neckband PUK around neck edge. Count stitches and adjust to an odd number on next row if necessary. *Row 1* (WS) **[K1, p1]** to last stitch, k1. *Row 2* (RS) P1, **[k1, p1]** to end. Repeat last 2 rows 4 times. Bind off in pattern.

Button band PUK along left front edge and Neckband. Work as for Neckband.

Buttonhole band Mark position of 7 buttonholes evenly spaced along right front edge with top and bottom buttonholes 1" from ends. Work as for Button band, beginning 3-row buttonholes on fourth row and centering each buttonhole over a purl rib. Sew on buttons.

Note *If your buttons are large and/or heavy, consider sewing a small shirt-style button to the WS of the button band, behind each large button, to provide support.*

RICK'S 3-ROW BUTTONHOLE

Row 1 (RS) Work to marked purl stitch, yo twice, k2tog, work to end.
Row 2 (WS) Knit into first yo, drop second yo.
Row 3 (RS) Purl into yo space in row below. Pull stitch off left needle and let it drop. Buttonhole will seem too small, but use it once and it will be perfect.

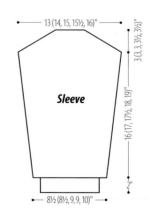

13 (14, 15, 15½, 16)"

3 (3, 3, 3½, 3½)"

16 (17, 17½, 18, 19)"

2"

8½ (8½, 9, 9, 10)"

Sleeve

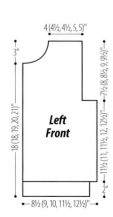

4 (4½, 4½, 5, 5)"

3"

7½ (8, 8½, 9, 9½)"

18 (18, 19, 20, 21)"

11½ (11, 11½, 12, 12½)"

2"

8½ (9, 10, 11½, 12½)"

Left Front

Neon river

Six related jewel-toned double-dyes and one Sandwashed solid play back and forth between entrelac and chevron stitch. Intarsia blocks of color follow angles formed by these stitch constructions.

Neon river

OTTO COLOR
ADVENTUROUS KNITTING

WHAT'S THE MAGIC?

Ramdonize and structure a group of double-dyed colors with intarsia worked in both entrelac and Chevron Stitch.

Notes 1 See page 164 for abbreviations and techniques. **2** Body is worked in 1 piece in Entrelac and Chevron stitch. Sleeves are worked in Entrelac. **3** Garment shaping and intarsia design both work with the **7** (**8, 9**)-stitch entrelac units and the **16** (**18, 20**)-stitch chevron repeats.

Color note: *River Twist is a double-dyed yarn: each of two strands has been dyed separately and then plied together with the colors unmatched. As the colors move through their repeats, some areas are mixed and appear tweedy while other areas are more closely aligned and stripe a bit more. Solid plum provides both a frame and punctuation.*

CHEVRON STITCH

MULTIPLE OF **16** (*18*, **20**) *+ 2*
RS rows Kf&b, [k6 (7, 8), S2KP2, k6 (7, 8), KOK] end last repeat), kf&b.
WS rows Knit for Garter Chevron; purl for Stockinette Chevron.
12-row color and stitch repeat Work 8 rows in Stockinette Chevron with intarsia colors. Work 4 rows in Garter Chevron with G.

KOK INCREASE (k1-yo-k1)
1 Knit 1, leaving stitch on left needle.
2 Bring yarn to front and over needle. **3** Knit into the stitch again.

Body

With smaller needle, cast on **168** (192, **216**). Work in K2, P2 rib for 1½". Change to larger needle and A, knit 1 row. *Next row* **[K1, k2tog]** to end — 112 (128, **144**) stitches.

Entrelac band
Tier 1 Work 16 BT (see instructions below). Cut yarn. *Tier 2* With A work LST, 15 Left-leaning Rectangles, LET. Cut yarn.
Attach G at beginning of RS and **[k7 (8, 9), PUK1 in top of triangle from Tier 1, PUK7 (8, 9) along side of next rectangle, PUK 1 in point]** 16 times — 256 (288, **320**) stitches. *Next row* Knit across to last stitch, Kf&b — **257** (289, **321**) stitches.
Begin Garter Chevron: *Next row* Kf&b, **[k6 (7, 8), sl 2 tog knitwise-k1-P2SSO, k6 (7, 8), (KOK)]** end last repeat with kf&b (rather than KOK). *Next row* Knit.
Establish intarsia blocks and begin Chevron stitch: Row 1 With C, work one **16** (18, **20**) repeat and next repeat to stitch before KOK; with D, KOK, work 5 repeats ending with KOK; with B, work 2 repeats; with F, work 4 repeats; with A work 1 repeat and work another repeat ending at stitch before KOK; with E, KOK, work to end. **Row 2** (WS) Purl in color established in previous RS row, twisting at color changes. **Row 3** (RS) Work in established colors to last KOK of D; with new ball of A, KOK, knit remaining D stitch on left needle; work all B stitches; then continue working across changing colors at F, A, and E.

BT   BASE TRIANGLE
Row 1 (WS) P2. **Row 2 and all RS rows** Knit stitches worked on previous row. **Row 3** Purl 1 more stitch than worked on previous row. Repeat last 2 rows to 7 (8, 9) stitches worked, end with a WS row.

LST   LEFT-LEANING STARTING TRIANGLE
Row 1 (RS) K2. **Row 2 and all WS rows** Purl stitches worked on previous row. **Row 3** Knit in front and back of stitch (kf&b), SSK to join (last stitch of triangle with stitch from base triangle). **Row 5** Kf&b, k1, SSK to join. **Row 7** Kf&b, knit to last stitch of triangle, SSK to join. Repeat last 2 rows, end kf&b, k**4** (5, **6**), SSK to join — all stitches of first base triangle have been joined. Do not turn.

LR   LEFT-LEANING RECTANGLE
With RS facing, pick up and knit (PUK) 7 (8, 9) stitches along edge of next unit (triangle or rectangle). **Row 1** (WS) P**7** (8, **9**). **Row 2** (RS) K6 (7, 8), SSK to join. Repeat last 2 rows until all **7** (8, **9**) stitches from previous unit have been joined.

LET   LEFT-LEANING ENDING TRIANGLE
With RS facing, pick up and knit (PUK) 7 (8, 9) stitches along edge of next unit (triangle or rectangle). **Row 1** (WS) P2tog, purl to end. **Row 2** (RS) Knit stitches worked on previous row. Repeat last 2 rows until 1 stitch remains. End with a WS row.

OVERSIZED
Size 1 (2, 3)
A 40 (44, **48**)"
B 23½ (25, **27**)"
C 27½ (29, **31**)"

10cm/4"
18 stitches and 28 rows
over stockinette stitch using **larger needles**

Medium weight
A, B, C, D, E, F
175 (200, **225**) yds each
G 425 (475, **550**) yds

4.5mm/US7,
AND
1 size smaller,
60cm (24") long or longer

8 16cm (5/8")

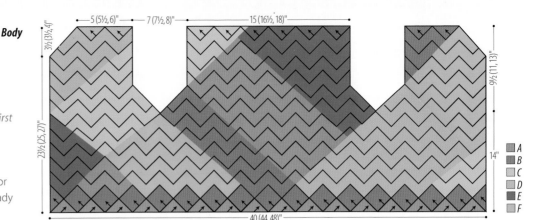

Body

5 (5½, 6)" — 7 (7½, 8)" — 15 (16½, 18)"

3½ (3½, 4)"

9½ (11, 13)"

23½ (25, 27)"

14"

40 (44, 48)"

- □ A
- ■ B
- □ C
- ■ D
- ■ E
- □ F

Rows 4–8 Work in established colors.

Note that color changes slant away from KOK increases in first few rows as Rule 5 states.

With G, work Rows 9–12.

Continue Chevron, shiftin the colors 2 stitches to the left or right on Row 1, as Rule 3 states. Use Body chart for color placement, to approximately 14" from beginning, end ready for Row 1.

Divide Fronts and Back

Notes 1 *Work Fronts and Back with separate yarns; attach additional yarns and colors as necessary for each section.* ***2*** *To shape the armhole, each KOK at underarms is replaced with 1 front edge stitch and 1 back edge stitch. Underarm shaping happens automatically by not increasing within the Chevron pattern at armhole edges.*

***Dividing row* Right Front** Work 4 repeats working last stitch as K1, do not drop stitch from left needle. **Back** K1 into stitch on left needle, work 8 repeats, replacing last KOK with K1, do not drop stitch from left needle. **Left Front** K1 into stitch on left needle to end. Continue in pattern, working no increases at armholes, until edge stitches are worked into **S2KP2 decrease.** ***Next WS row* Left Front** Work across; **Back** bind off **8** (9, **10**), work across; **Right Front** bind off **8** (9, **10**), work across. ***Next RS row* Right Front** Work to last stitch, kf&b; **Back** bind off **8** (9, **10**), kf&b, work to last stitch, kf&b; **Left Front** bind off **8** (9, **10**), kf&b, work in pattern to end. Armhole shaping complete. Place Fronts on hold.

Back

Work even for **7** (7½, **8½**)".

With appropriate colors, work 6 LTT — 1 across each **16** (18, **20**)-stitch repeat of Chevron.

Row 1 (RS) SSK, k**8** (7, **6**), SSK to join to side of Chevron. ***Row 2 and all WS rows*** Purl stitches worked on previous row. ***Row 3*** SSK, k**7** (6, **5**), SSK to join. Continue, working SSK at beginning of RS rows and 1 fewer stitch before SSK to join until 3 stitches worked on last WS row. ***Next RS row*** SSSK to join.

Right Front

Work even for **3½** (3½, **4½**)".

Shape neck

At beginning of row do not increase, (work k1, rather than kf&b) until edge stitch is worked into decrease. Next row (RS) Bind off **8** (9, **10**), kf&b, work to end. Work even placing Kf&b increases at edges, continue to same length as Back. Work LTT as for Back.

Left Front

Work as for Right Front EXCEPT work k1, rather than kf&b at **end** of row to shape neck. When neck edge stitch is worked into decrease, bind off **8** (9, **10**) at beginning of next WS row.

Intarsia notes and rules for this garment

1 *Work each stitch in color established in preceding row unless directed otherwise. The Chevron pattern will create diagonal lines as it is worked* ***2*** *Intarsia color flow is interrupted by the solid garter ridges, ALWAYS shift the intarsia colors 2 stitches to right or left to visually keep angles aligned.* ***3*** *It is not critical that every color block be started and stopped at precisely the same stitch as our model, BUT always add a new color at a KOK stitch to form the next color block.* ***4*** *Make sure to twist at color changes to avoid holes.* ***5*** *Color changes flow diagonally away from the KOK in the Chevron pattern; those diagonal lines will travel to the decrease dip of a chevron. AND when a color diagonal reaches and is worked into a decrease from the right, the following k7 (8, 9), KOK will be knit in that color. The next color is carried and woven behind those stitches, and then worked following the KOK. ALSO when a color diagonal reaches and is worked into a decrease from the left, you will complete the row as usual BUT IN the following WS row you will p8 (9, 10) after the decrease while carrying the adjacent color across those stitches to resume after those stitches.*

SSK
SSK

Size 2: MOUNTAIN COLORS River Twist in colors Whiskey Springs (A), Spring Creek (B), Grasshopper Falls (C), Glacier Lake (D), Stillwater River (E), and Firehole River (F); and 4/8's Wool in color Deep Purple (G)

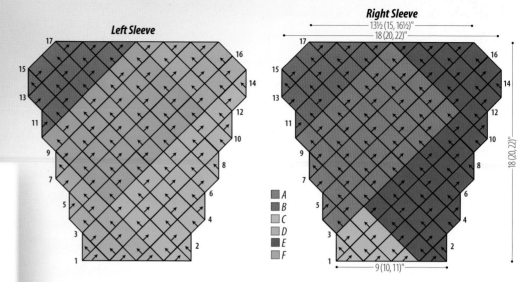

Left Sleeve

Right Sleeve
13½ (15, 16½)"
18 (20, 22)"
18 (20, 22)"
9 (10, 11)"

Legend:
■ A
■ B
■ C
■ D
■ E
■ F

RR   RIGHT-LEANING RECTANGLE

With WS facing, pick up and purl (PUP) **6** (**7**, **8**) stitches along edge of next unit — **7** (**8**, **9**) stitches on needle, 1 left from side triangle; after first Rectangle, PUP**7** (**8**, **9**). **Row 1** (RS) K**7** (**8**, **9**). **Row 2** (WS) P**6** (**7**, **8**), p2tog to join. Repeat last 2 rows until all **7** (**8**, **9**) stitches from unit in previous tier have been joined.

RST   RIGHT-LEANING STARTING TRIANGLE

Row 1 (WS) P2. **Row 2 and all RS rows** Knit stitches worked on previous row. **Row 3** Purl in front and back of stitch (pf&b), p2tog to join. **Row 5** Pf&b, p1, k2tog to join. **Row 7** Pf&b, purl to last stitch of triangle, p2tog to join. Repeat last 2 rows, end pf&b, p**4** (**5**, **6**), p2tog to join. Do not turn.

RET   RIGHT LEANING ENDING TRIANGLE

With WS facing, PUP **7** (**8**, **9**) stitches along edge of next unit in previous tier. **Row 1** (RS) Knit stitches worked on previous row. **Row 2** (WS) Purl to last 2 unit stitches, p2tog. Repeat last 2 rows until 2 stitches remain. **Next row** (WS) P2tog.

RTT   TOP TRIANGLE

With WS facing, PUP**7** (**8**, **9**) stitches along edge of next unit in previous tier — **8** (**9**, **10**) stitches on needle. **Row 1** (RS) K**7** (**8**, **9**). **Row 2** (WS) P2tog, purl to last stitch of unit, p2tog to join. Repeat last 2 rows until 2 unit stitches remain. **Next WS row** P3tog to join.

Sleeves

Note *Sleeves are worked in entrelac; follow charts for color placement.*

Right Sleeve

With smaller needle and G, cast on **42** (**48**, **54**). Work K2, P2 rib for 2". **Next row** Change to larger needle and **[k1, k2tog]** to end — **28** (**32**, **36**) stitches.

Tier 1 (WS) With C, work 3 BT; with E, work 1 BT.

Tier 2 With E, work 1 LST and 1 LR; with C, work 2 LR and 1 LET.

Tier 3 Following Right Sleeve color chart, work 4 RR.

Tier 4 Turn and cast on **7** (**8**, **9**) using cable cast-on; work 5 LR (last LR is not attached to tier below).

Tier 5 Work 1 RST, 4 RR, and1 RET.

Continue through Tier 15, casting on **7** (**8**, **9**) at beginning of Tiers 7, 10, and 13.

Shape cap

Tier 16 Bind off **7** (**8**, **9**). Work 7 LR.

Tier 17 Bind off **7** (**8**, **9**), Work 6 RTT. Fasten off final stitch.

Left Sleeve

Work as for Right Sleeve, following Left Sleeve chart.

Finishing

Sew shoulder seams. Sew sleeve seams. Set sleeves into armhole edge.

Neckband With G and smaller needle, beginning at right front neck edge, pick up and knit (PUK) **25** (**26**, **29**) to shoulder seam, 28 (30, 32) across back neck, **25** (**26**, **29**) to left front — **78** (**82**, **90**) stitches. **Next 5 rows** Work K2, P2 Rib, k2tog at beginning and SSK at end of each neck edge every other row twice. Bind off in pattern.

Left Front Band With G and smaller needle, PUK along left front edge at following rates: 3 stitches for every 4 rows along side of ribbing and 10 stitches for every 12-row repeat of Chevron pattern. Work 7 rows in K2, P2 Rib, adjusting to a multiple of 4 + 2 on first row, if necessary. Bind off in pattern. Mark for 8 buttons, beginning ½" from top edge and ending ¾" from bottom edge.

Right Front Band Work as for left front band, working buttonholes in 2nd row (see page 122). Sew on buttons.

Peaks & waves

Certain crochet stitches beg to be worked in hand-dyed yarns, and Spike Stitch is certainly one of those. While you could work this stitch in a single hand-dyed yarn, I like gathering a group of somewhat related colors, contrasting both in hue and color weight, and playing lighter colors against heavier ones.

Peaks & waves

OTTO COLOR

INTERMEDIATE CROCHET

WHAT'S THE MAGIC?

*Randomize a large group
of contrasting 64" repeats
with Spike Stitch.*

Color note *The Stripe Sequence allows
you to use the yarn called for without
purchasing additional skeins. If you vary
the sequence, simply make sure that, when
changing yarn, the next color selected has
some contrast so the pattern will show up.*

Notes 1 *See page 164 for abbreviations
and techniques.* **2** *Body and sleeves
are worked from side to side.*

Back

With larger hook and **A** (D, **C**, F, **E**), chain 45 (45, **45**, 51, **51**). Work Spike Stitch Set-up Row —
44 (44, **44**, 50, **50**) single crochet (sc). Work in pattern and Stripe Sequence until piece measures
approximately **1** (2, **2**, 3, **3**)", end with a WS row.
Shape first armhole *Row 1 or 7* Chain **31** (31, **37**, 37, **37**). Sc in second ch from hook and in each
ch across, then sc across body stitches — **74** (74, **80**, 86, **86**) sc. Continue as established until piece
measures approximately **16** (16, **18**, 18, **20**)" from armhole, end with a RS row.
Shape second armhole *Row 6 or 12* Ch 1, work in pattern across next **44** (44, **44**, 50, **50**)
stitches, turn, leaving remaining stitches unworked. Work even for **1** (2, **2**, 3, **3**)", end with a WS row.
Fasten off.

Left Front

Work as for Back until piece measures approximately **9** (10, **11**, 12, **13**)", end with a WS row.
Fasten off.

Right Front

With larger hook and H, ch **75** (75, **81**, 87, **87**). Work Spike Stitch Set-up Row — **74** (74, **80**, 86, **86**)
sc. Work in pattern until piece measures approximately **8** (8, **9**, 9, **10**), end with a RS row. Shape
armhole as for second armhole of Back.

Sleeves

Note *Work chain at end of RS row with a new color if next
pattern row is 6 or 12.*

With larger hook and **B** (B, **A**, A, **D**), chain 28. Work Spike Stitch
Set-up Row — 27 sc. Work in pattern and AT SAME TIME, shape as
follows: **[Ch7 at end of next RS row; turn, sc in second ch from
hook and in next 5 ch, work in pattern to end] 2** (2, **0**, 1, **2**)
times, working new stitches into pattern. **[Ch4 at end of next RS
row; turn, sc in second ch from hook and in next 2 ch, work in
pattern to end] 10** (10, **14**, 12, **10**) times, working new stitches into
pattern — 69 stitches. Work even until piece measures approximately
12 (12, **14**, 14½, **15**)", end with a WS row. **[Work 3 less than
previous row; turn, work 1 row even] 10** (10, **14**, 12, **10**) times.
[Work 6 less than previous row; turn, work 1 row even] 2 (2, **0**,
1, **2**) times — 27 sc. Fasten off.

5 (5, 6, 6, 7)"

6"

8 (8, 9½, 9½, 9½)"

12 (12, 13½, 13½, 13½)"

16 (16, 19, 19, 19)"

16½"

Left Front

Back

Sleeve

2"

2"

9 (10, 11, 12, 13)"

18 (20, 22, 24, 26)"

8 (8, 10, 10, 11)"

← *Direction of knitting*

10cm/4"

Small: PRISM YARNS *Symphony in colors Twilight (A),
Coral Reef (B), Autumn (C), Freesia (D), Thunderclap
(E), Highlands (F), Sapphire (G), and Deep Sea (H)*

STANDARD FIT
S (**M**, **L**, 1X, **2X**)
A 37 (41, **45**, 49, **53**)" (buttoned)
B 21½ (21½, **23**, 25, **25**)"
C 30½ (30½, **31½**, 31½, **32½**)"

15 stitches and
24 rows over
Spike Stitch, using
larger hook

Medium weight
A, B **350** (375, **450**, 500, **550**) yds each
C, D **225** (250, **300**, 325, **350**) yds each
E, F, H **110** (125, **150**, 160, **175**) yds each
G **450** (500, **575**, 625, **675**) yds

6.5mm/K-10½
5.5mm/I-9

5 25mm (1")

tapestry needle

Finishing

Notes 1 *Ch 1 at beginning of every row for turning chain. Beginning ch 1 does not count as a stitch.* **2** *Work bands with RS facing, smaller hook, and G.*

Sleeve Bands Join with a sl st in corner of bottom edge. Ch 1, work 1 sc in every other row across bottom edge; turn. Work 3 more rows sc, working in each sc across. Sc 2 rows with A, then 4 rows with G. Work 1 row rev sc with G. Fasten off.

Sew shoulder seams, leaving 6" or desired amount open for back neck. Set in sleeves. Sew side and sleeve seams. Mark Right Front for 5 button loops, with the first **10** (10, **10**, 12, **12**)" from bottom edge, the last 1" from bottom edge, and the other 3 spaced evenly between.

Bottom Band Join with a sl st in bottom corner of left front edge, ch 1, **[sc in each of next 2 rows, skip 1 row]** across bottom edge; turn. Continue as for Sleeve Band through fourth sc row of G. Do not fasten off.

Front, Lapel, and Neck Band Continuing with G, work 2 sc in corner, sc in every sc along Right Front, work 3 sc in top corner, **[sc in each of next 2 rows, skip 1 row]** across top of right front lapel, back neck, and left front lapel, work 3 sc in top corner, sc in every sc along Left Front to lower edge; turn. Work 2 more rows sc, working sc2tog at each shoulder seam on second row. *Next row* Sc around, working sc2tog 4 times evenly spaced across back neck. Sc 2 rows with A, then 1 row with G. *Button loop row* Work 1 row sc, working button loops at markers as follows: ch 3, skip 3 sc. Work 1 round rev sc around entire bottom, front, and neck edges, working 1 rev sc in every sc and 3 rev sc over each ch-3 loop. Sew on buttons. Fold lapels back and steam heavily. Allow to dry.

Stripe Sequence

	End:
D	— Back and Right Front **2X**, changing to E for last row
C	— Back and Right Front **1X**
B	— Back and Right Front **L**
A	— Back and Left Front **M**; Sleeve **2X**
D	— Back and Right Front **S**; Sleeve **L**, **1X**
C	— Sleeve **S**, **M**
F	
E	
B	Work 6 rows each color
A	following diagram, changing
D	color on Spike Single Crochet
C	(SSC) Row.
H	— End Left Front, Begin Right Front **All Sizes**
G	
B	
A	
F	
E	
D	
C	
B	Begin:
A	— Sleeve **S**, **M**
D	— Back and Left Front **S**; Sleeve **L**, **1X**
C	— Back and Left Front **M**; Sleeve **2X**
F	— Back, Left Front **L**
E	— Back, Left Front **1X**
	— Back, Left Front **2X**

Note *Last row of each piece is worked with next color in sequence.*

SC2TOG

Insert hook in stitch, yo and draw up a loop, insert hook in next stitch, yo and draw up a loop, yo and draw through all 3 loops on hook—1 stitch decreased.

SSC (SPIKE SINGLE CROCHET)

Insert hook the number of rows indicated below next stitch (example: SSC 5=5 rows below), yo, draw loop through and up to height of current row, yo, draw through both loops on hook.

SPIKE STITCH *MULTIPLE OF 6 + 2*

Note *Beginning ch 1 does not count as a stitch.*
Set-up row (WS) Sc in second ch from hook and in each ch across; turn.

Rows 1–5 Ch 1, sc in each sc across; turn. Drop yarn.

Row 6 (WS) With new color, ch 1, sc in first sc, **[sc in next sc, SSC 1 over next sc, SSC 2 over next sc, SSC 3 over next sc, SSC 4 over next sc, SSC 5 over next sc]** to last stitch, sc in last sc; turn.

Rows 7–11 Repeat Row 1. Drop yarn at end of Row 11.

Row 12 (WS) With new color, ch 1, sc in first sc, **[SSC 5 over next sc, SSC 4 over next sc, SSC 3 over next sc, SSC 2 over next sc, SSC 1 over next sc, sc in next sc]** to last stitch, sc in last sc; turn.

When instructed to end with RS row, end with Row 5 or 11; when instructed to end with WS row, end with Row 6 or 12.

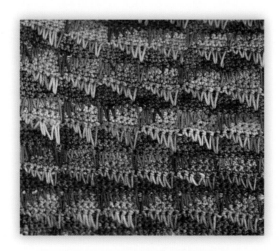

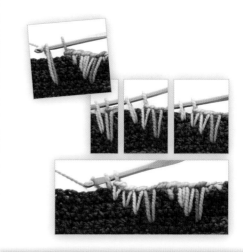

Contoured
color

Crème caramel

ATTENTIVE COLOR

INTERMEDIATE KNITTING

WHAT'S THE MAGIC?

Stack dyed-across 64" repeat on 2 times Magic Number. Shift colors in 1 tier by beginning in a different spot.

Color note Determine your Magic Number or adjust needle size to work with our Magic Number of 96. If your number is different, and when doubled is not a multiple of the stitch repeat, work as many repeats as possible, placing half the additional stitches on either side as garter borders. Then you will increase or decrease in final row before Yoke to get stitch count for yoke shaping. (2 × Magic Number = ___ + 1 = ___)

Knitting note See page 164 for abbreviations and techniques AND page 26 for Magic Number.

Vine Lace

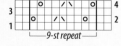

Stitch key
- ☐ Knit on RS, purl on WS
- ☉ Yarn over (yo)
- ╲ SSK
- ╱ K2tog

VINE LACE *MULTIPLE OF 9 + 4*

Rows 1 and 3 Purl.

Row 2 K3, [yo, k2, SSK, k2tog, k2, yo, k1] to last stitch, k1.

Row 4 K2, [yo, k2, SSK, k2tog, k2, yo, k1] to last 2 stitches, k2.

BUTTON LOOP

Slip 1 with yarn in front, **[slip 1 with yarn in back, psso]** 4 times; return last stitch to left needle. Place next stitch from right needle onto crochet hook, ch 7, move chain loop to left needle and k2tog.

A simple yet effective lace pattern showcases several different effects. The dyed-across yarn is carefully stacked in the top and bottom tiers, beginning at the middle of the side color. For the center tier, the colors are shifted so the side colors are in the middle, producing a different stack of colors with every-other-row subtleties. The entire capelet is framed in natural and is shaped at the top with decreases and at the front with short-row wedges. This allows shaping to occur without visually interrupting the stacks, and complements the cast-on edge.

Capelet

Determine your Magic Number or a needle size to work with our number of 96. With B, cast on 193 (or your Magic Number, adjusted for the pattern multiple, see Color note). Purl 1 row.

Tier 1 Beginning at middle of 1 side color of first skein of A, work Vine Lace to end of first skein — approximately 6½". Place stitches on hold on spare needle.

Tier 2 Beginning halfway between the 2 side colors so colors are offset, work in Vine Lace for 2".

Join Tiers

On next WS row, hold Tiers 1 and 2 together with WS facing and work across, purling together 1 stitch from each needle. Continue in pattern with second skein until piece measures 8" from Tier 1 cast-on; place stitches on hold on spare needle.

Tier 3 Begin as for Tier 1 and work pattern for 2" before joining to Tier 2. Continue in pattern for 1" more. Do not cut A.

Yoke

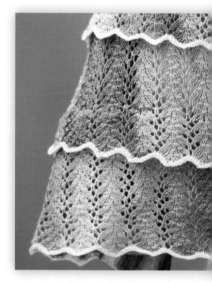

Join B and k24, place marker (pm), k22, pm, **[k2tog]** twice, **[k1, k2tog]** 31 times, **[k2tog]** twice, pm, k22, pm, k24 — 158 stitches. Knit 1 row.

Garter row 1 With A, **[knit to last 2 stitches before marker, k2tog, slip marker (sm), SSK]** 4 times, knit to end — 150 stitches.

Garter row 2 Knit 1 row. With B, repeat Garter Rows 1 and 2 — 142 stitches.

First eyelet band

With B, repeat Row 1 — 134 stitches. Purl 1 row. **Next row** With B, k1, **[yo, SSK]** 9 times, k2tog, sm, SSK, k1, **[yo, SSK]** 5 times, k1, k2tog, sm, SSK, k1, **[yo, SSK]** 13 times, k2, **[k2tog, yo]** 13 times, k1, k2tog, sm, SSK, k1, **[k2tog, yo]** 5 times, k1, k2tog, sm, SSK, **[k2tog, yo]** 9 times, k1 — 126 stitches. **Next row** Purl 1 row. Repeat Garter Rows 1 and 2 with B, then A, then B — 102 stitches.

10cm/4"

ONE SIZE

20 stitches and 34 rows over Vine Lace

 Fine weight
A 700 yds
B 250 yds

 4mm/US6 or size to make color repeat work, 60cm (24") or longer

 3.75mm/F-5

 2 spare circular needles

Second eyelet band

With B, knit 1 row, purl 1 row. **Next row** K1, **[yo, SSK]** 7 times, k2tog, sm, k1, **[yo, SSK]** 3 times, k1, sm, SSK, k1, **[yo, SSK]** 11 times, k2, **[k2tog, yo]** 11 times, k1, k2tog, sm, k1, **[k2tog, yo]** 3 times, k1, sm, SSK, **[k2tog, yo]** 7 times, k1 — 98 stitches. **Next row** Purl 1 row. Repeat Garter Rows 1 and 2 with B, then A, then B — 74 stitches.

Third eyelet band

With B, knit 1 row, purl 1 row. **Next row** K1, **[yo, SSK]** 5 times, k2tog, sm, k8, sm, SSK, k1, **[yo, SSK]** 9 times, k2, **[k2tog, yo]** 9 times, k1, k2tog, sm, k8, sm, SSK, **[k2tog, yo]** 5 times, k1 — 70 stitches. **Next row** Purl 1 row. Knit 2 rows with B, then A, then B — 70 stitches. Bind off.

Left Front

With B, RS facing, and beginning at neck edge, pick up and knit (PUK) 88 along left front edge, keeping edges of overlapping tiers free. Knit 1 row. With A, knit 2 rows.

Note No need to hide wraps.

Left B Wedge With B, knit 1 row. **Begin short rows: Rows 1–2** K75, wrap and turn (W&T); knit to end. **Rows 3–4** P66, W&T; k1, **[yo, SSK]** 32 times, k1. **Rows 5–6** P67, W&T; knit to end. Knit 1 row.

Left A Wedge

With A, knit 1 row. **Begin short rows: Rows 1–2** K66, W&T; knit to end. **Rows 3–4** K44, W&T; knit to end. **Rows 5–6** K22, W&T; knit to end. **Rows 7–8** K23, W&T; knit to end. **Rows 9–10** K45, W&T; knit to end. **Rows 11–12** K67, W&T; knit to end. Knit 1 row.

Work Left B Wedge, A Wedge, and B Wedge. With A, knit 2 rows. With B, knit 2 rows. With RS facing, bind off in purl.

LORNA'S LACES *Shepherd Sport in colors Monkey Shines (A) and Natural (B)*

Right Front

With B, WS facing, and beginning at neck edge, pick up and purl (PUP) 88 along right front edge, keeping edges of overlapping tiers free. Purl 1 row. With A, purl 2 rows.

Right B Wedge

With B, purl 1 row. **Begin short rows: Rows 1–2** P75, W&T; purl to end. **Rows 3–4** K66, W&T; p1, **[yo, p2tog]** 32 times, p1. **Rows 5–6** K67, W&T; purl to end. Purl 1 row.

Right A Wedge

With A, purl 1 row. **Begin short rows: Rows 1–2** P66, W&T; purl to end. **Rows 3–4** P44, W&T; purl to end. **Rows 5–6** P22, W&T; purl to end. **Rows 7–8** P23, W&T; purl to end. **Rows 9–10** P45, W&T; purl to end. **Rows 11–12** P67, W&T; purl to end. Purl 1 row.

Work Right B Wedge, A Wedge, and B Wedge. With A, purl 2 rows. With B, purl 2 rows.

Finishing

With WS facing, bind off in knit, inserting Button Loops as follows:
Bind off 2, work Button Loop; bind off 3, work Button Loop; bind off remaining stitches.

8 Pick up stitches and work front bands, leaving tier-overlap free.

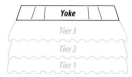

7 Work yoke. Bind off.

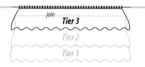

6 Join to second tier, then continue in pattern for 1" more.

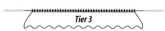

5 Tier 3 Begin third tier, and work pattern for 2".

4 Continue in pattern with second skein to 8", then hold on spare needle.

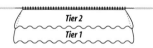

3 Then on next WS row, hold both pieces together with WS facing and work across, purling together 1 stitch from each needle to join layers.

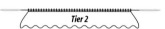

2 Tier 2 Begin next skein of A halfway between the two side colors, so stacks are offset. Work in Vine Lace for 2".

1 Tier 1 Beginning at middle of 1 side color of A, work Vine Lace to end of first skein - approximately 6½". Hold on spare needle.

Portofino spice

OTTO COLOR

INTERMEDIATE KNITTING

WHAT'S THE MAGIC?

Randomize 48" and 60" repeats by holding 2 strands together.

Notes 1 See page 164 for abbreviations and techniques. **2** To mimic princess seaming often found in ready-to-wear, Fronts and Backs are decreased along an interior dart line as well as at side seams.

INC 1

At beginning of RS rows or before marker K1, M1.
At end of RS rows or after marker M1, k1.

DEC 1

At beginning of RS rows K1, SSK.
At end of RS rows K2tog, k1.

Small: PRISM YARNS Merino Mia in color Spice (A); Saki in color Portofino (B); Symphony in color 307 (C)

Here, 2 sock-weight yarns with different skein repeats were held together to overcome any patterning tendencies. When the stitch counts change on this shaped sweater, only 1 of the 2 yarns nears its Magic Number while the other functions to block patterning. While a careful look might detect a bit of pattern, the overall appearance is simply a color story. The ruffled details add a nice frame to the sleek, shaped style, formed through side shaping and vertical darts on both back and front.

Back

With smaller needles and A and B held together, cast on **79** (87, **93**, 101, **107**). Knit 4 rows. Change to larger needles. Work in stockinette stitch until piece measures **1½** (1½, **2**, 2, **2½**)", end with a WS row.

Shape waist

Set-up row K1, SSK, k**22** (23, **25**, 28, **30**), place marker (pm), SSK, k**25** (31, **33**, 35, **37**), k2tog, pm, knit to last 3 stitches, k2tog, k1 — **75** (83, **89**, 97, **103**) stitches. **[Work 5 rows even; k1, SSK, work to first marker, SSK, work to 2 stitches before next marker, k2tog, work to last 3 stitches, k2tog, k1]** twice — **67** (75, **81**, 89, **95**) stitches. Work even until piece measures **6** (7, **7½**, 8, **8½**)", end with a WS row.
Next row **[Work to marker, slip marker (sm), Inc 1, work to last stitch before marker, Inc 1, sm, work to end; work 5 rows even]** 3 times, removing markers on last row — **73** (81, **87**, 95, **101**) stitches. Work even until piece measures **13½** (14, **14**, 14½, **15**)", end with a WS row.

Shape armholes

At beginning of next 2 rows, bind off **3** (3, **3**, 4, **4**), then Dec 1 each side every RS row **4** (6, **5**, 5, **6**) times — **59** (63, **71**, 77, **81**) stitches. Work even until armhole measures **7½** (8, **8½**, 9, **9½**)", end with a WS row.

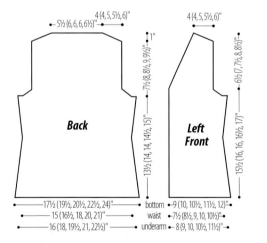

Shape shoulders

At beginning of every row, bind off **6** (6, **7**, 8, **8**) stitches 4 times, then **5** (6, **8**, 9, **10**) twice. Bind off remaining **25** (27, **27**, 27, **29**) stitches.

Left Front

With smaller needles and A and B held together, cast on **40** (44, **47**, 51, **54**). Work as for Back to beginning of waist shaping.

Shape waist and armhole

Set-up row K1, SSK, k**22** (23, **25**, 28, **30**), pm, SSK, knit to end—**38** (42, **45**, 49, **52**) stitches. Continue as for Back EXCEPT shape waist at beginning of RS rows and after marker only, and shape armhole at beginning of RS rows only—**30** (32, **36**, 39, **41**) stitches. Work even until armhole measures 2".

Shape front neck

Dec 1 at neck edge every other RS row **13** (14, **14**, 14, **15**) times—**17** (18, **22**, 25, **26**) stitches. Work even until piece measures same length as Back to shoulder. Shape shoulder at beginning of RS rows as for Back.

Right Front

Work as for Left Front to beginning of waist shaping.

Shape waist, armhole, and front neck

Set-up row K**13** (16, **17**, 18, **19**), k2tog, pm, work to last 3 stitches, k2tog, k1. Continue as for Back EXCEPT shape waist at end of RS rows and before marker only, and bind off armhole at beginning of WS rows and decrease at end of RS rows, and AT SAME TIME, when armhole measures 2", shape neck as for Left Front. Work even until piece measures same length as Back to shoulder. Shape shoulder at beginning of WS rows as for Back.

Sleeves

With smaller needles and A and B held together, cast on **43** (47, **49**, 53, **55**).

Knit 4 rows. Change to larger needles and stockinette stitch. Work 6 rows.

[Inc 1 each side on next RS row; work 5 rows even] **8** (8, **8**, 9, **10**) times—**59** (63, **65**, 71, **75**) stitches. Work even until piece measures **13** (14, **14**, 14½, **15**)", end with a WS row.

Shape cap

At beginning of next 2 rows, bind off 4. Dec 1 each side every RS row **15** (16, **18**, 20, **21**) times. Bind off remaining **21** (23, **21**, 23, **25**) stitches.

Finishing

Notes 1 Ruffles tend to spread the edge they have been worked onto, so these ruffles have fewer increases along the front edge than at sleeve, hem, and neck—otherwise the front ruffle would be too full. They won't look like much until the Fronts are sewn together, then the ruffles nest and fall gently into place. 2 Pick up and knit (PUK) with RS facing and at the following rates: 1 stitch in every cast-on stitch and 3 stitches for every 4 rows along front and neck edges. 3 For ease of knitting body and neck edge, use 1 circular needle for the bottom edge and 1 for the front and neck edges.
Block pieces.

Sleeve ruffle With larger needles and C, PUK along cast-on edge. Knit 1 row.
Next row **[Kf&b]** to end. *Next row* **[P1, pf&b]** to end.
Next row Knit. Bind off in knit.
Sew shoulder seams. Set in sleeves. Sew side and sleeve seams.

Ruffled edge Beginning at bottom corner of Left Front with circular needle and C, PUK along bottom edge to right front corner, pm; with second needle and C, PUK along front edge to beginning of neck shaping, pm, PUK along neck edge to beginning of neck shaping on Left Front, pm, PUK along front edge to bottom. Place marker and join to work in the round. Purl 1 round. *Next round* **[Kf&b]** across bottom to marker, sm, kf&b, **[k1, kf&b]** to neck marker, **[kf&b]** to next marker, sm, kf&b, **[k1, kf&b]** to end. Knit 2 rounds, Inc 1 each side of each marker. Purl 1 round. Bind off loosely in knit.
Sew center fronts together invisibly, inside ruffled edge. Steam ruffles if needed.

London fog

A classically styled jacket — with side decreases for a feminine fit, rounded front edges, and set-in sleeves — has lots of stitch-count changes and so poses challenges. Combining a strongly dyed sock-weight merino with 2 strands of lace-weight kid mohair softens and blurs the color changes and minimizes any tendency to pattern. The merino with its crisp color changes becomes a perfect choice for a bias-band trim.

London fog

OTTO COLOR

INTERMEDIATE KNITTING

WHAT'S THE MAGIC?

Randomize two 60" repeats by holding 3 strands together. Pattern 1 strand in stripes for narrow bias band.

Notes 1 *See page 164 for abbreviations and techniques.* **2** *Entire body is worked with 1 strand A and 2 strands B held together. Trim is worked with 1 strand A.*

INC 1

At beginning of RS rows K1, M1.
At end of RS rows M1, k1.
At beginning of WS rows P1, M1.
At end of WS rows M1, p1.

DEC 1

At beginning of RS rows K1, k2tog.
At end of RS rows SSK, k1.
At beginning of WS rows P1, p2tog.
At end of WS rows SSP, p1.

BIAS TRIM

Row 1 Kf&b, knit to last 2 stitches, k2tog.
Row 2 Purl.

Small: PRISM YARNS Merino Mia in color Coral Reef (A) and Gossamer in color Playa (B)

Back

With smaller needles and 1 strand A and 2 strands B, cast on **80** (90, **98**, 108). Knit 1 row.

Shape waist

Change to larger needles and stockinette stitch. ***Next row*** (RS) Knit. **[Work 7 rows even; Dec 1 each side on next RS row]** 4 times — **72** (82, **90**, 100) stitches. Work 7 (7, **9** 11) rows even. **[Inc 1 each side on next RS row; work 7 rows even]** twice — **76** (86, **94**, 104) stitches. Work even until piece measures **12** (13, **14½**, 15)", end with a WS row.

Shape armholes

At beginning of next 2 rows, bind off **4** (5, **6**, 7) stitches. Dec 1 each side every RS row **5** (6, **7**, 9) times — **58** (64, **68**, 72) stitches. Work even until armhole measures **7½** (8, **8½**, 9)", end with a WS row.

Shape shoulders

At beginning of every row, bind off **4** (5, **5**, 5) stitches 8 (6, **8**, 6) times, then **0** (4, **0**, 6) stitches twice. Bind off remaining **26** (26, **28**, 30) stitches.

Left Front

With smaller needles and 1 strand A and 2 strands B, cast on **20** (25, **29**, 34). Knit 1 row.

Shape center front

Change to larger needles and stockinette stitch. ***Next row*** (RS) Knit. At beginning of next 2 WS rows, using cable cast-on, cast on 4 once, then 3 once. Inc 1 at center front edge every row 10 times, every RS row twice, then every other RS row once and AT SAME TIME, shape waist at beginning of RS rows as for Back — **38** (43, **47**, 52) stitches. Work even until piece measures same as Back to underarm. Shape armhole at beginning of RS rows as for Back — **29** (32, **34**, 36) stitches. Work even until armhole measures 3", end with a RS row.

Shape neck

Dec 1 at neck edge every RS row **3** (3, **4**, 5) times, then every row 6 times. At beginning of next 2 WS rows, bind off 2 — **16** (19, **20**, 21) stitches. Work even until piece measures same length as Back to shoulder. Shape shoulder at beginning of RS rows as for Back.

Right Front

Work as for Left Front EXCEPT reverse shaping. Cast on for center front at beginning of RS rows. Shape waist at end of RS rows. Bind off armhole at beginning of WS rows and decrease at end of RS rows. Bind off neck at beginning of RS rows.

10cm/4"

STANDARD FIT
XS (S, M, L)
A **34** (38, **42**, 46)"
B **21** (22½, **24½**, 25½)"
C **28** (29½, **31**, 32½)"

18 stitches and **24 rows** over stockinette stitch with 1 strand A and 2 strands B held together, using **5mm/US8 needles**

Fine weight
A **1125** (1325, **1500**, 1650) yds
B **1325** (1525, **1725**, 1900) yds

For body,
5mm/US8
AND
2 sizes smaller
For trim, **3.25mm/US3**

2.25mm/B-1

Sleeves

With smaller needles and 1 strand A and 2 strands B, cast on **36** (38, **40**, 42). Knit 1 row. Change to larger needles, and stockinette stitch. *Next row* (RS) Knit. **[Work 5 rows even; Inc 1 each side on next RS row]** 15 times — **66** (68, **70**, 72) stitches. Work even until piece measure **17** (17½, **18**, 18½)", end with a WS row.

Shape cap

At beginning of next 2 rows, bind off **4** (5, **6**, 7). Dec 1 each side every RS row **13** (14, **16**, 17) times — **32** (30, **26**, 24) stitches. Bind off 5 at beginning of next 2 rows. Bind off **22** (20, **16**, 14) remaining stitches.

Finishing

Sew shoulder seams. Set in sleeves. Sew side and sleeve seams.
Pocket Flaps *MAKE 2* With smaller needles and 1 strand A and 2 strands B, cast on 20. Knit 1 row. Change to larger needles. Beginning with a knit row, work 3 rows in stockinette stitch. Bind off.

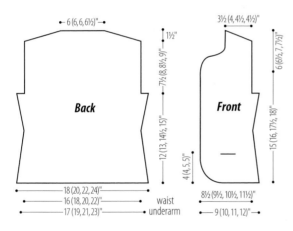

Trim

Notes 1 *Use smaller needles and A for trim.* ***2*** *It is better if body trim is slightly longer than needed, because extra fullness can be eased around the curved fronts. If it is too tight, the fronts will not lie flat.*

Trim for pocket flaps *MAKE 2* Cast on 2. **[Kf&b]** twice — 4 stitches. Work in stockinette stitch and Inc 1 each side every RS row 3 times — 10 stitches. Mark last row worked. Work Bias Trim until same length from marker as pocket flap, end with a RS row. **[Purl 1 row; SSK, knit to last 2 stitches, k2tog]** 4 times — 2 stitches. Bind off. With crochet hook and A, work reverse single crochet along each edge of pocket flap trim, working 1 stitch in every other row. With RS facing, pin trim along sides and cast-on edge of pocket flap, overlapping edge by approximately ¼". Tack invisibly in the ditch formed by the reverse single crochet. Fold trim in half to WS of flap and tack invisibly. Center pocket flaps **4** (4, **5**, 5)" from bottom edges of Fronts on RS. With trimmed edges at bottom, invisibly sew bound-off edges to Fronts.

Trim for sleeves and body With temporary cast-on, cast on 10 and work Bias Trim. For each sleeve edge, work trim for approximately **9** (9½, **10**, 10½)". For entire body, work trim for approximately **90** (96, **101**, 117)". Place each trim on hold. For each piece, graft live stitches to cast-on edge, removing waste yarn and being careful not to twist trim.

With crochet hook and A, work reverse single crochet along each

long edge of all trims, working 1 stitch in every other row. With RS facing, pin one sleeve trim to bottom of sleeve, overlapping edge by approximately ¼". Tack invisibly in the ditch formed by the reverse single crochet. Fold trim in half to inside and tack invisibly. Repeat for second sleeve. Pin body trim to body piece, easing fullness around curved edges so they lie flat. Tack as for sleeves. Block with steam.

Geisha

OTTO COLOR

INTERMEDIATE KNITTING

WHAT'S THE MAGIC?
*Randomize repeats of 56",
60", and 66" by alternating
1-row stripes A, B, C.*

Here is an A, B, C stripe combination that uses 3 very different yarns: sock-weight wool, doubled lace-weight Tencel, and thin rayon/metallic. There is a lot of both color and texture variation that hides side shaping and radical stitch-count changes. Details at the closure and collar use the subtle striping to define direction. Select colors that are similar in weight and feel, but don't worry about matching. Some accents and variation is desirable.

Back

With temporary cast-on and A, cast on **118** (126, **132**, 144, **156**).

Shape waist

Beginning with Row 2, work in Pat 1 and Stripe Sequence and AT SAME TIME, **[work 5 rows even; Dec 1 each side on next row]** 10 times — **98** (106, **112**, 124, **136**) stitches. Work even until piece measures **7½** (8, **8**, 8½, **8½**)", end with a WS row. **[Inc 1 each side on next row; work 7 rows even]** 6 times, working new stitches into pattern — **110** (118, **124**, 136, **148**) stitches. Work even until piece measures **13½** (13½, **14**, 14½, **15**)", end with a WS row.

Shape armholes

At beginning of next **2** (2, **2**, 2, **4**) rows, bind off 6. Dec 1 each side every RS row **5** (6, **6**, 10, **6**) times, then every other RS row **2** (3, **4**, 4, **5**) times — **84** (88, **92**, 96, **102**) stitches. Work even in pattern until armhole measures **7** (7½, **8**, 8½, **9**)".

Shape shoulders

At beginning of every row, bind off 5 stitches twice, 6 stitches 6 times, then **2** (3, **4**, 5, **7**) stitches twice. Bind off remaining **34** (36, **38**, 40, **42**) stitches.

STRIPE SEQUENCE

Cast on with A, then drop. Join B, work across, then drop. Join 2 strands of C, work across, then drop. A is waiting at edge, ready for next row. In this manner, alternate 1 row of each color over the 8 rows of pattern. To keep yarns from tangling, place 1 ball on either side of you and 1 ball in front. When you turn, lift the work up and look at how the strands lie — in one direction they twist, in the other they stay separate. You will occasionally need to move a strand over or under to keep the order.

Pat 1: Modified Half Linen

Rows 1 and 5 (RS) Knit.
Row 2 and all WS rows Purl.
Row 3 [K1, sl 1] to end.
Row 7 [Sl 1, k1] to end.
Row 8 Purl.

2-st repeat

Pat 2: Half Linen

Row 1 (RS) [K1, sl 1] to end.
Row 2, 4 (WS) Purl.
Row 3 [Sl 1, k1] to end.

2-st repeat

Stitch key

☐ Knit on RS, purl on WS
☑ Slip 1 with yarn at RS of work

Notes 1 Slip stitches purlwise with yarn at RS of work.
2 Change yarn at beginning of each row.

STANDARD FIT

XS (S, M, L, 1X)
A 37 (40, **42**, 45, **49**)"
B 21½ (22, **23**, 24, **25**)"
C 27 (28, **29**, 30½, **32**)"

10cm/4"

26 stitches and **38 rows** over Pat 1, alternating 1 row each color

Fine weight
A 650 (700, **775**, 875, **950**) yds
B 625 (675, **750**, 850, **925**) yds

Superfine weight
C 1100 (1175, **1300**, 1450, **1600**) yds

3.5mm/US4

3.5mm/US4, 60cm (24") or longer

1 25mm (1")

& stitch markers waste yarn

Alternate colorways,
from top to bottom:
Denali, Autumn, Embers, Jewels

Small: PRISM YARNS Merino Mia in color
Playa (A); Elise in color Harvest (B);
Delicato in color Sagebrush (C)

Notes 1 *See page 164 for*
abbreviations and techniques, page
138 for Inc 1 and Dec 1. **2** *When*
shaping, if a slip stitch falls at the edge,
work the stitch in stockinette stitch.
3 *For C, use 2 strands held together.*

141

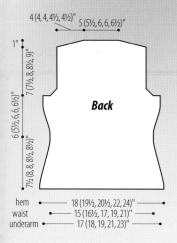

4 (4, 4, 4½, 4½)"
5 (5½, 6, 6, 6½)"

1"

6 (5½, 6, 6, 6½)"

7 (7½, 8, 8½, 9)"

Back

7½ (8, 8, 8½, 8½)"

hem • 18 (19½, 20½, 22, 24)"
waist • 15 (16½, 17, 19, 21)"
underarm • 17 (18, 19, 21, 23)"

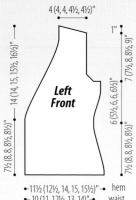

4 (4, 4, 4½, 4½)"

1"

14 (14, 15, 15½, 16½)"

7 (7½, 8, 8½, 9)"

6 (5½, 6, 6, 6½)"

Left Front

7½ (8, 8, 8½, 8½)"

7½ (8, 8, 8½, 8½)"

• 11½ (12½, 14, 15, 15½)" • hem
• 10 (11, 12½, 13, 14)" • waist
• 11 (12, 13, 14, 15)" • underarm

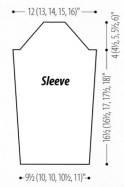

• 12 (13, 14, 15, 16)" •

4 (4½, 5, 5½, 6)"

Sleeve

16½ (16½, 17, 17½, 18)"

• 9½ (10, 10, 10½, 11)" •

Geisha

Left Front

With temporary cast-on and A, cast on **76** (82, **90**, 96, **102**). Work as for Back EXCEPT shape waist and armhole at beginning of RS rows only and AT SAME TIME, when piece measures 7½ (8, **8**, 8½, **8½**)", Dec 1 at neck edge every 3 rows **34** (37, **43**, 44, **45**) times — **25** (26, **27**, 28, **30**) stitches. Work even until piece measures same length as Back to shoulder. Shape shoulder at beginning of RS rows as for Back.

Right Front

Work as for Left front EXCEPT reverse shaping. Shape waist at end of RS rows. Bind off armhole at beginning of WS rows and decrease at end of RS rows.

Sleeves

With temporary cast-on and A, cast on **62** (64, **66**, 68, **72**). Beginning with Row 2, work in Pat 1 and Stripe Sequence and AT SAME TIME, **[work 7 rows even; Inc 1 each side on next row] 8** (11, **13**, 15, **16**) times, working new stitches into pattern — **78** (86, **92**, 98, **104**) stitches. Work even until piece measures **16½** (16½, **17**, 17½, **18**)" or desired length to armhole, end with a WS row.
Shape cap
At beginning of next 2 rows, bind off 6. Dec 1 each side every RS row **19** (21, **23**, 26, **28**) times. At beginning of next 2 rows, bind off 5. Bind off remaining **18** (22, **24**, 24, **26**) stitches.

Finishing

Sleeve I-cord edging Remove waste yarn from cast-on edge and place stitches onto needle, ready to work a RS row. Join A and cast 2 onto left needle (I-cord). **Next row [K1, SSK last stitch of I-cord with 1 stitch of sleeve, sl 2 back to left needle]** until all sleeve stitches are worked. Bind off 2 I-cord stitches.
Sew shoulder seams. Set in sleeves. Sew side and sleeve seams.
Left Front band With RS facing and A, pick up and knit (PUK) along Left Front edge from beginning of neck shaping to cast-on edge at a rate of 2 stitches for every 3 rows. Count stitches and adjust to an even number on next row if necessary. Beginning with Row 2, work in Pat 2 and Stripe Sequence for 9 rows, end with A and Row 2, and AT SAME TIME, Dec 1 at neck edge every RS row 4 times. Place stitches on hold.
Right Front band Work as for Left Front band EXCEPT PUK from cast-on edge to beginning of neck shaping and work for 10 rows, end with B and Row 3.

Collar With RS facing, circular needle and A, PUK along top of Right Front band, around neck, and along top of left front band at a rate of 2 stitches for every 3 rows along vertical and diagonal edges, and 1 stitch for every bound-off stitch. Count stitches and adjust to an even number on next row if necessary. Beginning with Row 2, work in Pat 2 and Stripe Sequence for 3" and AT SAME TIME, Dec 1 each side every RS row. Mark each side of last row for foldline. Continuing in pattern, Dec 1 each side every RS row for 3" more, end with A and Row 2.
Border Border will switch at foldline from RS to WS and back to RS, so that when Collar is folded, the RS of the border shows (RS of Body, WS of Border) With B, beginning with Row 2 of Pat 2, purl across Collar and place marker (pm) for corner; pick up and purl (PUP) an even number of stitches along collar edge to foldline marker, PUK an even number of stitches along remainder of collar edge, work Row 3 along left front band stitches from hold. *Next row* (WS Body) With C, work Row 4 to foldline, slip marker (sm), work Row 3 corner marker, M1, sm, k1, M1, work to last stitch, M1, k1, pm for corner, PUK an odd number of stitches to foldline marker, PUP an even number of stitches along remainder of collar edge, work Row 4 along right front band stitches from hold. *Next row* (RS Body) With A, work Row 1 to foldline marker, work Row 4 to next foldline marker, work Row 1 to end. Continue in pattern, changing rows at foldline markers, until Border along collar edge measures 1" from pick-up row, ending at bottom edge of Right Front and AT SAME TIME, on every RS row of Border (WS Body), work to corner marker, M1, sm, k1, M1, work to last stitch before corner marker, M1, k1, sm, M1, working new stitches into pattern.
Border I-cord edging Fold Collar along foldline and block heavily with steam. Try jacket on and mark for button and for beginning and ending of button loop. Loop should be just below foldline on RS. Work I-cord edging as for Sleeve, forming loop at Right Front marker as follows: work to beginning loop marker leaving 2 I-cord stitches on right needle, sl 1 from left needle, **[sl 1, psso]** 4 times or number of times needed for button. Sl 2 I-cord stitches to left needle, **[k2, sl 2 to left needle]** 4 times or until loop is same length as bind-off for button. Return to attaching I-cord as established and at each corner of Collar work **[k2, sl 2 to left needle]** once to ease corner. Work to bottom of Left Front — 2 I-cord stitches remain. Remove waste yarn from cast-on edge along fronts and Back and place stitches onto needle, ready to work a RS row. Sl 2 I-cord stitches to left needle. **[K2, sl 2 to left needle]** twice to ease bottom corner, return to attaching I-cord as established until 2 I-cord stitches remain, **[k2, sl 2 to left needle]** twice. Graft I-cord stitches to I-cord cast-on. Sew on button.

Boardroom

Alternating Spike Stitch is another in the family of ever-so-useful crochet stitches. Here, a hand-dyed yarn is worked on changing stitch counts for an ultra-feminine shaped jacket and pencil skirt. While the patterning changes as the stitch counts do, there is enough randomizing to work visually. The skirt is made from fine sock-weight wool, while the jacket is a thicker dk weight.

Boardroom

OTTO COLOR

INTERMEDIATE CROCHET

WHAT'S THE MAGIC?

Randomize repeats of 60" and 64" with Spike Stitch.

Color note *Choose a hand-dyed color with similar color weights for pleasing blending. More highly contrasting colors will make a visually busy surface.*

Notes 1 *See page 164 for abbreviations and techniques.* **2** *Jacket is worked in one piece to underarm, then divided and fronts and back are worked separately.* **3** *Skirt is worked back and forth in rows to top of back slit, then joined but worked back and forth in rounds to maintain pattern.* **4** *Fabric is reversible.*

DEC 1

[Insert hook in next stitch (or row below for SSC), yo and draw up a loop] twice, yo and draw through all 3 loops on hook — 1 stitch decreased. Work each decrease in pattern (sc or SSC).

DEC ROW

Work to 2 before marker, Dec 1, slip marker (sm), Dec 1.

INC 1

Work 2 sc in same stitch.

SSC (SPIKE SINGLE CROCHET)

Insert hook 1 row below next stitch, yo, draw loop through and up to height of current row, yo, draw through both loops on hook.

ALTERNATING SPIKE STITCH

MULTIPLE OF 2 + 1 (for turning chain)
Note *Beginning ch-1 does not count as a stitch.*
Set-up row Sc in second ch from hook and in each ch to end; turn. **Row 1** Ch 1, sc in each of first 2 sc, **[SSC over next sc, sc in next sc]** to end; turn.

JACKET
Body

With smaller hook, chain **149** (163, **173**, 189). Change to larger hook and work Alternating Spike Stitch Set-up Row — **148** (162, **172**, 188) stitches (sts). Work in pattern until piece measures approximately **4** (4, **4½**, 5)".

Shape waist [Work 15 (17, **18**, 20)**, Dec 1, place marker (pm), Dec 1]** 3 times; work **34** (36, **40**, 44), **[Dec 1, pm, Dec 1, work 15** (17, **18**, 20)**]** 3 times — 12 sts decreased, **136** (150, **160**, 176) sts: **33** (37, **39**, 43) for each front, **70** (76, **82**, 90) for back. **[Work 3 rows even; work Dec Row]** twice — **112** (126, **136**, 152) sts: **27** (31, **33**, 37) for each front, **58** (64, **70**, 78) for back. Work even until piece measures **9** (9, **9½**, 10)".
Next row [Work to 1 before marker, Inc 1, sm, Inc 1] 6 times, work to end — **124** (138, **148**, 164) sts: **30** (34, **36**, 40) for each front, **64** (70, **76**, 84) for back. Work 6 rows even, working new stitches into pattern.
Next row Work across, Inc 1 each side of first 2 and last 2 markers, removing 2 center markers — **132** (146, **156**, 172) sts: **33** (37, **39**, 43) for each front, **66** (72, **78**, 86) for back. Work even until piece measures **12** (12, **13**, 14)". *Next row* Work across, Inc 1 each side of first and last markers only, leaving remaining markers in place — **136** (150, **160**, 176) sts: **35** (39, **41**, 45) for each front, **66** (72, **78**, 86) for back. Work even until piece measures **14** (14, **15**, 16)".

Divide for Fronts and Back *Next row*

Mark as RS. Work to **2** (3, **3**, 4) before third (side) marker, turn (leaving remaining stitches unworked). *Next row* Work to **2** (3, **3**, 4) before next (side) marker, turn — **62** (66, **72**, 78) sts.

Back

Shape armholes Working across back stitches only, **[Dec 1 each side next row; work 1 row even]** 4 (5, **6**, 6) times, then **[Dec 1 each side next row; work 3 rows even]** 4 (4, **4**, 5) times — **46** (48, **52**, 56) sts. Work even until armhole measures **7½** (8, **8½**, 9)".
Shape shoulders [Work to last 4 (4, **4**, 5)**, turn]** 4 times. Work to last **4** (4, **5**, 5), turn. Work to last **4** (4, **5**, 5). Fasten off.

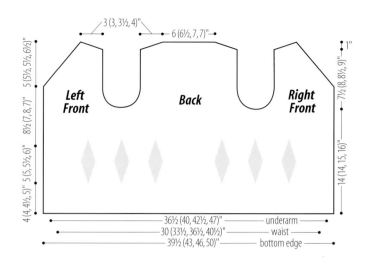

Schematic labels:

Left Front / Back / Right Front

- 3 (3, 3½, 4)"
- 6 (6½, 7, 7)"
- 5 (5½, 5½, 6½)"
- 8½ (7, 8, 7)"
- 5 (5, 5½, 6)"
- 4 (4, 4½, 5)"
- 1"
- 7½ (8, 8½, 9)"
- 14 (14, 15, 16)"
- 36½ (40, 42½, 47)" — underarm
- 30 (33½, 36½, 40½)" — waist
- 39½ (43, 46, 50)" — bottom edge

Skirt

- 30 (33, 36, 40)"
- 21 (21, 22, 23)"
- 9 (9, 9, 10)"
- 6½ (6½, 7½, 7½)"
- 5½"
- 17½ (19, 21, 23)"

Sleeve

- 13 (14, 15, 16)"
- 4½ (5, 5½, 5½)"
- 12 (13, 14, 15)"
- 10 (10½, 11½, 13)"

Left Front

With RS facing and larger hook, join yarn at left front armhole edge, **2** (3, **3**, 4) sts to left of side marker. Ch 1, work across in pattern. Shape armhole as for Back at beginning of RS rows only and AT SAME TIME, when armhole measures **3½** (3½, **4**, 3)", Dec 1 at neck edge every row **4** (4, **4**, 0) times, then every RS row **9** (11, **11**, 15) times — **12** (12, **13**, 15) sts. Work even until piece measures same length as Back to shoulder. Shape shoulder as for Back on WS rows only. Fasten off.

Right Front

With WS facing and larger hook, join yarn at right front armhole edge, **2** (3, **3**, 4) sts before side marker. Ch 1, work across in pattern. Continue as for Left Front EXCEPT reverse shaping. Shape armhole at end of RS rows. Shape shoulder as for Back on RS rows only.

Sleeve

With smaller hook, ch **39** (41, **45**, 49). Change to larger hook and work Alternating Spike Stitch Set-up Row — **38** (40, **44**, 48) sts. Work in pattern and AT SAME TIME, **[work 11 rows even; Inc 1 each side on next row] 5** (6, **6**, 6) times, working new stitches into pattern — **48** (52, **56**, 60) sts. Work even until piece measures **12** (13, **14**, 15)", or desired length to underarm.
Shape cap [Work to last 2 (3, **3**, 4) **stitches, turn]** twice — **44** (46, **50**, 52) sts. Dec 1 each side every other row **12** (12, **14**, 14) times. **[Work to last 2, turn] 4** (6, **6**, 6) times — **12** (10, **10**, 12) sts. Fasten off.

Finishing

Sew shoulder and sleeve seams. Set in sleeves. Place markers for 5 button loops on Right Front, with top marker 6" below beginning of neck shaping, bottom marker 5" from bottom edge, and the other 3 spaced evenly between. Try jacket on to confirm that button placement is hitting correctly at bust and waist.
Front and Neck Band With smaller hook, join yarn in lower right front edge, ch 1, **[sc in each of next 2 rows, skip 1 row]** along right front edge, working 2 sc at beginning of neck shaping, sc in each sc across back neck, **[sc in each of next 2 rows, skip 1 row]** along left front edge, working 2 sc at beginning of neck shaping; turn. Work 4 more rows sc, working 2 sc at beginning of neck shaping on each front. *Button loop row* Work 1 row sc, working button loops at markers as follows: ch 2, skip 2 sc. Work 1 round rev sc around entire bottom, front, and neck edge, working 1 rev sc in every sc and 2 rev sc over each ch-2 loop. Work 1 round rev sc around bottom of sleeves. Sew on button

SKIRT

With larger hook, ch **195** (211, **231**, 253). Work Alternating Spike Stitch Set-up Row — **194** (210, **230**, 252) sts. Work in pattern until piece measures approximately 5½". *Joining round* Work to last 10 stitches. Hold first 10 stitches behind last 10 stitches. Sc in each of next 10 sc, working through both layers to join at center back — **184** (200, **220**, 242) sts. Mark end of round. Continue working in rounds, joining

every round with a sl st to beginning ch-1; then turn, moving marker up. Work even until piece measures **12** (12, **13**, 13)".
Shape hips [Dec 1 at beginning and end of round; work 13 rounds even] 2 (1, **2**, 1) times. Work even until piece measures **15** (15, **16**, 17)" — **180** (198, **216**, 240) sts. Change to smaller hook and work even until piece measures **21** (21, **22**, 23)". Fasten off.

Finishing

Cut elastic to waist measurement with a ½" overlap. Use needle and thread to sew ends together. Pin elastic inside top edge. With a long length of yarn and darning needle, lace over elastic as shown. Or, work a crochet chain following a similar pathway and joining with slip stitch on either side of elastic. With larger hook, chain to bottom edge of elastic, then slip stitch into skirt. Work another chain and slip stitch into top edge, moving over 4 stitches. Continue around, creating a casing with zig-zag chains. Join at center back. Work 1 round rev sc around top edge. Work 1 round rev sc around hem and slit. Fasten off.

Carnivale

ATTENTIVE COLOR

INTERMEDIATE KNITTING

WHAT'S THE MAGIC?

Argyle repeat of 51" on half Magic Number; add shape with solids and short rows.

Color notes 1 *Argyle panels will pattern on about 40 stitches with Essential's 51" repeat. It is a firm yarn with no elasticity, so adjusting for tension variation is more difficult. These argyles may therefore be less precise, with more movement of the colors. This should not be considered a flaw. Careful attention and adjustment on every row will help maintain a precise pattern.* **2** *One skein of Essential will make one patterned panel, so skirt or top can be shorter, but not longer, without joining new yarn.* **3** *For either piece, determine needle size that gets both stitch and row gauge as close as possible to specified gauge. Use this needle size to determine your Magic Number, then use Half Magic Number for argyle panels.* **4** *Patterned panels are the same for all sizes. Adjustments in size are made through short-row sections that are worked between patterned panels.*

Knitting notes *See page 164 for abbreviations and techniques AND page 26 for Magic Number*

INC 1
At beginning of RS rows K1, M1.
At end of RS rows M1, k1.

DEC 1
At beginning of RS rows K1, k2tog.
At end of RS rows SSK, k1

STANDARD FIT

Top, S (M, L, 1X)	
A **34** (40, **46**, 52)"	
B **24**"	

Skirt, S (M, L, 1X)	
D **36** (40, **44**, 48)"	
E **24**"	
F **33** (35, **37**, 39)"	

Intentional patterning of a boldly colored hand-dye creates argyles—perfect with coordinating semi-solid stripes. Sizing is a snap—simply work more or fewer of the solid-colored rows, as needed. Add a garter section to draw the waist in slightly and short rows for a flounced hem, and this tank and skirt are ready for summer fun.

TOP
Back
Argyle panel
Determine your Magic Number (see color note 3).

With C, cast on 36 (or half your Magic Number). Knit 4 rows, increasing 4 evenly spaced across last row—40 stitches. Change to A and work in stockinette stitch until piece measures 24" from beginning when held upright to allow for downward stretch. Bind off.

On Left and Right Panels, all stitches above waistband are stockinette; all waistband and peplum stitches are garter EXCEPT on rows worked with E, when all stitches are garter.

Left panel
With RS facing, E, and beginning at bind-off pick up and knit (PUK) along side of Argyle panel at a rate of 2 stitches for every 3 rows, placing marker (pm) after 15" and 17" for waistband. Make note of number of stitches picked-up. Knit 1 row. Work **Wedge 1** for **58** (74, **88**, 98, **106**) rows, end with Row **58** (16, **30**, 40, **58**) of Wedge 1. **Shape armhole** Continuing in pattern, at beginning of RS rows, bind off 26 once, then 2 once. Dec 1 at beginning of RS rows **8** (10, **12**, 14, **16**) times. Work even until piece measures approximately **4** (5, **6**, 7, **8**)" from pick-up row, end with Row **58** (27, **58**, 27, **58**). Place on hold.

Right panel
Pick up same number of stitches as for Left panel along opposite side of Argyle panel EXCEPT pick up and purl (PUP) with WS facing. Purl 1 row. Work **Wedge 2** for **58** (74, **88**, 98, **106**) rows, end with Row **58** (16, **30**, 40, **58**) of Wedge 2. Shape armhole as for Left panel EXCEPT bind off and decrease 1 at beginning of WS rows.

Front
Work Argyle Panel as for Back until piece measures 20" when held upright to allow for downward stretch. Place on hold for neck.
Right panel
Beginning at top edge, PUK as for Back Left Panel, pm after 11" and 13" for waistband. Count stitches and adjust to 20 fewer stitches than picked up for Back Left Panel on next row if necessary. Work as for Back Left Panel and AT SAME TIME, Inc 1 at neck edge at beginning of RS rows 6 times. At beginning of RS rows, cable cast on 2 twice, then 10 once, marking first cast-on stitch for neckband shaping—20 stitches total increased.

10cm/4"

20 stitches and 32 rows to 10cm/4" over stockinette stitch

3

Light weight
Top
A **250** (275, **300**, 350) yds
B **75** (85, **100**, 110) yds
C, E **200** (225, **250**, 300) yds
D **150** (170, **190**, 210) yds

Skirt
A **375** (400, **425**, 450) yds
B **125** (135, **150**, 160) yds
C, D **250** (275, **300**, 325) yds
D **175** (190, **205**, 220) yds

3.25mm/US3

2.75mm/C-2

stitch markers

WEDGE 1 (WEDGE 2)

Row 1 (RS) (WS) With C, knit (purl).

Rows 2, 3 Knit (purl) to 1 stitch before first marker, wrap next stitch and turn (W&T); knit (purl) to end.

Rows 4, 5 K16 (P16), W&T; knit (purl) to end.

Rows 6, 7 K8 (P8), W&T; knit (purl) to end.

Row 8 Knit (Purl) to second marker, purl (knit) to end.

Row 9–16 Repeat Rows 1–8.

Rows 17–24 With D, repeat Rows 1–8.

Rows 25 With B, knit (purl).

Rows 26 Repeat Row 8.

Rows 27–28 Repeat Row 3.

Rows 29–32 Repeat Rows 25–26 twice.

Rows 33–40 With D, repeat Rows 1–8.

Rows 41–56 With C, repeat Rows 1–16.

Rows 57–60 With E, knit (purl).

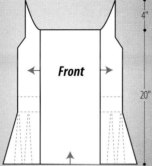

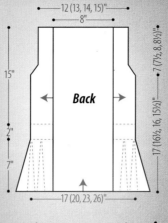

Approximate measurements when piece is held up in direction of knitting.

Left panel

Beginning at bind-off, pick up along opposite side as for Front Right panel EXCEPT PUP with WS facing. Purl 1 row. Work *Wedge 2* and AT SAME TIME, shape as for Right Front panel EXCEPT increase neck at end of RS rows and cast on at beginning of WS rows AND bind off and Dec 1 for armhole at beginning of WS rows.

Finishing

With RS together, join sides using 3-needle bind-off with same color as last row worked. Align shoulders at armhole edge, and sew shoulder seams.

Neckband *Note 1* *Band is worked in garter stitch back and forth. W&T at end of each row allows you to work garter stitch with no jog and no seam, as you are working back and forth and locking the seam at the same time. 2 Pick up stitches at the following rates: 1 stitch for each bound-off and cast-on stitch and 2 stitches for every 3 rows along vertical edges.* With RS facing and C, PUK along back neck, pm, PUK

along front cast-on stitches to marked stitch, pm, PUK along side panel to argyle panel, pm, knit front panel stitches from hold, pm, PUK along side panel to marked stitch, pm, PUK along cast-on stitches to Back neck, pm for beginning of round, W&T. *Next row* (WS) Knit, decreasing 4 evenly spaced across both center front and back panels, W&T—8 stitches decreased. *Dec row* (RS) SSK, knit to 2 stitches before marker, k2tog, slip marker (sm), SSK, **[knit to next marker, sm, k2tog]** twice, **[knit to 2 stitches before marker, SSK, sm]** twice, knit to last 2 stitches, SSK, W&T—8 stitches decreased. *Next row* Knit, W&T. Repeat last 2 rows 5 more times. Change to E and repeat these 2 rows once. *Next row* Knit, W&T. Bind off.

Edging With E and crochet hook, work 1 round sc and 1 round rev sc around bottom edge. Repeat for each armhole.

*Small: TWISTED SISTERS Essential in HandPaint 86 (A),
Calendula (B), Black Gold (C), Topaz (D), and Plum (E)*

Carnivale

SKIRT

Notes *Skirt has 3 Argyle panels identical to those in top and 3 short-row shaped sections. Additional short-row shaping is worked into Sections 2 and 3 to define hips and waist.*

Argyle Panels *MAKE 3*
Work as for Argyle Panel of Top.

Short-row section 1
Beginning at top edge of an Argyle panel, PUK as for back Left panel of Top. Make note of number of stitches picked-up. Knit 1 row. Work **Wedge 1** twice, ending with Row 58. Place on hold.

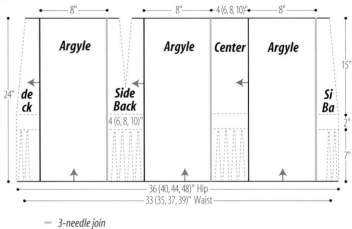

— 3-needle join
⟶ Direction of knitting

Approximate measurements with piece held upright.

WEDGE 3

Row 1 (RS) With C, knit.

Rows 2, 3 Knit to 1 stitch before first marker, wrap next stitch and turn (W&T); knit to end.

Rows 4, 5 K16, W&T; knit to end.

Rows 6, 7 K8, W&T; knit to end.

Rows 8, 9 Knit to second marker, purl to last 12, W&T; knit to end.

Ro;s 10, 11 K8, W&T; knit to end.

Rows 12, 13 K16, W&T; knit to end.

Rows 14, 15 Knit to last stitch before first marker, W&T; knit to end.

Row 16 Knit to second marker, purl to end.

Rows 17–23 With D, repeat Rows 1–7.

Row 24 Knit to second marker, purl to end.

Row 25 With B, knit.

Rows 26, 27 Knit to second marker, purl to last 20, W&T; knit to end.

Rows 28, 29 Knit to 1 stitch before first marker, W&T; knit to end.

Rows 30, 31 Knit to second marker, purl to last 24; W&T; knit to end.

Row 32 Knit to second marker, purl to end.

Rows 33–39 With D, repeat Rows 1–7.

Row 40 Knit to second marker, purl to end.

Rows 41–56 With C, repeat Rows 1–16.

Row 57 With E, knit.

Rows 58, 59 Knit to last 30 stitches, W&T; knit to end.

Row 60 Knit.

Short-row sections 2 and 3

Beginning at top edge of second Argyle panel, PUK same number of stitches as for Center panel. Knit 1 row. Work **Wedge 3** 2 (**3**, 4, **5**) times, end with Row 57. With E, knit 2 rows. Place on hold. Repeat for third Argyle panel. Join sections following diagrams 1–5b.

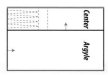

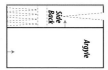

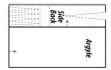

Finishing

With crochet hook and E, work 1 round sc around top edge of skirt. Do not fasten off. Cut elastic to fit around waist with a ½" overlap. Sew ends together. Pin elastic inside top edge. With crochet hook, chain to bottom edge of elastic, then slip stitch into skirt. Work another chain and slip stitch into top edge, moving over 4 stitches. Continue around, creating a casing with zig-zag chains. Join at center back. Work a second round, offset. Fasten off. With crochet hook and E, work 1 round sc and 1 round rev sc around bottom edge. Fasten off.

JOIN SECTIONS

With WS facing, PUP same number of stitches as are on hold. Work from bind-off to cast-on along argyle edge.

1 PUP along Section 1.

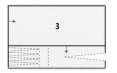

2 Flip Section 1 to RS. Place Section 2 on top of Section 1, with RS together, and align held stitches with PUP stitches. Work 3-needle bind-off to join sections.

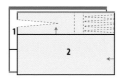

3 PUP along Section 3.

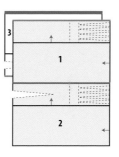

4 Flip Section 3 to RS. Place joined sections on top of Section 3, with RS together, and align held stitches with PUP stitches. Work 3-needle bind-off to join.

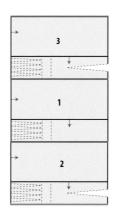

5a PUP along Section 3.

5b Fold with RS together so held stitches align with PUP stitches. Work 3-needle bind-off to join.

— held sts
— PUP on WS
— 3-needle bind-off with RS tog

Playful color

Nautilus

Our Nautilus wrap uses short rows paired with increases and a softly rounded end to wind round and round your shoulders. The narrow end can be pinned and allowed to hang free for a ruffled effect like Color Waves. Worked in subtle related colors of similar weight, the wrap is a quiet statement of elegance. Select a more highly variegated color combination, and the short-row wedges serve to define ever-changing lines of color.

EASY + KNITTING

OTTO COLOR

WHAT'S THE MAGIC?

Randomize dyed-around 66" repeat with short-row wedges.

Notes 1 *See page 164 for abbreviations and techniques.* **2** *Wrap is worked in one piece from side to side, beginning at small end of front. Shaping is achieved both through short rows and increases.* **3** *You may find it helpful to place markers at each W&T. No need to hide wraps.*

Scarf
Cast on 4.
Row 1 (RS) Knit, knitting in front and back (kf&b) of first and last stitch — 2 stitches increased.
Row 2 Knit. Repeat last 2 rows 3 more times — 12 stitches.

Wedges
Note *Short-row wedges will add extra length at the beginning of RS rows (the bottom edge of scarf). Mark the RS to help maintain your place.*

4-row Wedge [**Work Rows 1–4; work Increase Band**] twice — 16 stitches.
6-row Wedge [**Work Rows 1–6; work Increase Band**] twice — 20 stitches.
8-row Wedge [**Rows 1–8; work Increase Band**] twice — 24 stitches.
10-row Wedge [**Rows 1–10; work Increase Band**] twice — 28 stitches.
12-row Wedge [**Rows 1–12; work Increase Band**] twice — 32 stitches.
14-row Wedge [**Rows 1–14; work Increase Band**] twice — 36 stitches.
16-row Wedge [**Rows 1–16; work Increase Band**] twice — 40 stitches.
Mark edge for reference.
18-row Wedge [**Work Rows 1–18, knit 2 rows even**] 18 (24) times — 40 stitches.
Bind off.

SHORT ROWS
Rows 1, 2 Knit to last 4, wrap next stitch and turn (W&T); knit to end.
Rows 3, 4 Knit to last 8, W&T; knit to end.
Rows 5, 6 Knit to last 12, W&T; knit to end.
Rows 7, 8 Knit to last 16, W&T; knit to end.
Rows 9, 10 Knit to last 20, W&T; knit to end.
Rows 11, 12 Knit to last 24, W&T; knit to end.
Rows 13, 14 Knit to last 28, W&T; knit to end.
Rows 15, 16 Knit to last 32, W&T; knit to end.
Rows 17, 18 Knit to last 36, W&T; knit to end.

INCREASE BAND
Knit 4 rows, knitting in front and back (kf&b) of first stitch of RS rows.

PRISM YARNS Indulgence in color Smoke or Orchard

10cm/4"

TWO SIZES
Approximately **100** (114)" long at outside edge × 12" deep

14 stitches and 28 rows over garter stitch

Medium weight
325 (350) yds

6mm/US10

locking stitch markers

Color waves

Short rows worked in repeated wedges create a softly ruffled scarf whose arc sits cleanly on your shoulders. Add a semisolid contrasting stripe between each wedge, and show off the structure even more!

EASY + KNITTING

OTTO COLOR

WHAT'S THE MAGIC?

Randomize dyed-around 64" repeat with short-row wedges and contrasting color.

Notes 1 *See page 164 for abbreviations and techniques.*
2 *Carry colors not in use loosely along side edge.* **3** *Short-row wedges add extra length at the beginning of RS rows. Mark RS to help maintain your place.* **4** *Since scarf is worked in garter stitch, there is no need to hide short-row wraps.*

With A, cast on 24.
Rows 1–4 WIth A, knit 4 rows. *Row 5* (RS) With B, knit. **Work short-row-wedge**: *Rows 6–7* K**22**, wrap next stitch and turn (W&T); knit to end.
Rows 8–9 K**20**, W&T; knit to end. *Rows 10–27* Continue as established, knitting 2 fewer stitches before W&T every WS row, end last RS row with k2 — half of wedge complete. *Rows 28–29* **K4**, W&T; knit to end.
Rows 30–31 **K6**, W&T; knit to end. *Rows 32–48* Continue as established, knitting 2 more stitches after W&T every WS row until all stitches have been worked, end with WS row — wedge complete. Repeat Rows 1–48 to desired length, end with Row 28. Cut B. With A, knit 3 rows. Bind off, but do not fasten off.

Finishing

Insert crochet hook in last loop and work 1 row reverse single crochet along short side, from bound-off edge to cast-on edge. Fasten off.

PRISM YARNS Angora in color Blue (A); Symphony in color Garden (B)

10cm/4"

&

Approximately
5" x 54"

19 stitches and **38 rows** over garter stitch

Medium weight
A 90 yds
B 350 yds

5.5mm/US9

4mm/G-6

stitch markers

Windowpanes

ATTENTIVE COLOR

INTERMEDIATE KNITTING

WHAT'S THE MAGIC?

Stack 54" repeat on
Magic Number in Boxes
Pattern. Slip stitch pattern
allows larger width.

OTTO COLOR

Structure layered
colors with strong
geometric pattern.

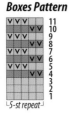

Notes 1 See page 164 for abbreviations and
techniques. **2** Instructions are the same for
both hats, the only differences are the yarn
used and whether you pattern or not.

K1, P1 RIB
All rows or rounds [K1, p1].

BOXES PATTERN
MULTIPLE OF 5
Slip stitches purlwise with yarn at
WS of work.
Rounds 1–3 With B, knit.
Round 4 With A, [sl 2 , k3] around.
Round 5 With B, [k2, sl 3] around.
Rounds 6–11 Repeat Rounds 4 and
5, three more times.

Boxes Pattern

⌐5-st repeat⌐

Color key
- ■ A
- ▨ B

Stitch key
- ☐ Knit
- ☑ Slip stitch with yarn at WS

Slip-stitch boxes are worked circularly with a semisolid outline and a highly
colored dyed-around skein that has been designed to pattern. The colors
shifting behind the window frames have a magical look, and the pattern
continuity is maintained by working a specially designed 3-needle bind-
off shaped crown. I-cord is looped together for a playful top-knot. Without
the added solid stitches, the hand-dyed yarn would have produced a
circumference too small for a hat.

With B and larger circular needle, cast on 110.
Hem
Change to smaller circular needle, place marker (pm), and join to work in the round, being careful not
to twist the stitches. Work K1, P1 Rib for 3". ***Turning round*** [**Yo, k2tog**] around. With larger needle
and B, begin Boxes Pattern on Round 2. Repeat Boxes Pattern 8 times, decreasing 6 stitches on last
round as follows: k2tog at beginning of first repeat, then every fourth repeat 5 times—104 stitches.
Next round [**K13, pm**] 7 times, k13.

Finishing
Finish with Crown Bind-off and I-cord
Tassle. Turn band to inside and tack
invisibly to hat body.

SIZING OPTIONS
If your Magic Number is different,
you may be able to add or
subtract a repeat and still have a
proper-sized hat. Or, instead of 2
stitches between boxes, you may
reduce it to 1 stitch or increase
it to 3 stitches. Remember: if the
repeat is larger, you will need
more A stitches; if it is smaller,
you will need fewer A stitches.

10cm/4"

&

ONE SIZE
22" circumference,
unstretched

20 stitches and **26 rows**
Needle size may have to be
adjusted to make colors flash

Medium weight
A 115 yds
B 225 yds

5mm/US8
AND
1 size smaller,
50cm (20") or shorter

Two 4mm/US6

stitch markers

The same Windowpane hat gets a more tailored, classic treatment with the selection of 2 layered colors. The lighter color shows hints of gray and beige with an overall reading of taupe, while the deeper color is blue tinged with undertones of warm khaki.

PRISM YARNS Symphony in colors Freesia (A) and 704 (B), at left; Layers version in colors Mushroom (A) and Lapis (B), above

I-cord tassel With double-pointed needles and A, cast on 5. Work I-cord as follows: k5, slide stitches to other end of needle, pull yarn tightly along back and k5 again. Repeat to 32". Graft live stitches to beginning of I-cord, leaving tail. Wrap cord 7 times around 3 fingers, distributing loops evenly. Wrap remaining tail tightly through bottom of loops several times, capturing all loops. Stitch cluster to top of hat.

Crown bind-off Turn work inside out and work 4 sections of 3-needle bind-off: **[Align the needle tips, and join stitches with 3-needle bind-off to first markers on each needle (if necessary, pull needle cable out at one of the markers — or over bind-off area in subsequent repeats — to separate stitches so they effortlessly slide to needle tips). Remove marker(s) (rm). Fasten off by pulling ball through last bind-off loop and, with back needle tip, purl to next marker, rm]**; repeat, knowing next 2 repeats are worked to a single marker, and no markers will exist when completing fourth repeat. Break yarn, leaving a 12" tail. Sew on I-cord tassel or just neaten center of 4 bind-off sections.

A dyed-across yarn in an openwork stitch with a picot edge is worked circularly at twice the Magic Number. This simple lace stitch can be worked as either yo, k2tog or yo, SSK, whichever the knitter prefers. The stitch's diagonal is in opposition to the colors' spiral for a nice push-pull contrast. Begin with a temporary cast-on, leaving a very long tail to bind off with later in a picot edge. On this number of stitches, the colors will naturally pull out of order on either the cast-on or the bind-off, so opt for a decorative edge that takes advantage of this natural phenomenon.

Worked with less even tension, this cowl could easily flash. The pattern stitch won't allow increasing or decreasing, so tension adjustments would be needed to move the color.

EASY + KNITTING

MINDFUL COLOR

WHAT'S THE MAGIC?

Spiral dyed-across 56" repeat on twice the Magic Number minus 2.

Note *See page 164 for abbreviations and techniques AND page 26 for Magic Number.*

Determine your Magic Number in Lacy Stitch (ours was 66).
With a temporary cast-on, cast on twice your Magic Number minus 2 (if necessary, adjust to an even number; we cast on 130). Place marker and join to work in the round, being careful not to twist stitches. Work Lacy Stitch until piece measures 9". Remove temporary cast-on and work Faux-picot Edge.

MALABRIGO Silky Merino in color 478 Viena.

LACY STITCH
OVER AN EVEN NUMBER OF STITCHES
All rounds [Yo, k2tog] around.

FAUX-PICOT EDGE
Yo, k1, pass yo over k1, **[(yo, pass stitch over yo) twice, k1, bind off stitch]**, around.
In essence, you are making 2 chains between each worked stitch. Another way to do this is with a crochet hook: Ch 1, **[sl st into next stitch, ch 2]** to end, fasten off.

10cm/4"

One size

 18 stitches and **32 rows** over Lacy Stitch

 Medium weight 225 yds

 5.5mm/US9 or size to make color repeat work, 60cm (24") long

 waste yarn for temporary cast-on stitch marker optional crochet hook

Trader's bag

OTTO COLOR

INTERMEDIATE KNITTING

WHAT'S THE MAGIC?

Randomize 52" repeat with Linen Stitch and a solid color.

Note 1 *See page 164 for abbreviations and techniques.* **2** *Bag begins with a flat rectangular bottom. Stitches are then picked up around the rectangle and worked circularly to the top.*

Full Linen Stitch, which forms an extremely dense fabric, is perfect for a carry-all market bag. A highly colored multicolor is randomized by alternating 2 rows with a tonal, layered semisolid that imparts an overall blended tone. A leather strap polishes the look.

Bag

With A, cast on 52. Work Linen Stitch flat for 4", alternating 2 rows A with 2 rows B. On next RS row, work across 52 stitches, pull cable out to facilitate turning corner, pick up and knit (PUK)18 stitches along short edge of rectangle; pull cable out and PUK52 along cast-on edge (picking up into first row of B to ensure edge is firm); pull cable out and PUK17 along next short edge—139 stitches. Place marker and join to work in the round.

Work Linen Stitch in the round, alternating 2 rounds A with 2 rounds B, to 12" from bottom rectangle. Bind off.

Edging

With larger crochet hook and B, work 1 round sc around top edge, working 1 stitch in every other bound-off stitch. With smaller crochet hook, work 1 round reverse sc around top edge. Sew strap to sides.

LINEN STITCH

This bag takes advantage of Linen Stitch's ability to compress very tightly; hence a large needle will produce a tight fabric. To improve the appearance of Linen Stitch: every few inches of progress, grasp the fabric at the bottom and at the needles and pull apart very hard, then tug horizontally. You will see the stitches drop under the floats, producing a flatter, more refined fabric. Working Linen Stitch in the round produces a tiny vertical line between rounds — this is not considered a flaw.

Note: *Slip stitches purlwise with yarn at RS of work.*

LINEN STITCH
WORKED IN THE ROUND
Round 1 (RS) **[K1, sl 1]** to last stitch, k1.
Round 2 (WS) **[Sl 1, k1]** to last stitch, sl 1.

LINEN STITCH
WORKED FLAT
Row 1 **[K1, sl 1]** to end.
Row 2 **[P1, sl 1]** to end.

Stitch key
☐ Knit on RS, purl on WS
☑ Slip 1 with yarn at RS

ONE SIZE	**17 stitches** and **30 rows** over Linen Stitch, alternating 2 rows A and 2 rows B	**Bulky weight** A and **B** 225 yds each	**8mm/US11**, 60cm (24") or longer	**5.5mm/I-9** AND 2 sizes smaller	48" leather strap
12" wide × 4" deep × 12" high					

10cm/4"

PRISM YARNS Merino 12 in color Prairie (A); Athena in color Highlands (B)

157

Aegean dream

EASY + KNITTING

OTTO COLOR

WHAT'S THE MAGIC?

Two contrasting textures dyed in the same Layers colorways.

Note *See page 164 for abbreviations and techniques.*

BODY PATTERN

Row 1 (RS) Knit.
Row 2 K3, p54, k3.

INSERTING B STRANDS

At random, cut A and tie to a strand of B, leaving approximately ½" tails; tie other end of B to A.

PRISM YARNS Gossamer in color Aegean; Constellation in color Aegean

The contrast here is simply one of scale: classic lace-weight kid mohair and wide ribbon flashed through with metallic are both dyed in a layered color of sea-green and blue. The technique is simple: very fine-weight yarn has random sections of large scale ribbon knitted in. The effect is of waves of color on a gauze background. Need we say more?

Preparation

Open skein of B and carefully cut through all strands at one end. Remove 3 strands. Fold remaining strands in half and carefully cut again. Reserve 30 strands for fringe.

With A, cast on 60. Knit 6 rows. Work Body Pattern for approximately 79", inserting B strands as desired and spacing 3 longer B strands throughout. Knit 6 rows. Bind off. Block with steam.

Fringe

With WS facing, insert crochet hook through first cast-on stitch from WS to RS and pull loop of fringe through, then pull tails of fringe through loop, remove hook, and tighten loop. Repeat in every fourth stitch across. Repeat across bound-off stitches. Lightly steam fringe to release wrinkles: don't put any weight on fringe, simply wave steam at it. Take one tail from each of first two fringes and tie together: to maintain spacing, insert thumb into space between fringes and snug knot lightly to thumb, making sure each side is equal. Take remaining tail from second fringe and tie to one tail of next fringe. Repeat across, taking care that knots are spaced equally. Hang fringe over table or ironing board. Align edge and place several heavy books on top of wrap to keep it from shifting. With sharp shears, trim fringe to approximately 8".

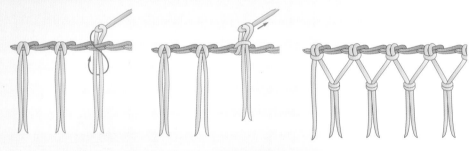

ONE SIZE approximately 20" x 80"	**12 stitches and 20 rows** over stockinette stitch with A	**Fine weight** A 550 yds	**Bulky weight** B 50 yds	6.5mm/US10½ 5.5mm/J-9

10cm/4"

159

Stitches in color

In the same way an artist will sketch, a knitter can swatch, and I find making swatches half the fun of any project. Swatches provide endless information, not only about how colors look, but also about hand, drape, and suitability for a particular project. Make a good-sized swatch — at least 6" square — and then don't be surprised if it looks different in a garment width. Larger swatches are more accurate, and knowing the Magic Number also helps, as it can steer you toward or away from patterning.

The following stitch patterns have been used in swatches and projects throughout this book — be sure to look through the projects for more choices. I know them to be very useful for randomizing colors, so use them as a resource of first resort when faced with a difficult hand-dye. A good stitch dictionary will include many similar stitches, so you can do your own investigation.

Applying a stitch pattern is easy: once you have a pattern stitch whose effects you like, simply find a basic garment pattern whose gauge is the same. You can now adapt that pattern to the pattern stitch's repeat, and use the stitch to create your own successful project. Learn to love your swatch, and happy knitting!

Stripe with twisted bars

STRIPE WITH TWISTED BARS
MULTIPLE OF 6 + 1
Row 1 (RS) K1, **[yo, k1, k3tog, k1, yo, k1]** to end.
Row 2 P1, **[k5, p1]** to end.

Rambler

RAMBLER PATTERN
OVER AN ODD NUMBER OF STITCHES
Rows 1, 3, 5, 7 (WS) K2, **[p1, k1]** to last stitch, k1. *Rows 2, 4, 6, 8* K1, **[knit next stitch in row below (k1b), p1]** to last 2, k1b, k1. *Rows 9, 11, 13, 15* K1, **[p1, k1]** to end. *Rows 10, 12, 14, 16* K1, p1, **[k1b, p1]** to last stitch, k1.

Jaquard stitch

JACQUARD STITCH *MULTIPLE OF 6 + 4*
Slip stitches with yarn at RS of work. *Row 1* (RS) K1, **[sl 2, k4]** to last 3, sl 2, k1. *Row 2* P1, sl 1, **[p4, sl 2]** to last 2, p2. *Row 3* K3, **[sl 2, k4]** to last stitch, k1. *Row 4* P4, **[sl 2, p4]**. *Row 5* K5, **[sl 2, k4]** to last 5, sl 2, k3. *Row 6* P2, **[sl 2, p4]** to last 2, sl 1, p1. *Row 7* Repeat Row 1. *Rows 8, 9, 10, 11, 12* Repeat Rows 6, 5, 4, 3, 2.

Cartridge-belt rib

CARTRIDGE-BELT RIB *MULTIPLE OF 4 + 3*
Slip stitches with yarn in front of work (wyif) at RS on RS rows and at WS on WS rows. *Row 1* (RS) K3, **[sl 1, k3]** to end. *Row 2* K1, **[sl 1, k3]** to last 2 stitches, sl 1, k1.

Swag stitch

SWAG STITCH, OR SCALLOP STITCH *MULTIPLE OF 5 + 2*
Slip stitches with yarn at RS of work. *Row 1 and all WS rows* Purl. *Row 2* Knit. *Rows 4, 6* P2, **[sl 3, p2]** to end.

Dice stitch

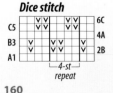

DICE CHECK *MULTIPLE OF 4 + 2*
Slip stitches with yarn at WS of work. *Row 1* (WS) With A, purl. *Row 2* With B, k1, sl 1, **[k2, sl 2]** to last 4, k2, sl 1, k1. *Row 3* With B, p1, sl 1, **[p2, sl 2]** to last 4, p2, sl 1, p1. *Row 4* With A, knit. *Row 5* With C, p2, **[sl 2, p2]** to end. *Row 6* With C, k2, **[sl 2, k2]** to end.

Two-tone lattice

TWO-TONE LATTICE *MULTIPLE OF 6 + 2*
Slip stitches with yarn at WS of work. Cast on with A and knit one row. *Row 1* (RS) With B, k1, sl 1, **[k4, sl 2]** to last 6, k4, sl 1, k1. *Row 2* With B, p1, sl 1, **[p4, sl 2]** to last 6, p4, sl 1, p1. *Row 3* With A, repeat Row 1. *Row 4* With A, k1, sl 1, **[k4, sl 2]** to last 6, k4, sl 1, k1. *Row 5* With B, k3, **[sl 2, k4]** to last 5, sl 2, k3. *Row 6* With B, p3, **[sl 2, p4]** to last 5, sl 2, p3. *Row 7* With A, repeat Row 5. *Row 8* With A, k3, **[sl 2, k4]** to last 5, sl 2, k3.

Woven diagonal herringbone

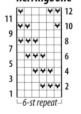

WOVEN DIAGONAL HERRINGBONE *MULTIPLE OF 6*
Slip stitches with yarn in front of work (wyif) at RS on RS rows and at WS on WS rows. *Row 1 and all WS rows* Purl. *Row 2* **[Sl 3, k3]** to end. *Row 4* K1, **[sl 3, k3]** to last 5, sl 3, k2. *Row 6* K2, **[sl 3, k3]** to last 4, sl 3, k1. *Row 8* **[K3, sl 3]** to end. *Row 10* Sl 1, **[k3, sl 3]**, end k3, sl 2. *Row 12* Sl 2, **[k3, sl 3]** to last 4, k3, sl 1.

French weave, fancy

FRENCH WEAVE, FANCY *MULTIPLE OF 5 + 4*
Rows 1, 5 (WS) With A, purl. *Row 2* With B, k1, sl 1 wyib, **[k1, sl 1 wyif, k1, sl 2 wyib]** to last 2, k2. *Row 3* With B, k1, p1, **[sl 1 wyif, sl 1 wyib, p3]** to last 2, sl 1 wyif, k1. *Row 4* With A, k3, **[sl 1 wyib, k4]** to last stitch, k1. *Row 6* With B, k2, **[sl 2 wyib, k1, sl 1 wyif, k1]** to last 2, sl 1 wyib, k1. *Row 7* With B, k1, sl 1 wyib, **[p3, sl 1 wyif, sl 1 wyib]** to last 2, p1, k1. *Row 8* With A, k5, **[sl 1 wyib, k4]** to last 4, sl 1 wyib, k3.

Stitch key
- ☐ Knit on RS, purl on WS
- ▨ Purl on RS, knit on WS
- Ⓞ Yarn over (yo)
- ◿ K3tog on RS, p3tog on WS
- ↓ Knit in row below
- ⩔ Slip 1 with yarn at RS
- ⩒ Slip 1 with yarn at WS

LINEN STITCH

Row 1 (RS) **[K1, sl 1]** to end.
Row 2 (WS) **[P1, sl 1]** to end.

Linen Stitch

2-st repeat

HALF LINEN STITCH

Row 1 (RS) **[K1, sl 1]** to end.
Rows 2 and 4 (WS) Purl.
Row 3 **[Sl 1, k1]** to end.

Half Linen Stitch

2-st repeat

STRING OF PURLS *MULTIPLE OF 12*

Slip stitches with yarn at WS of work.

Rows 1, 3 (WS) With A, purl. *Row 2* With A, knit. *Row 4* With B, k11, **[turn; sl 1, k3, turn; p4, k12]**, end last repeat k1. *Row 5* With B, k5, **[turn; p4, turn; k3, sl 1, k12]**, end last repeat k7. *Row 6* With A, k8, **[sl 2, k10]** end last repeat k2. *Rows 7, 8, 9* With A, repeat Rows 1, 2, 3. *Row 10* With B, k5, **[turn; sl 1, k3, turn; p4, k12]**, end last repeat k7. *Row 11* With B, k11, **[turn; p4, turn; k3, sl 1, k12]**, end last repeat k1. *Row 12* With A, k2, **[sl 2, k10]**, end last repeat k8.

String of purls

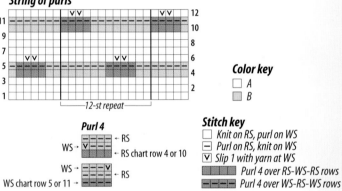

12-st repeat

Color key
- ☐ A
- ▨ B

Purl 4

WS → RS
← RS
← RS chart row 4 or 10

WS → RS
← RS
WS chart row 5 or 11 →

Stitch key
- ☐ Knit on RS, purl on WS
- — Purl on RS, knit on WS
- ☒ Slip 1 with yarn at WS
- ▨ Purl 4 over RS-WS-RS rows
- ═ Purl 4 over WS-RS-WS rows

LITTLE BUTTERFLY *MULTIPLE OF 10*

Slip stitches with yarn at RS of work.

Rows 1, 3, 5 (RS) K1, **[k5, sl 5]** to last 6, k6. *Rows 2, 4* Purl. *Row 6* P8, **[insert right needle under 3 strands on RS of work; yo needle and draw up a gathering loop; p1, pass gathering loop over p1, p9]** end last repeat p8. *Rows 7, 9, 11* K1, **[sl 5, k5]** to last 6, sl 5, k1. *Rows 8, 10* Purl. *Row 12* P3, **[lift 3 strands with gathering loop, p1, pass loop over p1, p9]**, end last repeat p3.

Little butterfly

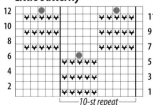

10-st repeat

Stitch key
- ● Lift 3 strands with gathering loop, purl next stitch, slip loop over purl stitch
- ☐ Knit on RS, purl on WS
- ☒ Slip 1 with yarn at RS

In other words for charts

SAMPLER JACKET, PAGE 89
PAT 1: QUILTED CHECK
MULTIPLE OF 6 + 2

Slip stitches purlwise with yarn at RS of work (wyif on RS rows and wyib on WS rows).
Use 5mm/US8 needles and B and G.
Row 1 (WS) With G, p1, **[sl 3, p3]** to last stitch, p1.
Row 2 With B, **[k5, sl 1]** to last 2, k2.
Row 3 With B, p2, **[sl 1, p5]** to end.
Row 4 With G, **[k5, insert left needle under G strand of Row 1; lift strand over point of left needle and k2tog-b (strand and first F stitch on needle]** to last 2, k2.
Row 5 With G, p4, **[sl 3, p3]** to last 4, sl 3, p1.
Row 6 With B, k2, **[sl 1, k5]** to end.
Row 7 With B, **[p5, sl 1]** to last 2, p2.
Row 8 With G, k2, **[insert left needle under G strand of Row 5, and k2tog-b as in Row 4, k5]** to end.

PATS 2–4, see page 160 for
RAMBLER, 2-TONE LATTICE, and WOVEN DIAGONAL HERRINGBONE

PAT 5: SLIP-STITCH SMOCKING
MULTIPLE OF 8 + 7

Slip stitches purlwise with yarn at WS of work (wyib).
Use 6mm/US10 needles and J.
Row 1 (RS) K1, **[sl 1, k4, pass slipped stitch over 4 knit stitches (psso), p3]** to last 6, sl 1, k4, psso, k1.
Row 2 K1, p1, **[k1, k1 under running thread between stitch just worked and next stitch, k1, p5]** to last 5, k1, k1 under running thread, k1, p1, k1.
Row 3 K2, **[p3, k5]** to last 5, p3, k2.
Row 4 K1, p1, **[k3, p5]** to last 5, k3, p1, k1.
Row 5 K2, **[p3, sl 1, k4, psso]** to last 5, p3, k2.
Row 6 K1, p1, **[p5, k1, k1 under running thread, k1]** to last 6, p5, k1.
Row 7 K1, **[k5, p3]** to last 6, k6.
Row 8 K1, **[p5, k3]** to last 6, p5, k1.

SUN SHADOWS, PAGE 82
PAT 1: BROKEN DIAGONAL RIB PATTERN *MULTIPLE OF 8*

Rows 1–4 **[P4, k4]** to end. *Rows 5, 7* K2, **[p4, k4]** to last 6, p4, k2. *Rows 6, 8* P2, **[k4, p4]** to last 6, k4, p2. *Rows 9–12* **[K4, p4]** to end. *Rows 13, 15* P2, **[k4, p4]** to last 6, k4, p2. *Rows 14, 16* K2, **[p4, k4]** to last 6, p4, k2.

PAT 2: CHECKERBOARD PATTERN
MULTIPLE OF 8

Rows 1–6 **[K4, p4]** to end. *Rows 7–12* **[P4, k4]** to end.

PAT 3: SEEDED RIB CHECK *MULTIPLE OF 4 + 3*

Row 1 K3, **[p1, k3]** to end. *Row 2* K1, **[p1, k3]** to last 2, p1, k1. *Rows 3, 5* Repeat Row 1. *Rows 4, 6* Repeat Row 2. *Rows 7, 9, 11* Repeat Row 2. *Rows 8, 10, 12* Repeat Row 1.

161

Project Yarns

 **Across**  **Around**  **Hand-painted**  **Double-dyed**  **Kettle-dyed, sandwashed** **Layered**

1
Super Fine

BLUE MOON FIBER ARTS *Marine Silk Lace* 51% silk, 29% merino, 20% Sea Cell® rayon; 100g (3.5oz); 793m (868yds)

PRISM YARNS *Delicato* 100% Tencel®; 112g (4oz); 576m (630yds)

PRISM YARNS *Lace Wool* 100% merino wool; 100g (3.5oz); 1335m (1460yds); 66" repeat

2
Fine

BLUE MOON FIBER ARTS *Socks that Rock® Lightweight* 100% superwash merino; 155g (5.5oz); 370m (405yds); 62" repeat

KOIGU YARNS *KPPPM* 100% merino wool; 50g (1.75oz); 155m (170yds)

LORNA'S LACES *Shepherd Sport* 100% superwash merino wool; 56g (2oz); 183m (200yds); 64" repeat

PRISM YARNS *Merino Mia* 100% merino superwash; 56g (2oz); 174m (190yds); 60" repeat

PRISM YARNS *Saki* 75% merino wool, 25% nylon; 100g (3.5oz); 402m (440yds); 48–50" repeat

PRISM YARNS *Elise* 85% rayon, 15% metallic polyester; 43g (1.5oz); 183m (200yds); 56" repeat

PRISM YARNS *Gossamer* 80% kid mohair, 20% nylon; 100g (3.5oz); 855m (935yds) 60" repeat

3
Light

BLUE MOON FIBER ARTS *Marine Silk Worsted* 51% silk, 29% merino, 20% Sea Cell® rayon; 100g (3.5oz); 222m (243yds)

BLUE MOON FIBER ARTS *Socks that Rock® Mediumweight* 100% superwash merino; 170g (6oz); 370m (405yds)

PRISM YARNS *Tencel® Tape* 100% Tencel®; 56g (2oz); 110m (120yds); 65" repeat

TWISTED SISTERS *Essential* 60% hemp, 40% silk; 50g (1.75oz); 123m (135yds); 51" repeat

4
Medium

BLUE MOON FIBER ARTS *Gaea* 100% organic wool; 226g (8oz); 278m (305yds)

LORNA'S LACES *Shepherd Worsted* 100% superwash merino wool; 112g (4oz); 206m (225yds); 64" repeat

MALABRIGO *Silky Merino* 50% silk, 50% baby merino wool; 50g (1.75oz); 137m (150yds); 56" repeat

MOUNTAIN COLORS, INC *River Twist* 100% merino wool; 100g (3.5oz); 219m (240yds)

MOUNTAIN COLORS, INC *4/8's Wool* 100% wool; 100g (3.5oz); 229m (250yds)

PRISM YARNS *Indulgence* 68% silk, 15% wool, 12% kid mohair, 5% nylon; 56g (2oz); 84m (92yds); 66" repeat

PRISM YARNS *Symphony* 80% merino, 10% cashmere, 10% nylon superwash; 56g (2oz); 108m (118yds); 64" repeat

SCHAEFER YARNS *Miss Priss* 100% merino wool; 113g (4oz); 256m (280yds); 45" repeat

Yarn weight categories

Yarn Weight

1	2	3	4	5	6
Super Fine	**Fine**	**Light**	**Medium**	**Bulky**	**Super Bulky**

Also called

Sock Fingering Baby	Sport Baby	DK Light-Worsted	Worsted Afghan Aran	Chunky Craft Rug	Bulky Roving

Locate the Yarn Weight and Stockinette Stitch Gauge Range over 10cm to 4" on the chart.
Compare that range with the information on the yarn label to find an appropriate yarn.
These are guidelines only for commonly used gauges and needle sizes in specific yarn categories.

Stockinette Stitch Gauge Range 10cm/4 inches

27 sts to 32 sts	23 sts to 26 sts	21 sts to 24 sts	16 sts to 20 sts	12 sts to 15 sts	6 sts to 11 sts

Recommended needle (metric)

2.25 mm to 3.25 mm	3.25 mm to 3.75 mm	3.75 mm to 4.5 mm	4.5 mm to 5.5 mm	5.5 mm to 8 mm	8 mm and larger

Recommended needle (US)

1 to 3	3 to 5	5 to 7	7 to 9	9 to 11	11 and larger

Bulky

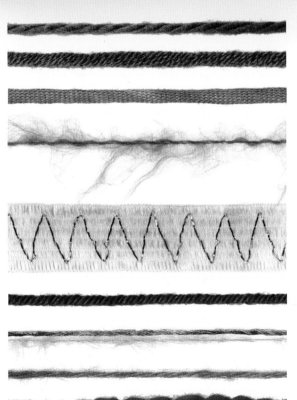

LORNA'S LACES *Shepherd Bulky* 100% superwash merino wool; 112g (4oz); 128m (140yds); 62" repeat

PRISM YARNS *Merino 12* 100% merino wool; 100g (3.5oz); 108m (118yds); 52" repeat

PRISM YARNS *Athena* 80% cotton, 20% nylon; 56g (2oz); 69m (76yds)

PRISM YARNS *Big Kid* 78% kid mohair, 13% wool, 9% nylon; 454g (16oz); 905m (990yds); 67" repeat

PRISM YARNS *Constellation* 95% nylon, 5% metallic polyester; 56g (2oz); 49m (54yds)

PRISM YARNS *Madison* 75% merino wool, 15% cashmere, 10% silk; 100g (3.5oz); 155m (170yds); 47–48" repeat

PRISM YARNS *Kid Slique* 66% rayon, 26% kid mohair, 8% nylon; 56g (2oz); 80m (88yds); 68" repeat

PRISM YARNS *Angora* 100% angora; 28g (1oz); 82m (90yds)

SCHAEFER YARNS *Elaine* 99% merino wool, 1% nylon; 227g (8oz); 274m (300yds); 45" repeat

Techniques

BASICS

YARN OVER (YO)

Bring yarn under the needle to the front, take it over the needle to the back and knit the next stitch.

KNIT THROUGH THE BACK LOOP (K1 TBL)

1 With right needle behind left needle and right leg of stitch, insert needle into stitch…

2 …and knit.

PICK UP & KNIT

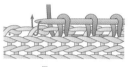

With right side facing and yarn in back, insert needle from front to back in center of edge stitch, catch yarn and knit a stitch. (See stockinette above, garter below.)

PICK UP & PURL

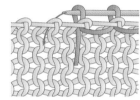

With wrong side facing and yarn in front, insert needle from back to front in center of edge stitch, catch yarn, and purl.

Specifications
at a glance

Use the charts and guides below to make educated decisions about yarn thickness, needle size, garment ease, and pattern options.

centimeters	0.394	inches
grams	0.035	ounces
inches	**2.54**	**centimeters**
ounces	28.6	grams
meters	**1.1**	**yards**
yards	.91	meters

centimeters × inches (conversion)

CONVERSION CHART

¾	oz		20 g
1	oz		28 g
1½	**oz**		**40 g**
1¾	oz		50 g
2	**oz**		**60 g**
3½	oz		100 g

EQUIVALENT WEIGHTS

NEEDLES/HOOKS

US	MM	HOOK
0	2	A
1	2.25	B
2	2.75	C
3	3.25	D
4	3.5	E
5	3.75	F
6	4	G
7	4.5	7
8	5	H
9	5.5	I
10	6	J
10½	6.5	K
11	8	L
13	9	M
15	10	N
17	12.75	

Measuring

A Bust/Chest
B Body length
C Center back to cuff
arm slightly bent

Measure around the fullest part of your bust/chest to find your size.

Children	2	4	6	8	10	12	14
Actual chest	21"	23"	25"	26½"	28"	30"	31½"

Women	XXS	XS	Small	Medium	Large	1X	2X	3X
Actual bust	28"	30"	32–34"	36–38"	40–42"	44–46"	48–50"	52–54"

Men	Small	Medium	Large	1X	2X
Actual chest	34–36"	38–40"	42–44"	46–48"	50–52"

STANDARD FIT
bust/chest
plus 2–4"

ONE SIZE FIT
actual bust/chest
size plus 1–2"

OVERSIZED FIT

CAST-ONS

LONG-TAIL LOOP CAST-ON

1 Hold needle in left hand and tail of yarn in right hand (allowing about 1" for each stitch to be cast on).
2 Bring right index finger under yarn, pointing toward you.

3 Turn index finger to point away from you.
4 Insert tip of needle under yarn on index finger (see above); remove finger and draw yarn snug, forming a stitch. Repeat Steps 2–4. After every few stitches, allow the yarn to hang freely to restore its original twist.

TUBULAR CAST-ON

  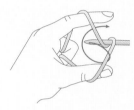

1 Leaving a tail approximately 4 times the width of the cast-on, fold the yarn over a needle 3–4 sizes smaller than main needle (1–2 sizes smaller than ribbing needle). Bring yarn between fingers of left hand and wrap around little finger as shown.

2 Bring left thumb and index finger between strands, arranging so tail is on thumb side. Open thumb and finger so strands form a diamond. Take needle **over index yarn, then under it.**

3 Bring needle **over thumb yarn** then **under it and under index yarn,** forming a purl stitch on needle.

4 Bring needle toward you, **over thumb yarn, under it**, and up between the two yarns.

5 Bring needle **over and under** the **index yarn**. Bring index yarn **under thumb yarn,** forming a knit stitch on the needle.

6 Take needle over index yarn, then under it. Repeat Steps 3–6.

7 End with Step 3. Note that knit stitches alternate with purl stitches.

8 Work 2 rows double knit as follows: *Row 1* * Knit 1 in back loop, slip 1 purlwise with yarn in front; repeat from *.
Row 2 * Knit 1, slip 1 purlwise with yarn in front; repeat from *.
9 Change to larger needles and work knit 1, purl 1 rib or repeat Row 2 for double-knit fabric.

CABLE CAST-ON

1 Start with a slipknot on left needle (first cast-on stitch). Insert right needle into slipknot from front. Wrap yarn over right needle as if to knit.

2 Bring yarn through slipknot, forming a loop on right needle.

3 Insert left needle in loop and slip loop off right needle. One additional stitch cast on.

4 Insert right needle **between** the last 2 stitches. From this position, knit a stitch and slip it to the left needle as in Step 3. Repeat Step 4 for each additional stitch.

BUTTERFLY

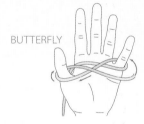

Wrap yarn in figure-8 fashion around fingers 6–8 times. To start knitting, pull butterfly, and yarn will feed from center of ball.

Make small butterflies when using short lengths (less than 5 yards) of yarn for colorwork.

CROCHET & CUT STEEK

 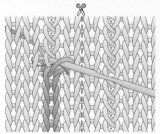

1 Prepare for the crochet steek by knitting through the back loop of the first and last steek stitch of every round.
2 Holding yarn on the WS and crochet hook on the RS, chain through each twisted stitch as shown.
3 Cut through the center of the steek to form an opening.

INCREASES

MAKE 1 (M1)

Knit

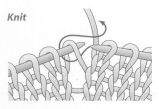

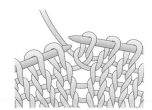

Insert left needle from front to back under strand between last stitch knitted and first stitch on left needle. Knit, twisting strand by working into loop at back of needle.

KNIT INTO FRONT AND BACK (KF&B)

1 Knit into the front of next stitch on left needle, but do not pull the stitch off the needle.

2 Take right needle to back, then knit through the back of the same stitch.

3 Pull stitch off left needle. Completed increase: 2 stitches from 1 stitch. This increase results in a purl bump after the knit stitch.

DECREASES

K2TOG

1 Insert right needle into first 2 stitches on left needle, beginning with second stitch from end of left needle.

2 Knit these 2 stitches together as if they were 1.

The result is a right-slanting decrease.

P2TOG

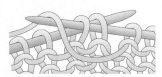

1 Insert right needle into first 2 stitches on left needle.

2 Purl these 2 stitches together as if they were 1.
The result is a right-slanting decrease.

SSK

1 Slip 2 stitches **separately** to right needle as if to knit.

2 Slip left needle into these 2 stitches from left to right and knit them together: 2 stitches become 1.

The result is a left slanting decrease.

SSSK

Work same as **SSK** EXCEPT:
1 Slip **3** stitches….
2 Slip left needle into these 3 stitches… 3 stitches become 1.
.The result is a left-slanting double decrease.

S2KP2, SL2-K1-P2SSO

A centered double decrease
1 Slip 2 stitches together to right needle as if to knit.

2 Knit next stitch.

3 Pass 2 slipped stitches over knit stitch and off right needle: 3 stitches become 1; the center stitch is on top.

The result is a centered double decrease.

BIND-OFFS

3-NEEDLE BIND-OFF

Bind-off ridge on wrong side

1 With stitches on 2 needles, place **right sides together**. * Knit 2 stitches together (1 from front needle and 1 from back needle, as shown); repeat from * once more.

2 With left needle, pass first stitch on right needle over second stitch and off right needle.

3 Knit next 2 stitches together.

4 Repeat Steps 2 and 3, end by drawing yarn through last stitch.

Bind-off ridge on right side

Work as for ridge on wrong side, EXCEPT, with **wrong sides together**.

I-CORD

Make a tiny tube of stockinette stitch with 2 double-pointed needles:

1 Cast on 2 or 3 sts.
2 Knit. Do not turn work. Slide stitches to opposite end of needle. Repeat Step 2 until cord is the desired length.

ATTACHED I-CORD

1 K3 (or 4), SSK (last stitch of cord together with next stitch on left needle).

2 Slip 4 (or 5) stitches back to left needle.

SHORT ROWS, WRAP & TURN (W&T)

Each short row adds 2 rows of knitting across a section of the work. Since the work is turned before completing a row, stitches are usually wrapped at the turn to prevent holes. Wrap and turn as follows:

Knit side

1 With yarn in back, slip next stitch as if to purl. Bring yarn to front of work and slip stitch back to left needle (as shown). Turn work.
2 With yarn in front, slip next stitch as if to purl. Work to end.

3 When you come to the wrap on a following knit row, hide the wrap by knitting it together with the stitch it wraps.

Purl side

1 With yarn in front, slip next stitch as if to purl. Bring yarn to back of work and slip stitch back to left needle (as shown). Turn work.
2 With yarn in back, slip next stitch as if to purl. Work to end.

3 When you come to the wrap on a following purl row, hide the wrap by purling it together with the stitch it wraps.

KNIT IN ROW BELOW (k1b)

1 Instead of working into next stitch on left needle, work into stitch directly below it.

2 Pull stitch off left needles and let it drop.

INTARSIA

Color worked in areas of stockinette fabric: each area is made with its own length of yarn. Twists made at each color change connect these areas.

Right-side row

Wrong-side row

INTERLOCKING THE COLORS

Work across row to color change, pick up new color from under the old and work across to next color change.

CROCHET

CHAIN STITCH (CH ST, CH)

1 Make a slipknot to begin.
2 Catch yarn and draw through loop on hook.

First chain made. Repeat Step 2.

BACKWARD SINGLE CROCHET

1 Insert hook into a stitch, catch yarn, and pull up a loop. Catch yarn and pull a loop through the loop on the hook. **2** Insert hook into next stitch to right.

3 Catch yarn and pull through stitch only (as shown). As soon as hook clears the stitch, flip your wrist (and hook). There are 2 loops on the hook, and the just-made loop is to the front of hook (left of old loop).

4 Catch yarn and pull through both loops on hook; 1 backward single crochet completed.

5 Continue working to the right, repeating Steps 2–4.

SINGLE CROCHET (SC)

1 Insert hook into a stitch, catch yarn and pull up a loop. Catch yarn and pull through the loop on the hook.
2 Insert hook into next stitch to the left.

3 Catch yarn and pull through the stitch; 2 loops on hook.

4 Catch yarn and pull through both loops on hook; 1 single crochet completed. Repeat Steps 2–4.

SLIP STITCH (SL ST)

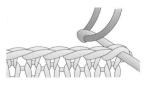

1 Insert the hook into a stitch, catch yarn, and pull up a loop.

2 Insert hook into the next stitch to the left, catch yarn and pull through both the stitch and the loop on the hook; 1 loop on the hook. Repeat Step 2.

GRAFTING

STOCKINETTE STITCH

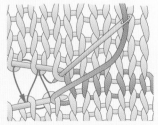

1 Arrange stitches on 2 needles as shown.

2 Thread a blunt needle with matching yarn (approximately 1" per stitch).
3 Working from right to left, with right sides facing you, begin with Steps 3a and 3b:
3a *Front needle:* bring yarn through first stitch as if to purl, leave stitch on needle.
3b *Back needle:* bring yarn through first stitch as if to knit, leave stitch on needle.

4a *Front needle:* bring yarn through first stitch as if to knit, slip off needle; through next stitch as if to purl, leave stitch on needle.
4b *Back needle:* bring yarn through first stitch as if to purl, slip off needle; through next stitch as if to knit, leave stitch on needle.
Repeat Steps 4a and 4b until 1 stitch remains on each needle.

5a *Front needle:* bring yarn through stitch as if to knit, slip off needle.
5b *Back needle:* bring yarn through stitch as if to purl, slip off needle.
6 Adjust tension to match rest of knitting.

Index

Visit knittinguniverse.com/artfulcolor

Colophon
Laura's Layers

"Oh, I love _koulourákia_!"

Laura Bryant's mom, Kanella, in a black-and-white lace sweater that complements her salt and pepper classic bob, smiles as she reminisces about her childhood growing up in Chicago's Greektown.

"I still have my mother's recipe," she says. "Where did you get them?'

In another Greek Town, Tarpon Springs, where I am staying while in Florida. In fact, my Mini Cooper is stuffed for the road with _koulourákia_, sweet _tsourékia_ bread, and my favorite pastries, _kourambiéthes_.

"With the ground almonds, a pound of butter, and the powdered sugar?" Kanella asks. "Another of my favorites! What about _dolmáthes_? I remember my mom sending us out to the fields to pick grape leaves before the Fourth of July, because after that she said they would be too tough. This was before the freezer, and mom would string them high in a dark closet to let them dry. You had to immerse them — very slowly — into hot water to bring back the softness before using them.

"Mom always talked about Greece, and I was so happy to visit her village in the Peloponnese. I spent one night in Psari

(Opposite page) Turning white into magical color.

and slept in the bed that my mom had slept in: a wood frame with ropes for a spring. I remember the rooster waking us up at five in the morning."

Psari? In the valley below my village by the train tracks, a few kilometers from my childhood home? What a coincidence! And Laura's mom shares with my mother the name Kanella, which means cinnamon. And, like my mother, Kanella was a weaver.

"But I had to give it up about 10 years ago," she says. "I just couldn't crawl under a loom anymore. I treasure one of my mom's weavings, an orange-and-blue overshot coverlet, so stiff and so scratchy.

"My mom also crocheted — not with a pattern, but by feel, as she did when she baked, saying, 'We need to put some more flour in.'"

"It's the same way I make color!" says Laura, laughing. She's been enjoying listening to her mom and me reminisce. In a black dress and short, curly, dark hair, Laura would fit right in, in the old country. But we're a world away, in St. Petersburg, Florida. We step out into the courtyard where 2 large stainless steel pots are steaming. Her grandma would have had to haul wood from the forest on her back for their cauldrons, but this is America, and a blue gas flame does the job.

Laura takes a pinch of red dye, throws it into the pot, and stirs the mixture with a long wooden dowel. As the surface of the dye bath steams, she slowly lowers a hank of yarn into the pot, and the magic I remember seeing as a kid happens: pristine white turns into brilliant color.

"I'm doing the first color for Layers — our new style of dyeing," Laura explains. "These are 4-ounce skeins, and I turn them so they can take the dye, then I flip them and turn them again. You can see that the dye is taking unevenly, on purpose, although it is distributed throughout each skein.

"That's the whole point of Layers — we're exploiting the natural tendency of dye to absorb unevenly. After a skein is dyed, it gets washed and goes on racks to dry. The process is fairly simple and takes about 45 minutes for each dye bath."

What was your concept behind Layers?

"Take a look at this gray and beige skein, one of the more subtle Layers colors. Overall, it's taupe, but when you really look you can see that some of it is a little browner, some a little grayer, because the dye takes unevenly. You do your first color, it comes out, it drips off, it gets — not dry, but drier. When you put it into the second color, it also takes the dye unevenly: stronger in some places and less strong in others. Overall, it's a *combination* of the two, with notes that are higher and lower.

How did Layers come about?

"That's a good question. In 2008 I did a show of my weavings, and they ended up being combined with painting, in lots and lots of layers. So I started thinking about under-painting, because when we dye, where color overlaps you get that equivalent. So I was thinking of melded colors.

"Textiles were definitely an early part of my education from mom. She was our Brownie Troop Leader and taught us all how to knit. I was 8, kept knitting, made doll clothes and learned to sew. My Greek grandmother, Georgia, came to visit and taught me how to crochet. Mom was a full-time housewife, but she took painting, weaving, ceramic, and sculpture courses. When she started taking classes at the Art Institute, I took classes there myself.

"When I was in my teens, crochet had a huge resurgence. All my mom's women's magazines were filled with crochet articles, working with enormous hooks and 4 strands of knitting worsted held together. There were afghans and jumpers, tunics and sweaters.

"Crochet was so fast that I stopped knitting for a while. I was crocheting mini skirts, making ceramic beads, putting them on purses, and selling them to the local boutique when I was 14 years old. But in my late teens I went back to knitting.

Laura Bryant with mom Kanella in St. Petersburg.

A palette of dying yarns, blended knits.

"In college, at first I was interested in the theater and fine art. But the practical side of me was saying maybe you should be a lawyer. In my second semester, I took one 2-credit-hour art class for which I spent 20 hours a week doing homework — by choice. That's when I said to myself, 'This is your passion, this is what you need to do.'

"I transferred to the art school and, even though I thought I'd paint, I ended up doing ceramics. But, interestingly, all my ceramics looked like fabric! So I finally took a textiles class, and the funny thing is, my mother had also zeroed in on weaving and had bought a big loom. But I resisted it for a while, because I didn't want to do what my mom did. Eventually, when I took that weaving course, that's what spoke to me. I guess it's in the genes.

"So into weaving I went. And, at the time, the art school didn't require you to take a color course, so I concentrated on pattern weaves and 3-dimensional structures: double-weave with weighted warps, pleats that were sculptural. And I have to mention this because it's such an integral part of my story: all the weavings I made were *white*. Because I didn't know what to do with color — didn't have an innate color sense.

"So I took a color course. And I always tell my students: color *absolutely* can be taught. That color course, which I struggled mightily with, changed my life. My work changed phenomenally. I've always had good observation skills, but I struggled with this course for 2 months before I had an 'Aha!' moment. Then it was like the whole world opened up to me."

What made color make sense to you all of a sudden?

"This method of teaching color was developed by Josef Albers. It's really eye training, a set of exercises that can seem mind-numbingly dull. The human eye is capable of discerning something between 3 and 10 million different colors — but most people see the 256 on their computer screen, or the 314 that's in my box of silk screen papers. It's all about training your eyes to see all of that nuance, then it's about embracing those millions of colors. All about not just learning color theory, but how to discern color weight. The way colors interact is all about contrast. The more contrast there is, the less the colors interact. The sharper boundaries are between colors, the more you see shapes.

"Pattern is enhanced by highly contrasting colors. Color stories are enhanced by colors closely related in weight. Weight isn't exactly the same thing as value, but it equates. Value is a gray scale, white at the top and black at the bottom, with all the shades of gray in between. And highly saturated colors might have neither black nor white in them, so they don't really fit into a gray scale.

"All colors aren't created equal: pure, bright yellow is much lighter than blue or red, even though they're all primaries. Color weight defines space and is how we make sense of the world — light colors move forward, visually; heavy colors recede. The Chaos Board is great because it shows what's moving forward: white, gray, and yellow. The colors that are punching back are black, blue, and, to some degree, red.

"So that's the definition of what color weight is. Functionally what it means is that, when you have a bunch of colors arranged randomly [see photo, below], it's hard to imagine using them all together. But when you take the exact same yarns and arrange them by weight, now you have total visual sense [see photo, above].

"For colors to work together, it doesn't matter what the colors are — it only matters what their weights are. In other words, those dirty greens are going to look just great with that lavender. The problem most people have is where to put bright colors. Where does this orange go? It doesn't go here and not there. See how it shifts? Here it looks light and bright and here it looks too heavy. Eventually you get to a spot where it lives, and now you know that it's the same weight.

"For the first few years after I had the color course, for every weaving that I did I labored over every single color combination, every thread, every shot of the shuttle. I had to analyze, in terms of color weight, what I was trying to achieve: Is it advancing? Receding? But as with any practice, be it meditation or athletics or language, the more you do it, the more you internalize it. Trainers talk about muscle memory. I think that's what intuition is — the memory of everything that you've done before, that you access without having to think about it. It's there.

"If you analyze a golf swing — stop and think every time you swing a club — you're not going to play good golf. You have to do it, and do it, and do it, until you get it right and can do it automatically.

"I don't think I started to internalize color until, in the late 1980s, I had an opportunity to teach it at the State University College at Buffalo. No longer was I analyzing my own work — I was analyzing everything that my students were doing as I passed my eye training to them. Having to look

"Our brains don't like chaos; they like to see patterns," says Laura Bryant — Laura's color course in two photos: colors arranged at random (below) or by weight (above).

173

(From left, above) Yes, it all starts out white; cheerleader? and Shipping Clerk in Chief? Matt Bryant packaging color. (Opposite page) Laura posing for her author's photo; Crossings VI, 20" × 20".

at their work and say something sensible — articulate — about it was very difficult. But it made me so much better with color. They often say: 'To really learn something, try teaching it.' I really leaned color to the point I almost can't tell you how I do it anymore.

"This was the color training that opened up my whole world. I was selling my weavings well enough that it could be a second income for our family. I had moved to Buffalo in 1980 because I married Matt, and then the 1982 recession hit. And the first thing that goes is art, so my little weaving business suffered.

"I was working part-time in a yarn store at the time, doing finishing and clerking, and sales reps would come in and show their wares. When a rep who was an underemployed engineer found a job in his field, he came in and said, 'Laura, you should take my lines.' He was representing Tahki and Berocco, so in 1982 I became a sales rep.

"My new job got me into the market, the national scene, and industry shows. I walked down the aisles of my first wholesale show and there was hand-dyed yarn. I thought, 'I can do that. I know how to do that!' I had just concentrated in textiles and color. So I talked Dianne Friedman of Tahki into letting me hand dye their yarn. She sent me five bags — and that's how Prism was born. I had to come up with a name and a logo, and Prism is a nice, clear, crisp name, an encapsulation of what I did, which is taking white yarn and creating color, which is what a prism does to white light. Then I came up with a nice color line.

How did you start developing a color line?

"Between being in the yarn store and being a sales rep, I knew you had to have a balanced color line. I knew I needed a neutral, something in the blue tones, something in the rosy tones, something in the sagey-green tones,

and I went on from there. We were only talking about five multicolors. I knew enough to understand that they were not going to be highly contrasting colors, but tonal, and similar in weight, because if you're knitting, those are the most beautiful hand dyes. Unless you want to do self-patterning, or some really particular effects, highly contrasting colors within the same yarn give you that messy look.

"My hand-dyed yarns sold well but, after a few seasons, Tahki was on to other things and I started sourcing my own yarns. The first thing I found was really nice mohair from England. Of course, when you source from a mill, you're talking about hundreds and hundreds of pounds of yarn! It was thousands of dollars of yarn and I said, 'What if it doesn't work?' — and my dear husband Matt encouraged me, saying, 'The worst thing that happens is that you sell it at cost. So let's do it.'

"And I did it, in our basement in Buffalo, with mohair. My mother, who at the time was living in Florida, was a yarn rep. I would send her boxes full of these big mohair balls that would each make a sweater, and she would take them and leave them on consignment in stores. She gave ten balls to a yarn shop in Sarasota on Saturday, and by Tuesday morning they were calling her, wanting more.

"That's how it started. I was sourcing other yarns, but Matt got tired of coming home and smelling acetic acid, so we moved the company from the basement to his machine shop — to a 2-room unheated garage. We put a small wall heater in, but there was no plumbing, so we ran hoses from the main building over to sinks at Matt's shop. But this was Buffalo, and they would freeze in the winter, so every night we'd undo the hoses, empty them, roll them up, and the next day roll them back out.

"How much I could grow in that garage was limited, but it was there that I invented Wild Stuff — our crazy, everything-tied-together yarn — and that absolutely involved Mom. Like every other hand dyer on the planet, you wind up with odds and ends, all this leftover stuff. I was talking to Mom about coming up with something to use all these odd skeins, and she said, 'There's this great project going around Florida — the Chinese Menu Sweater.'

"You did it with random stripes, so I picked eight yarns that would go together color-wise, gave the pattern to my sample knitter, and said, 'Just do stripes wherever you think.' Mom happened to be visiting me when the sweater came back. It looked good. Mom, who's very creative, looked at it and said, 'Wouldn't it be neat if you could unknit that sweater now and take all those stripes and all those yarns, and put them in a skein so everybody could knit it just like that?'

"I said that was a crazy idea, because every knitter is different and the knots wouldn't wind up in the same place; the stripes wouldn't be even. And as I'm saying that, another part of my mind is saying, 'But maybe we don't care. The knots don't have to line up with the side seam. Maybe there's something to this.'

"That was the spark that started my exploration of making yarns that were tied together. We had to go through a lot of experiments to find out the optimum lengths — minimum and maximum — and the rest of it has been my color sense: putting similar-weight colors together.

"That's how I did the first few balls of Wild Stuff, until I found out how much was too much — how little was too little. At that time, doing your colors was all the rage, so we did a Spring palette of pastels, a Summer palette of jewel-tone brights, an Autumn palette of earth tones with some jewel tones in it, and a Winter palette of dark brights.

"This was in 1991, and during the six months of development we kept saying, 'What are we going to call this wild stuff? Finally one day we realized Wild Stuff is the perfect name, and from that we got Cool Stuff, Light Stuff, Neat Stuff, and now we have Layers Stuff, because we're now doing our Layers colors in a new style of Stuff.

"Because these are fashion, textured yarns, the knots stay put on the wrong side and, typically, you go back and weave them in or just trim them and let them be. Some knitters choose to untie the knots and bury the ends. But sometimes people choose to leave them on the outside as part of the design.

How did the book come about?

"As in much of my life, it all came together: I started teaching at STITCHES where I have great synergy with my vendors, became a sponsor, did Opening Day. When the idea started to form 2 years ago I approached Elaine, who took my Intentional Patterning class at STITCHES South: how to take a multicolored yarn and force it to create a pattern by itself.

When I first talked to Elaine, it was a book just about that. But we really clicked — I love working with Elaine, bouncing things off her — and the book became so much more. The more we thought about it, the bigger the book got. And it also got to be a better book. I've always loved your books, with those beautiful photos, and you at XRX were the only ones I wanted to do this with — the only ones who I thought could understand where I was going with it and what it needed to be.

"Color and intention is what it really comes down to. There's a large up-front portion about color, and we're adding to that, because if you don't understand how color works, how will you understand how the color in that hand-dyed yarn is going to work?

"And then it's about the intention: either you're going to intentionally harness the colors to pattern, or you want to randomize them. Your intention towards that is what's critical. And so the book is about those two approaches in working with hand-dyed yarns.

"You have a highly contrasting multicolor and want to make this really wild argyle pattern? Here's how you do it — how you incorporate it into a garment, how you make it look purposeful. You don't want that? You want to show

the beautiful Monet's garden of colors that are happening without that nasty pooling, striping, and blotching? Here's how you do that as well.

"It's trying to give knitters ultimate control over those skeins that we all love. I ask every single class, 'How many of you have knit with hand-dyed yarns?' Every hand comes up. 'How many of you have had bad experiences with how they look?' And every hand stays up. The tendency is to think, 'This is so beautiful, all I need is stockinette stitch.' And, most often, it's the worst thing you can do, because it doesn't show hand-dyed yarns to their best advantage. That's what the book is about.

"I'm fond of saying that there aren't any bad color combinations, there are just bad ways of using those colors together. It has to do with the color weight and the quantity of each color. The right balance means all is well with the world, because our brains don't like chaos — they like to see patterns."

Time to take a break, munch on some more *koulourakia,* and ask Laura: Have there been any disasters?

"Got some leftovers? Turn them into Wild Stuff!" she says. And you can always overdye — if something doesn't work, you can always just make it darker."

Kanella nods her head in approval. And I wonder — what has it been like watching Laura grow into a fine hand dyer?

She says, "From 2 pots on the stove in the kitchen? It's unbelievable!"

— Alexis Xenakis
December 2012, Sioux Falls, SD

ACKNOWLEDGEMENTS

They say it takes a village, and I know this to be true. *Artful Color, Mindful Knits* became so much more than what I was able to put into words and knitting. The creative force that is XRX — Elaine, Alexis, and Rick — was invaluable in giving form to my vision, to completing it in a way that I might not even have imagined. This was by far the most collaborative project I have worked on, and I treasure the effort you expended on my behalf. Elaine in particular — thank you for saying "yes" every time I suggested we needed to add something more, and for your patience and encouragement in giving voice to my color concepts. Sarah, Traci, Rick, and Ginger were adept and vigilant in translating my sometimes intuitive patterns into clear directions that any knitter can follow—thank you. To my many test knitters—Kay, Martha, Bobbi, Karen, Candice, Karla, Judy, Myra, Orna, Lynn, Marilyn, Carol, and Meg—it was a lot of knitting and I couldn't have done it without you — thank you for your lovely work. Thanks to the many hand-dyers who contributed yarn for research and projects — you helped to make my approach more universal. Thanks to Bejewelled & Bedazzled Buttons for the perfect finishing touch on Neon Rivers. The production team at XRX did a superb job of realizing the final book — a special thank you goes to Natalie for her beautiful design. Editorial support and logistics were handled efficiently and ably by Karen — thank you for putting up with my deluge of e-mails. Benjamin, I didn't have to bug you much about this one, but thanks for always being there.

And lastly, this book would not have been possible without the support of my staff at Prism, and particularly that of my dear and loving husband, Matt. Thanks for having my back.